One Man's Medicine

One Man's Medicine

Charles Harris, M.D.

HARPER & ROW, PUBLISHERS

New York   Evanston

San Francisco

London

Acknowledgment is gratefully made to the University of Chicago Press for permission to reprint "The Autopsy of C" by Horton Johnson from *Perspectives in
Biology and Medicine,* Volume 13, No. 4, Summer, 1970. © 1970 by The University
of Chicago.

FIRST EDITION

Designed by Dorothy Schmiderer

Library of Congress Cataloging in Publication Data

Harris, Charles, date
   One man's medicine.
   1. Harris, Charles, date.   2. Physicians–Correspondence, reminiscences, etc., I.
Title. R154.H263A33 1975   610′.92′4[B]   74–1813
ISBN 0–06–011761–3

75 76 77 78 79 10 9 8 7 6 5 4 3 2 1

An Appreciation

THE BOOK is dedicated to the memory of my parents, and to three physicians who, as I grew to know each of them, inspired me to pursue a career in medicine:

Leon Harris, M.D., D.D.S.
Joseph H. Hersh, M.D.
Stanley S. Lamm, M.D.

My life, of which this book is a small part, is dedicated to my wife, Rachel, whose critical comment, born of a fine sense of literary style, helped form the book and provide the title, and to my children, Hana, Susan and Leon, who were quick to detect flaws in characterization. Their love and support made the project worthwhile.

I thank my editor, the quite remarkable Virginia Hilu, for her crisp, pertinent judgments.

AUTHOR'S NOTE

Whoever sees him- or herself in these pages pays homage to the universality of human traits, the multiplicity of human faults and virtues; the events and characters portrayed are a composite, drawn to describe the changing mode of medicine during thirty years, and to evoke the satisfying memory of arduous tasks and bittersweet time well spent.

Prologue

THIS IS A fictionalized memoir about medicine. It is true to the mood of the thirty years it spans, during which medicine and science have abolished or learned to control most of the old scourges, have advanced or regressed, as the case may be, to the stage of genetic tinkering, and, in so doing, have imposed their own unique stresses on society.

As we struggle to attain a higher plane of social organization, the physician becomes increasingly subordinate to organizations, governments, institutions, and men of neither license nor tradition in medicine, who have vaulted into positions of power in the newly created health syndicate: businessmen, lawyers, accountants, car salesmen, bankers and the new breed, the hospital administrator; paper doctors who treat paper. They see to the health of the by-laws, procedure manuals, bills, accounts, debits and insurance forms, beguiled by the delusion that if the records are neat and orderly, institutional care of the patient is neat and orderly.

The doctor, as their hireling, is forced to use the tools and services they provide, which may not be the best available; urged to consider the community as a whole when treating his patient; coerced into violating the confidentiality of the doctor-patient relationship by monitoring the utilization of hospital beds by his colleagues.

Nurses resent being "handmaidens" to the doctor, and strive to become an independent profession.

There is a hue and cry for doctors to divest themselves of the elite position they have held so long in medicine. Who, then, should be the elite?

Clearly the precious bond that exists between a patient and his doctor is being riven by unqualified intruders with unlimited power. The physician, in his spiritual and serving role, may be the commodity that is squandered in this struggle.

The medical profession is increasingly in bondage. Like the point of an inverted pyramid it is being pressed deeper into the ground by the weight of an enlarging, expensive bureaucracy. If the profession of medicine is shattered by this burden, would it be asking too much for Aesculapius to be reborn?

1

I DID NOT DECIDE to be a doctor. I did not appraise various pursuits, or evaluate pros and cons, or measure fine points to choose a career. There was no uncertainty. From the pit of my memory I know that I always expected to be a doctor.

My father was a doctor. His colleagues flocked to our house, where discussions in the fascinating patois of medical men raged long past my bedtime hour, loudly enough to penetrate the confines of my room where I caught aural glimpses of fabled scenes spun out of contemporary adventure. By listening carefully, despite mysterious words like "diagnosis," "prognosis," "etiology," "myelitis," "angina," one could sense even in the cloistered world of the child that a desperate human drama was being revealed. *Hospital* conjured up apparitions in white, moving silently in a white dream world. *Ether* became a dance of diaphanous scarves that undulated until the patient fell asleep, and the gauzy surgeon could make his *incision,* a mighty sweep with a scimitar that would rend asunder the sick flesh to reveal a pool of amorphous muddy-red ooze, from which he would *excise* something called an *appendix*, then strut away heroically. *Brain* meant a bugle-shaped coil of bloody bones, and *heart* was confused with the red knave of a deck of cards.

My father and his friends recorded the horror of the great flu epidemic: endless house calls and sudden deaths, truckloads of empty caskets clattering horse-drawn to the funeral parlors, interminable processions to the cemeteries, and never once was it mentioned that any of the doctors had suffered even a sniffle. Doctors were never ill, I thought. They refereed the outcome of disease. If not angels, they were on the side of the angels, and exempted from mortal perils.

For a child growing up in the guise of a doctor, life has other perils. It is one thing to hear tell of sickness, disease and death, and another to confront them. It is one thing to detect the faint and romantic smells of iodine and other antiseptics lingering on the hands of a returning father, and another to greet them first-hand, more pungent, more odious when mingled with the sticky-sap smell of blood in the calamitous atmosphere of a humid operating suite.

Once, traveling in a foreign country, my father, with me belt-high at his side, visited the local hospital. Suddenly I was in the busy hallways of an operating suite, being hoisted aloft by my father to peer through steamy windows at the draped figures in the operating rooms. In one, a leg was held aloft by an assistant while blood seeped into white towels that bound the limb above and below an open wound. I struggled to get down. At that moment an orderly emerged from another room carrying a large bloody mass suspended from tongs. My stomach lurched, and soon I lay in a pool of vomit. For weeks I pushed the scene and the sinking feelings from my memory. If this was the real world of medicine, it wasn't for me.

Many evenings after being sent to bed I would sneak back to sit on the upstairs landing, my legs dangling between the balusters, and eavesdrop on the fascinating recitations of my father and his doctor friends. I could see Francine, her face blue, struggling for the breath that could prevent pneumonia from strangling her, or Mrs. Horton in bed with cancer (whoever that might be); or the Proctor kid, who expired from meningitis. When I asked my father what expired meant, he told me it was the act of letting all your breath out.

I guessed that Dr. Green was a surgeon because he always smelled of iodine. Dr. Cooper carried a stethoscope, and tongue depressors protruded from his breast pocket. Whenever ears hurt, Dr. Strecker would come to the house, open a small black case, remove appliances which he would then screw together into one piece that would light up, and then jam it painfully into my ear. Dr. Ruben treated throats. When he visited, he would make me say "Ahhh," and peer along a wooden stick thrust into my throat.

Dr. Barrow probably was a urologist. He dealt with tubes and parts of the body that were mentioned only *sotto voce* in my presence. My mother once told me that my father had been to Dr. Barrow once, and hadn't been very brave about it.

Then there was Gwathmey, who would shake his head while he told stories about his duties during the First World War. He told how he sat on a small stool in a tent, and swung his anesthesia machine from patient to patient in a large circle while operations were being performed, and that when he had returned to the place from which he had started another wounded soldier had already been rolled into place, so he just kept going round and round for days at a time without rest.

I remember shivering when my father described Ludwig's angina. Although I didn't know what it meant, nor learn till later that it was a suffocating cellulitis of the neck that usually started after the extraction of a tooth from the lower jaw, I did know that the unfortunate people who had it usually died. Berman survived, but only after he had been taken to the operating room, and, without anesthesia, his bulging neck had been incised and the pus drained. My father described how brave Berman had been. But when Berman recovered, and the drains had to be pulled from his raw tissues, he screamed in pain. My father then wondered whether he had been brave, or so sick, the tissues so full of pain, that they weren't able to transmit additional pain signals.

In those days of no antibiotics many who died were very young. What might have started as a frivolous problem could end fatally, and blood poisoning was more serious and immediate than cancer. Today, the diseases that then killed children can be cleared up overnight with nothing more than a single prescription.

3

Max Chester, who was tall, and a serious dentist, came to the house one night with his thumb bandaged. A patient had bitten it while he was doing an extraction. We all laughed about it. But Max died of blood poisoning three weeks later after a terrible struggle. I couldn't imagine him dying.

Dr. Zingher had helped develop the Schick test and knew how to give injections. Every so often on Sunday we would take a long drive to his house, where I would have to roll up my sleeve while he put a needle into my arm. I agreed not to cry if he would take the needle out when I yelled "That's enough!" By the time I could get the words out he had finished what he had to do and withdrawn the needle, as if my command had forced his hand. That gave me a sense of control. After the injections I was rewarded by being allowed to play with the Zingher children, the pleasure of which was limited by Joey, twice my size, who took delight in hitting me. I would shout "That's enough!" but he kept hitting me anyway. Dr. Zingher died in his laboratory. At the funeral I watched Joey standing over the open grave crying uncontrollably, reduced to the lonely despair of a child who had lost his father. I understood for the first time the remote finality of death that gave meaning to the concept of life.

When the doctors came to the house, they would greet me briefly, or tousle my hair and say "Hello, Harry," and then turn to talk to each other. One doctor was different. Dr. Lapius, a large man with wild black hair and a long black mustache, not only shook my hand but also introduced himself to me. When the other doctors were engrossed in heated discussions in medical language, he would take me on his lap, and take pains to translate things I didn't understand. His real name was Simon Quentin Lapius, but the doctors called him "S.Q." or just "Lapius."

Lapius explained that the word "febrile" meant the patient had a temperature. Septicemia was what happened when germs got into the blood stream.

"Couldn't you kill the germs with iodine?" I asked. "No, Harry, you can't put iodine into the blood stream, but someday we hope to have medicine that will be put into the blood stream to kill germs."

When, at bedtime, pajama-clad I would sit surreptitiously on the landing and eavesdrop on the wondrous tales unfolding below, I was invariably discovered and sent back to bed. Years later

I realized that my huddled form threw a large shadow on the wall that caught my father's eye. Lapius would often rescue me and accompany me to the bedroom. "Don't be long, Simon," my father would call after him. "We haven't heard from you yet about the remarkable rheumatoid."

"Will you tell me about the rheumatoid too, Dr. Lapius?" I might ask.

"Surely, Harry," Lapius chuckled. "But now I have other stories to tell you."

He would tuck me fast beneath the quilts, then sit on the end of the bed and tell me stories, while shadows on the wall mimed paraphrases of his tales.

During these cloistered moments I learned about Apollo, the son of Zeus who was physician to the gods, and about his son Asclepius and how he went to school in the cave of Chiron the Centaur, and grew up to be so great a doctor that he became regarded as the god of medicine. The Romans called him Aesculapius. At Epidaurus and its surroundings he built many temples for healing the sick. My slumber dreams raced across the sky in the fiery chariot of Apollo as he took his family for a Sunday outing, and the children Hygeia, Panacea, Machaon and Podalirius giggled and laughed and threw things over the side. I was in love with Hygeia because she was beautiful and clean, and hated her when I had to wash my face at night.

I wept when Aesculapius died. It was unfair. Because Aesculapius had saved so many people there weren't enough of the dead to populate Pluto's kingdom. Pluto wanted Zeus to kill Aesculapius. Apollo pleaded with Zeus to give Aesculapius another chance. But then Pluto lied, saying that Aesculapius took money for bringing someone back from the dead. That clinched it and Zeus killed Aesculapius with a thunderbolt.

"You see, Harry," Lapius said, "Zeus may have had a point. After all, if doctors cured everybody and no one died, the world would certainly be very crowded, wouldn't it?" But I couldn't then bring myself to believe that people would hate doctors for saving their lives, or that anyone could hate someone who had the power to bring Dr. Zingher back to Joey.

But Lapius also explained that it was the gods who killed Aesculapius; and he pointed out that gods are immortal and not concerned about dying.

5

As I grew older, Lapius told stories of real doctors, Hippocrates, Rhazes, Galen, Vesalius, Paré, Malpighi, Descartes, Jenner, Hunter, Scheele, Laënnec, Purkinje, Henle, Morton, Semmelweis, Koch, Pasteur, Pavlov, and what they did to free us from disease. How they descended through the millennial fires of plague and pestilence, guardian heroes to mankind. They were all the descendants of Aesculapius, medical gods to me, and hovered as immortal shadows on the storied walls of my bedroom.

"But Aesculapius wasn't really a god, Harry," Lapius pointed out. "The Greeks deified him, but he died, as all mortals must."

Lapius lived nearby, and he became my tutor in many things. His house was filled with bric-a-brac of the medical world. One room contained a table with a microscope, a metal rack with glass tubes, a sink and above it a shelf lined with bottles of red, purple, blue and colorless liquids. Another room had a desk, a typewriter and pads of paper. He then was on the editorial staff of a medical journal. He signed all his editorials "S. Q. Lapius."

His basement was filled with tools, and Dr. Lapius would make many things out of wood, metal or even wet paper, which he molded to look like heads and masks. I spent hours watching him work. He gave me tools and taught me the use of them.

At a certain age a child may develop an alter ego, a friend whom he keeps chained to his imagination and calls forth to fill a lonely moment, to test an idea or to supply confidence in the enactment of an errant scheme. Lapius became my imaginary friend. He confided once that it was my father who had inspired him to go into medicine, so I would lie abed at night, picturing Lapius as a youngster being schooled by my father. It was then that S. Q. Lapius became my friend, teacher and surrogate medical father for life.

Eventually, under the tutelage of one Lapius or another I became conversant, in advance of my years, with the magisterial vocabulary of medicine.

The sugar-coated frames of fantasy that magically can catapult the child into the doctor's chair behind the walnut desk in a paneled consulting room are false. The grinding truth is that the doctor stands in the presence of illness, blood, pus, misery and a host of things that afflict people, all a mirror to his own ultimate destiny.

2

———————◆———————

IN THE EARLY FORTIES it was said that the medical schools classi-fied Jews as aggressive, Italians as lazy, and the Irish as ambi-tious, and since ambition was the preferable quality, more Irish were accepted by medical schools than Italians or Jews.

One of the standard questions on medical-school applications, or posed at the interview, was "Why do you want to become a doctor?" The obvious answer, "Because I want to help people," was unacceptable to the dons. Possible answers flooded my dreams.

"Medicine is a path to independence."

"Trivial. Rejected."

"Medicine is the most interesting way to spend the rest of my life."

"Shallow. Rejected."

"It's a good way to make a living."

"Lacks idealism. Rejected."

"Because medicine is the crossroads of the mind and the spirit. It is the fusing of the intellect and its immediate physical application to the benefit of the patient. It is a field of study which enables one to expand one's cultural horizons; it is a broad-based profession which embraces the fine qualities of art and blends them with the precision of science. A doctor can be a scientist, healer, guide, friend, counselor. What more fulfilling way to spend one's life? How better to serve society?"

"How noble—accepted."

In looking back I would answer the question with a question: "What better way to serve?"

The medical school I attended consisted of two antiquated buildings facing each other across a busy, narrow downtown street.

Maudlin dreams of serving humanity were shattered by the Formalin smell of salty dead bodies in the anatomy room. Thirty bodies covered by cracked oilskins lay on gray slabs with gutters on the side and a drain centrally located near the foot of the table. They represented a small part of the city's daily harvest of the dead. They had died on street corners, in lodging houses, in hospital wards, unclaimed derelicts who had names but were unknown. Assigned from city morgues, they were brought to this place, embalmed by a small gray man in a striped apron, then suspended by their ears from ice hooks in a cold room, a hung jury that could bear no witness.

Four of us were assigned to each body. Starting with a complete man, we reduced him methodically, daily for six months, to a disemboweled carcass, then to dismembered bones and the shriveled shavings of dissected tissues. In the process we elucidated the course of nerves and arteries and struggled with the mnemonics that helped us to memorize the relationship of anatomical minutiae. *"On Old Olympus Towering Top . . ."* and so forth spun out the cranial nerves: Olfactory, Ophthalmic, Oculomotor, Trochlear, Trigeminus, etc.—otherwise known as cranial nerves I, II, III, IV and V. Or "NAVEL" to indicate the position of the *Nerve, Artery, Vein, Empty space* and *Lymph nodes* beneath the inguinal ligament. Or:

> The lingual nerve it took a swerve
> And crossed the hyoglossus.
> "Well I'll be fucked," said Wharton's duct,
> "The lingual nerve has crossed us."

Little by little my stiff disappeared in direct proportion to how much of him I had memorized. We were supposed to learn the protuberances on the surfaces of the long bones, their names and which ligaments attached to them. Each of us trustingly believed that this massive collection of trivia was the stuff from which doctors were made. And indeed it was, for if nothing else, it was indoctrinating, and taught the structural equivalent of strange words like "occiput," "aorta," "parietal," "sphenoid," "sella turcica," the "wandering vagus," "thalamus," "hypothalamus," "amygdala" and "cor." We intoned these Greco-Latin incantations weekly in oral quizzes, so that in unison it sounded like the friars' chorus of a monastic service.

Medical school is a trade school, where the nuts and bolts are provided to enable you to assemble new sets of knowledge into some type of meaningful structure. It is the kindergarten of medicine, prelude to the twenty years it takes for the whole thing to come together. In thirty-six months the student has to amass a working vocabulary in anatomy, embryology, histology, physiology, neuroanatomy, biochemistry, and the clinical subdivisions of medicine—ophthalmology, otolaryngology, dermatology, gastroenterology, gynecology, obstetrics, the complexities of surgical technique. . . .

The war years imposed a stringent schedule. Thirty-six months of schooling were run consecutively, without the customary summer vacation. Of the one hundred and twenty students who started, only one hundred would graduate. The days became a stylus that burnt a procession of details into our memories, a hood that guarded our medical privacy from extraneous influences in the outside world; and they became a cave of medical sights and smells, from which one could move only into the den of night, lighted by a small lamp with a single bulb that illuminated the glaring pages of medical tomes filled with the undigested material that we had to assimilate before the morrow. Sleep was a black plane between two edges of light, a brief corridor between the days.

Vacation was but a week between semesters. I would borrow a car and drive to the mountains, where I would make a bed of my meadows and a bath of the cold springs that fed the quarries. I rolled my musty odors off in the morning dew, and hoped the smell of fresh-cut grass would last till I got back. I baked in the sun, hoping to store enough of its healing light to take me through the winter.

Eventually we entered the clinics and the hospitals. The stiff in the dissecting room bore no horrors for us. The body was passive, and despite the destructive scars there were no signs of struggle.

The hospital was different. Everything, even the dying, lived. Chemical and physiological function visibly fought to survive life-quenching toxins.

A hospital is a maelstrom of turbulent but controlled activity measured in terms of beds. Patients are in bed three or bed seven. The ward has twenty beds. So-and-so is in a two-bedded room. The hospital has three thousand beds. Bed is the universal measure, much as feet or yards are used on the outside. And for each bed there is a patient and a waiting list of prospective patients, some of whom don't realize that soon they will be sick.

The corridors are conduits for lifelines drawn or pushed by doctors, nurses, orderlies and aides. Medical students dressed in white often were mistaken for doctors. Young single nurses, not unmindful that we soon would become doctors, flattered us with their obeisance and readiness to serve. And young visitors on the distaff side eyed us appreciatively, while their mothers, appraising us for the marriage mart, would say, "Stand up, Jennie, and show the doctor how tall you are!"

Because of the shortage of doctors during the war, we were impressed into service on the wards. When called to emergencies, I recall the panic with which I would try to select and assemble the appropriate facts that flooded my mind, then fled like vanishing credits from a movie screen; the uncertainty with a dying patient, never sure that you had done all that could be done, or had not overlooked something. The closer the patient came to death, the more frantic the attempt to cull some nonexistent memory. There was guilt when the patient died until, as you reflected on the episode during the course of the next few days, you assured yourself that everything possible had been done. You found yourself relating the details of the case at lunch with your classmates, in an offhand professional way.

"What happened?"

"She died," you said indifferently, then forked a large piece of apple pie as if that were the most important deed of the day, while listening carefully for any critical statements in the comments that your story might have elicited.

We learned to accept death, but never got used to it. Although it is an inevitable sequel of life, in our role as doctors we felt that we had to oppose it, stave it off, establish ourselves as the mortal enemies of death, whereas in truth death could only be conquered by an immortal enemy.

Fran Brown's death was inevitable but premature. She was a secretary in the dean's office, and each of us knew her well because she was the intermediary for every message, memo, schedule, change of curriculum imposed on us by the faculty. She was impish, and smiling, and, for all her attractiveness, unmarried at twenty-eight. She was discreet, polite and helpful. She was the kid next door.

When I first saw her as a patient, she was in a wheelchair. She waved me down and smiled.

"What's going on, Fran?"

"Nothing much. A little trouble with my eyes."

The "little trouble" magnified when my classmate Garth, assigned to the laboratory, came to lunch later and told us her urine was thick as pudding. "Protein," he said.

One by one the function of each of her muscles failed. Medical students were assigned special duty with her round the clock. Important professors from the school flooded the place to see Fran, and she must have suffered ten examinations in a two-day period while she grew progressively worse.

I always regretted that when she winked at me, while they were putting the respirator around her, I didn't wink back, or squeeze her hand, or smile. I just stood numbly trying to appear professional while the Chief of Medicine and the dean were relaying our assignments. She deserved better than that from me. But at that time I wasn't quite sure what constituted being a doctor.

It soon became apparent that the great doctors attending her were as puzzled and helpless as the students. Fran finally lost consciousness, and soon even the respirator couldn't help, as the mysterious malady that afflicted her brain finally destroyed its vital centers.

We were forced to attend her autopsy as a matter of medical protocol. We were ashamed because Fran had been a modest girl and now she was nude on a white enamel slab. A doctor in an apron cut her fair skin. Rivulets of blood seeped from the wound under her breasts to the table. The pathologist worked efficiently and rapidly. He tried to keep the field as clean as possible while removing the various organs. After a while I became intrigued by the anatomical puzzle, and when they opened the skull, Fran no longer existed, only the memory of her death.

Weeks later her case was presented at a pathology seminar. We listened disinterestedly to the recitation of the clinical history and laboratory findings, all of which we knew by heart. Finally all that was medically important about Fran had been reduced to a microscopic slide of brain tissue that was projected on the screen. It didn't look like her at all. The pathologist aimed a pointer at the screen. "Here in the perivascular spaces are collections of lymphocytes. The only diagnosis we can come up with is some nonspecific encephalitis," he said lamely. Fran had finally become a case.

Horton Johnson wrote "The Autopsy of C." It could have been the autopsy of Fran.

> And now the academic question dies
> As I, the white-gowned priest, must
>   helpless stand
> (I pause with neatly opened heart
>   in hand)
> To watch the soul of brave Adonis rise:
> This thin and anguished spirit stripped
>   so soon
> Of precious [wo]manhood, seeing its
>   dream congeal
> In shapeless pools on sterile stainless
>   steel,
> Runs off into the empty afternoon.
> We were such willful [youth] not long ago
> I might have caught her flying shirt tails
>   then
> And dragged her crashing down: "Come back!
>   You know
> It's just a game." And shaking hands like
>   men
> We would have wandered home beneath a sky
> Where time being quiet, only clouds passed by.*

* *Perspectives in Biology and Medicine*, Vol. 13, No. 4, Summer, 1970.

The word "case" depersonalizes the patient. "I saw a case the other day . . ." or "I had a case in the office . . ." or "It was the most complicated case . . ." Case is neuter and takes an *it*. Perhaps doctors neuterize their patients to preserve an anonymity that helps relieve the burden of misery. The embryo doctor learns to do this in medical school. It takes only a few weeks on the wards to force a medical student to confront his own mortality. We realize that there but for a space of time lie I. We learn to inspect ourselves minutely, and invariably find enlarged lymph nodes, pathognomonic or Hodgkin's disease, or the pallor of nephritis, or a funny cell in our blood smears that sends us scurrying to the hematologist for assurance it doesn't mean leukemia. Then suddenly we know that to survive, we must separate ourselves from our patients and their disease. At that moment they become "cases." Much later, when we have survived the minimum number of crises, the "cases" become patients again, and we are less afraid, and of course more human.

For pulmonary edema due to a failing heart the interns in the hospital taught us how to make a cardiac cocktail and inject it intravenously. It consisted of a mercurial diuretic, a digitalis preparation that could be served parenterally, aminophyllin, that worked its wonders mysteriously, and morphine. The concoction was to be injected slowly, and even then, due to the nature of the substances and the precarious condition of the patient, the cocktail wedded to the medical moment produced its share of mortality.

I used it once. A bearded old man in the ward was huffing and puffing, with a rapid heart rate. He had recently entered the hospital. The intern, after he had made rounds, ordered me to administer the cocktail. As I approached the bed, the old man gasped, "Help me, Doctor, help me out of my misery."

"Don't worry," I said loudly, brandishing the giant syringe and rapier needle, while waiting for his veins to bulge under the restrictions imposed by the tourniquet. "I'll help you out of your misery."

I administered the potion a milliliter at a time every thirty seconds, intent on the second hand of my watch. When finished I extracted the needle slowly from the vein, plugged the leak with cotton and said, "There now, you should be feeling better shortly." I looked up for the first time. The patient was dead.

13

Whenever I showed up on the ward thereafter, some wag would be sure to call out, "Watch out for Harry, he'll put you out of your misery."

The deed is done. You find that you don't slink back to your room and cut your throat, nor leap dramatically from the eighth-floor window, in full sight of witnesses, as an expiation (although one of our classmates did just that). Rather, you replay the scene to yourself a number of times, and either decide that those things are bound to happen or modify your approach to the problem. After that I administered the drugs in different syringes, pausing for several minutes between injections. If the patient died, at least I would know which medication I was giving when he expired. Because patients die, every doctor at one stage of his training and career must have a hand in the death of a patient, and must come to grips with his conscience and his worth as a physician at that moment.

Illness causes physiological instability and disequilibrates the complex chemical processes of living matter. The job of the physician is to create the conditions that permit the manifold interrelationships to resume their steady state. The physician must learn to proceed warily where angels do not fear to tread.

3

IN MY SENIOR YEAR I was assigned a two-month externship in a small hospital devoted entirely to the treatment of tuberculosis. At that time the only medical treatment for the disease was bed rest. Occasionally attempts were made to place the diseased lung at rest by injecting air into the pleural cage of the diseased side, and collapsing the lung until healing occurred. When to let the lung expand again was a matter of judgment, because X-rays of the collapsed lung were unrevealing. When adhesions between the lung and the chest cage prevented the lung from collapsing, the surgeons would resort to a mutilative procedure called thoracoplasty. The supportive ribs on that side of the chest were removed and the lung collapsed when the chest caved in.

Most of the patients at the small hospital were female, and most of these were either Irish or Italian (Jews seemed generally more resistant to the ravages of tuberculosis because, it was felt, they had descended from the European ghettos, where death had eliminated those genetically susceptible).

The nurses were elderly, graying, seasoned, bustling women, kindly and efficient. Their excellent clinical judgment had been refined by years of experience, and they wasted no energy misleading the patients about their chances of recovery. Thus the patients, most of whom were dying, adjusted to the shrunken boundaries of their lives, and learned to live with this disease as if it were a companion. The question most often asked of the new doctor learning their charts and examining them was not "When will I get well?" but "How long do I have to live?"

At first I shook my head helplessly, not knowing what to say, wondering whether this was simply a cruel, macabre institutional joke used to haze the new staff. But finally I learned that it was a serious question, and was soon able to mention the unmentionable and talk to them directly about death.

Tuberculosis was commonly called consumption because it wasted the lungs and other tissues of the body. When so much lung tissue was destroyed that the patient could no longer gather sufficient oxygen to support life from normal respirations, the wealthier patients could buy a few months of life by purchasing oxygen. The cumbersome cylinder would be rolled to the bedside and the mask placed over the patient's nose and mouth. Instantly the heaving chest's stertorous attempts to breathe would be stilled, the agonized facies would relax, and pink would again suffuse the cheeks. Those unable to afford the oxygen would persist in their final agonies until they became unconscious, and soon died.

Sweet Ellen Price couldn't afford oxygen, and daily she found living more difficult. She had the full-cheeked baby face of a doll, and her blond hair fell in curly ringlets. She was afraid of the dark and at night we kept a light burning in the goose-necked lamp in one corner of her room. During the evening rounds she would grasp my hand and look up and ask, "Am I going to die tonight, Doctor?"

I wanted to say, "No, Ellen, not tonight. You'll never die, Ellen, you can't die, Ellen, because I love you." But all I did say was "No, Ellen, not tonight."

Each of my girls, as death approached, would fade into a pallid tableau of innocent angels surrounded by the cloud image of pillows and white sheets. It was not our practice to lacerate their veins with needles and cutdowns or to attempt any futile preser-

16

vation of life. We merely tucked them in and kissed them good-bye. I learned that from Ellen, because one night when she asked me the terrible question, I said, "Yes, Ellen, maybe tonight." And she said, "Tuck me in and kiss me good-bye, Doctor."

When Betty Ryan started to die, I became apoplectic with fright. She was hemorrhaging. The wise old nurses, noting my agitation, gave me a bucket of ice and an ice bag. "Place the ice on her chest, it will help, and give her some morphine. Sometimes the bleeding stops." They knew it wouldn't help Betty, but would calm me, give me something to do, allow me to appear as if I were helping to treat medically an untreatable condition.

Betty, older and more seasoned than the other patients, had been steeling herself to experience the anoxic death of wasted lung, and thus was quite aghast when one of her profound coughs brought blood welling into her mouth. When she spat it out to keep from strangling, it created a starburst splash of claret on her white bed cover, and by the time she got done plucking rubbery clots and mucus from her lips and mouth, her face had become a bloody mask. I brought an emesis basin to her bedside, and a wet towel to clean her face. The nurses rushed in with new bedsheets, and soon she was clean and cozy, except for the racking cough that kept producing blood. I placed the ice on her chest and stayed with her for hours as steadily she grew weaker. We would not postpone this by giving her blood transfusions, for there was no way we could stop the bleeding. Or so I was told. But when I approached with the needle of morphine, Betty raised her hand.

"Doctor, before you give me that, promise me that you won't let them do an autopsy. I promised my husband that I would come to him clean and unscarred."

"I promise, Betty."

"Thank you, Doctor." I gave her the morphine, and she became soporific. The bleeding continued inexorably, until, depleted, her breathing and heart slowed to a standstill, and her skin, before my eyes, whitened to the color of an embalmed corpse.

The patients unfortunately were sick, and the good gray nurses were there to serve and care for them. They showed no pity. They were never idle and eschewed no task. They dressed the most indelicate chore in scrupulous elegance. An enema was performed

17

in white gowns and rubber gloves, and with assistants, the leader quietly issuing crisp commands, while encouraging the patient to believe that an enema properly performed was one of the modern medical miracles. "There now, this will clear you out and you will be one hundred percent better. See if it doesn't do wonders."

They carried bedpans with the majesty of a courtier bearing a crown to a coronation. Temperatures were taken four times daily with the precision of a general inspecting his troops, and medications were handed out like medals, an award to each for being so good a patient. They turned the day into a sequence of expectations; chores became events the patients could look forward to. And when the doctor hove into view to make rounds, they announced his presence in hushed, respectful tones, and rallied to his side.

They were instantly attentive and respectful. They turned him into an invincible conqueror of dread diseases, not because they believed he was, but because they knew it was important for the patients to believe in him.

They kept a supply of fresh white coats for me and insisted I be spotless. They would interrupt what they were doing to straighten my tie. When I protested, they said, "If you fail to instill confidence in the patients, you have betrayed them."

One of them always accompanied me to every bedside, for they were unanimous in the belief that tuberculosis made all the young females wanton, and that I must be protected.

"It's the lack of oxygen, you know. Does funny things to their brains. They are young girls, after all."

The fire in the linen room one beautiful spring night brought thirty rugged handsome men to the hospital heralded by bells and sirens. They evacuated patients from the ward and one wing until the fire could be contained, and some of the girls, too frail to walk, were carried in the arms of the firemen to the safety of the street. They were placed on the grass of the small park that fronted the institution, while their heroes returned to extinguish the flames. Afterward, they were brought back to their beds the same way they had left, but now they snuggled against the manly chests of the burly firemen, and when they reached their beds, many had to be separated by the force of a flying wedge of nurses from their saviors, to whom they clung for dear life. For the girls it was a moment of dear life, and they giggled about it for days afterward, threatening to set more fires, it had been such fun.

When a pretty blond young R.N. joined their force, the nurses surrounded her like a gaggle of geese and took pains to introduce us. Her name was Tracey. I don't know whether it was her first name or last, but we developed a nodding acquaintance for several weeks. Then one night she came to me and asked whether I would examine her, that she had a severely malfunctioning rheumatic heart. I agreed, since it was inconceivable that a body so beautifully formed could conceal a damaged organ.

I signaled one of the nurses to come with us, but she lagged behind, and Tracey and I arrived at the examining room alone.

Tracey unfastened her blouse and lay supine on the examining table, then wriggled to unsnap her bra. Her chest heaved, with every heartbeat imparting a quivering motion to her breasts that made concentration difficult. But when I placed my hand on her chest, I knew she hadn't lied. The palpable rumbles were confirmed as murmurs by the stethoscope, and I became interested in the dynamics of her damaged heart.

"Would you like to fluoroscope me?" she asked. Indeed I would. We went to the fluoroscope room across the hall, and no sooner had I shut the door and turned on the red light than I felt her completely naked body pressed against me, her face turned up expectantly.

I struggled vainly to invoke the proscriptions of the Hippocratic Oath, when suddenly someone was calling my name right outside the door. "Here," I said, breaking her embrace and throwing some of her garments at her. "Put these around you and get behind that screen."

I turned on the fluoroscope and peered intently at the screen. "I'll be right out," I called professionally.

Her heart was indeed enlarged, but more horrifying was the occlusion of penetrating rays by a totally diseased upper lobe of her left lung. I snapped on the lights. She blinked in the brightness, pale and beautifully nude.

She stepped out from behind the screen and once again flung her arms around my neck. "Kiss me," she moaned. I held her close, averting my head.

"I can't," I said, "there's something wrong. You're sick."

19

"That heart's been that way all my life—"

"Not your heart, Tracey, your lungs. I think you have tuberculosis."

"Tuberculosis! What kind of a joke are you playing? What is it with you? Don't you like girls? Tell me nonsense like that! I wouldn't kiss you if you were the last man on earth."

"Tracey, for God's sake, listen to me. Your entire left upper lobe is black on fluoroscopy. You have to get an X-ray in the morning. You have to get sputum examinations. You have to go on sick leave."

"I'm not sick. I'm not going on sick leave."

"You have to, Tracey. You can't run around here with an open lesion. You'll reinfect any patient that is recuperating. You're a visiting plague." I came to a decision. "If you don't voluntarily go on sick leave, I'll report you."

That brought her to a standstill. "You bastard. You report me and I'll scream bloody murder, that you tried to rape me in the fluoroscopy room. And then when that X-ray shows you're wrong, they'll throw your sweet ass out of here."

She frightened me. "Please, Tracey, be reasonable. It's for your own good. If you are sick, the disease is well advanced. If you don't get treated, you'll be dead in a year. Volunteer for an X-ray first thing in the morning.

"Screw you," she said, running down the hall.

Two days later she still hadn't gone for an X-ray, so I reported her to the charge nurse. They ordered Tracey to take an X-ray, but she quit instead. I reflected that maybe the old nurses were correct about the libidinous effects of tuberculosis.

Some years later, while eating a quick lunch at a dingy café across from another hospital, a slim girl slipped suddenly into the booth beside me. I turned; it was Tracey. She peeled the left shoulder of her blouse down far enough to show me the mutilated remnants of her chest. "You were right, Harry. They did a thoracoplasty on me." She readjusted her blouse and, without another word, rose and left.

After the tuberculosis hospital I spent a month in pediatrics, then some time in surgery. Our class, parceled in small staggered groups, scattered to hospitals throughout the city. Each week a new schedule was posted on the bulletin board, then suddenly a clean page on which a single word appeared: "Graduation."

It ended suddenly, with little fanfare. Parents and relatives gathered happily in a large auditorium while we assembled in gown and mortarboard on stage. A judge, no less, welcomed us into the community of medicine, an eminent physician extolled our successful efforts to become physicians, the dean told how proud he was of this class in a speech that would be read again the following year. Then before descending to the podium to accept our diplomas and a cold handshake, we rose to recite the Hippocratic Oath.

I swear by Apollo, the Physician, and Aesculapius and Health and All-Heal and all the Gods and Goddesses that, according to my ability and judgment, I will keep this oath and stipulation:

To reckon him who taught me this art equally dear to me as my parents, and to share my substance with him and relieve his necessities if required: to regard his offspring as on the same footing with my own brothers, and to teach them this art if they should wish to learn it without fee or stipulation, and that by precept, lecture and every other mode of instruction. I will impart a knowledge of the art to my own sons and to those of my teachers and to disciples bound by a stipulation and oath, according to the law of medicine but to none others.

I will follow that method of treatment which, according to my ability and judgment, I consider for the benefit of my patients, and abstain from whatever is deleterious and mischievous. I will give no deadly medicine to anyone if asked, nor suggest any such counsel; furthermore, I will not give to a woman an instrument to produce abortion.

With purity and with holiness I will pass my life and practice my art. I will not cut a person who is suffering with a stone, but will leave this to be done by practitioners of this work. Into whatever houses I enter I will go into them for the benefit of the sick and will abstain from every voluntary act of mischief and corruption, and further from the seduction of females or males, bond or free.

Whatever, in connection with my professional practice, or not in connection with it, I may see or hear in the lives of men which ought not to be spoken abroad, I will not indulge, as reckoning that all such should be kept secret.

While I continue to keep this oath unviolated may it be granted to me to enjoy life and the practice of the art, respected by all men at all times but should I trespass and violate this oath may the reverse be my lot.

HIPPOCRATES 460–377 B.C.

I knew it well, memorized from the parchment copy Lapius had given me, lettered in Old English script, the first letters of each paragraph embossed in gold, and accompanied by a note that said: "Medicine is a great nation without boundaries. The caduceus is its emblem, the Hippocratic Oath its constitution."

4

THE INTERNS IN NEW STARCHED WHITES gathered in the auditorium. Shoulder-buttoned white cossack blouses draped over the belt line of starched white pants. These were covered by short single-breasted coats starched to cardboard consistency. We had drawn uniforms from the laundry that morning—two uniforms, as specified in the contract. We would supply our own white shoes and keep them clean. We would supply our white socks and underwear, but the hospital would launder them in conjunction with our uniforms. After each month of service we would pick up our paychecks, "$12.50" typed under the Great Seal of the City. Small private hospitals paid more in a month than the $150, plus room and board, that we would receive in a year, but they weren't The County. The County was legend. Every city has its County.

A doctor traveling in a foreign land, mute in the language of strangers, and deaf to the syntactical babel wrought by distance, would find instant sanctuary in any of the Counties of the world.

The stench alone would be like the aroma of a friendly kitchen, the grimy halls with their traffic of stretchers, the wards lined by white enameled beds, the single beam of sunlight probing these dingy rooms like a linear halo, all this a familiar chapel to a medical stranger in a distant land.

These hospitals are the funnels for the misery of the teeming cities; baskets collecting the mutilations dispatched by the guillotine of tragic events. Their admitting wards are bloody concentrations of fractures, stab wounds, bullet holes and coma; a colloquy of cries, moans, vituperations, gurgling breath sounds and the giggles of drunks. Young Jesuits scurrying to comfort the sick or pray for the dying, cops assigned to guard the criminals, eager crew-cut heroes from the district attorney's office, competed with doctors and nurses to be first at the bedside. Clinical material was the living legend of The County. One year of County experience taught more than thrice the time in a private hospital, in return for which a 90 percent loss of salary seemed a fair equation.

In the auditorium a group of eminent doctors sat in a semicircle on the stage. A microphone was centrally placed. The audience in unsoiled whites was like a layer of virgin snow in the age-stained hall. The reverse of graduation, which dispatched us, this convocation welcomed us into the world of medicine.

Seated on the stage, his black hair sprinkled with gray, his gray mustache sprinkled with black, hands folded across his ample belly, cheeks puffing slightly with each breath and with twin shafts of light ricocheting from his highly polished glasses, was S. Q. Lapius, M.D. That was how he signed his editorials as editor of the *Annals of Medicine*. But as Medical Director of The County, we learned, to avoid confusion, to think of him as Lapius. Except for Lapius, each of the other doctors on the stage wore long white coats, some with stethoscopes protruding from the pockets, each with a pencil light in the breast pocket.

Lapius moved to the fore. There was a gradual hush.

"Gentlemen, my name is Simon Quentin Lapius, and as Medical Director I want to welcome you to The County. You are privileged to be here, and we look forward to teaching and training you for the many productive years ahead. Your predecessors have fanned out into communities all over the nation and, by their prowess in medicine and success in its many specialties, have enhanced our reputation as a training ground for young doctors. You will be proud to have trained at The County, and no doubt, in the years ahead, we will point with pride and boast that we trained you here. On either side of me are seated the department heads, and I would like to introduce them to you. First, Dr. William Pier, Chief of Medicine."

Pier was tall and angular, with a lean, sparse frame. He had a high forehead and thin jutting nose. His lips were thin, the lower thrust forward. He walked lightly to the microphone.

"Welcome, gentlemen. Your next years will be arduous indeed. You are entering a profession which today has possibly just passed the crest of its popularity. It is not ordained that doctors will always be held in high esteem. As Ambrose Bierce said, a physician is one upon whom we set our hopes when ill and our dogs when well. Pliny the Elder was scathing in his criticisms of doctors, a trend reversed briefly by the triumphs of Galen. But in the sixteenth century the docs were in the trough again simply because they couldn't fool all of the sick all of the time. It is recorded that Louis XIII of France in a single year took 288 purges, 224 enemas and was bled on 42 occasions, which may have prompted Montaigne to say, 'I notice no man as soon sick or as late cured as the one who persists in a physician's care.' But medicine was rescued by the brilliant advances of the seventeenth, eighteenth and nineteenth centuries, prompting Whittier to cast the doctor in the hero's role:

> Smite down the dragons fell and strong,
> Whose breath is fever fire;
> No knight of fable or of song
> Encountered foes more dire.

Finally Martin Arrowsmith became legend, and there is no doubt in my mind that at least some of you in this audience were inspired to go into medicine after reading his famous story. Well, there will be no heroes at The County. It's just work and more work. Exhausting hours. You will lose more patients than you save. You will, I hope, become humble men, because here you will be tested in the service of medicine, and when you leave you will have learned what it takes to be a doctor, and to earn the respect of the community."

He sat down abruptly. "That's my kind of doctor," the man next to me whispered. I turned for the first time, to see a lean, ascetic, almost gaunt, face, with shell glasses, slim nose and hollow cheeks. His name, I later learned, when he introduced himself as my roommate, was Wilkie Rush.

A small man with the face and body of a Buddha strode to the microphone. His long white coat almost swept the floor. "My name is John Shaver, Chief of Surgery. In my department you'll save more than you'll lose. But it's a ball-breaking job. You are going to be awake for thirty-six hours out of every forty-eight, and then you'll be too tired to sleep. You will admit patients through the night. You will do your own blood counts and urines on all admissions. You'll be walking on your knees by the time the night is over—right to the operating theater, where you will assist at surgery for eight hours or so. You will be physically tested, gentlemen. We will be certain when you leave here that you have the physical stamina to meet the challenge of medicine. You will know, gentlemen, that you can go without sleep days at a time and still do a creditable job. If you can't learn that, you won't survive our service. We'll cut you," he drew his finger across his throat, "but if you survive, you'll thank us for it. That's all I have to say."

The next speaker arose.

"I'm Dr. Andrew McCrae, head of obstetrics and gynecology. You each will have delivered about one hundred babies into this world by the time your three-month service with us ends. The deliveries will occur mainly at night, possibly because, as someone said, it takes exactly nine months to make a baby. You will be supervised by your resident. When it's time for a delivery, don't call us, we'll call you. It is an arduous service. But very rewarding. You are assisting the last stages of the most noble of God's creations, the birth of a baby. I look forward to meeting each of you, and hope you enjoy your County experience. The next doctor you will meet is Dr. Bernard Caspar, the director of pathology."

Dr. Caspar walked to the microphone. He was smiling. "Welcome. Pathology is a quiet service." He paused to allow the ripple of laughter to subside. "There is little night duty and few emergencies. After listening to my colleagues, we are not sure in what condition you will reach the morgue. Hopefully you will not be too tired to help us with our chores. We hope that pathology service will enable you to consolidate the knowledge you have gained in medicine, surgery and obstetrics-gynecology. It is a studious service, a contemplative service and a funny service, because here is where you have the last laugh. In pathology we will show you the misdiagnosed coronaries, the surgical errors and the botched deliveries. We don't have too many of this sort of thing at The County, but it is the threat of exposure that keeps my colleagues on their toes, and minimizes the incidence of medical error."

Lapius dug his hands into his coat pockets and rocked slowly.

"Gentlemen, not too long ago, the doctors to the right and left of me sat where you sit now, listening to attending physicians welcome them. They felt, as you do now, like members of the Light Brigade, being welcomed into the valley of death. For Willie Pier, Johnnie Shaver, Andy McCrae, Bernie Caspar were awed by The County, and intimidated by their responsibilities, until, that is, they started to work. That is when the range and depth of The County's experience become apparent. The County offers you medical experience at an alarming rate. But experience is the memory of error. As Da Costa said, 'What we call experience is often a dreadful list of ghastly mistakes.' It is sad but true that your experience will be gained at the expense of the patients who will flock here in the year ahead. Your careers will thrive on their misery. If you understand this, you won't resent the long hours, the scoldings, the sleepless nights, but rather accept them with grace as tokens of the privilege to serve. Overcome by exhaustion, you will be asked to rise again and again to the occasion of human need. Doctors who learn to accept this as a mission rather than a chore become physicians. I could say much more, but in deference to my colleagues, Dr. Pier, Dr. Shaver, Dr. McCrae and Dr. Caspar, all of whom are accustomed to having the last word, I will restrain myself. Gentlemen, you will meet your residents on the respective wards at 7 A.M."

Suddenly the beginning had ended.

Rush, my roommate, and I were up at six, and by 6:45 had toileted, dressed and breakfasted on scrambled eggs, bacon and coffee. We walked slowly through the hospital grounds, along a stone path that led from the house-staff quarters to the main hospital building, past the ramshackle psychiatric unit, the

27

morgue, a balconied four-story building for skin and cancer that dealt mainly with venereal disease. We entered the main pavilion through the emergency area, its halls heavily trafficked by orderlies pushing stretchers, and nurses hustling with intravenous solutions, with young doctors following in their wake. The walls, ceilings, uniforms, blankets and sheets were a monotony of white relieved only by the cop in blue and the Jesuit in black. We strode briskly, as doctors should, into the barren halls that separated the three pavilion wings of the building, heading for the surgical wards. A large, fleshy man with a pulpy nose and soft features, his hair parted in the center and combed back slickly on each side, stopped us at the nurses' station. "Hi. My name is Paul Cushing. I'm the resident on surgery. You'll be working for me."

We introduced ourselves and shook hands. "We meet at 7 A.M. daily except Sunday for ward rounds. Then you two will alternate on the following schedule. Eight A.M. in the operating room. We do five or six cases daily, and you'll be finished by about 3 P.M. Grab a quick bite and follow your patients back to the wards, scan the orders and make necessary corrections or additions. Then you will admit patients from the receiving ward till the following morning. New admissions will be completely worked up. When indicated, traction and casts will be applied immediately. If you get a chance, grab an hour's sleep. There are beds in the residents' quarters of this building reserved for you so you won't have to trek back and forth to the interns' building. The following morning you will meet for rounds at seven, and spend the remainder of the day doing procedures assigned during rounds. If you're lucky, you should be finished by five, free till morning. Essentially, you're on your feet thirty-six hours and off twelve."

After rounds, Rush and I flipped a coin. He went to the OR and I remained on the ward. That was how it began.

The wards at The County had windows on three exposures to trap as much yellow light as possible from the rotating sun. This compensated in part for the paint that peeled from the walls.

Thirty, forty, sometimes sixty patients were aligned in a single barnlike room, the beds scarcely three feet apart when the census was low. A small dressing table in scuffed enamel stood at bedside. Privacy consisted of bedclothes and a bedside curtain. It was a collegium of the sick, a cooperative of illness. The patients kept an eye on each other, and the ambulatory were neither too proud to fetch a bedpan to a bedridden compatriot nor too vain to carry it away and dispose of the contents. There were never enough nurses or orderlies, especially in the night. Then, in the dark and eerie silence, the tunneled corridors, cavernous and brooding in the soft glow of a solitary yellow bulb, shadowy figures of patients attending each other would glide to and fro between the ward and the utility room. There were always one or two watchdogs among the patients, husky, physical men defying the strangeness of their incapacity by assuming responsibilities they were not assigned. "Nurse, get the doc. Shimkin's stump is bleeding." "Nurse, Kelly is vomiting. It stinks in here." Bedpans materialized and doctors gathered.

Where today is this surveillance? Who watches over these prisoners in the darkness, who governs their suffering, who sees when they beckon, who scurries when they call? Today, if well enough, the patient presses a button and somewhere a light flashes. The nurse sits at a large console pressing buttons that activate an intercom.

"Do you need a sleeping pill tonight, Mr. Jones?"

"Do you need a laxative tonight, Mr. Swenson?"

If she presses the wrong button, some unsuspecting patient will get an enema.

The wards were training grounds for good, sometimes great, doctors. The system was disciplined according to a hierarchy of training. The attending physicians, unpaid for this service, demanded skill, and the contrary qualities of independence and subservience from their residents. They demanded loyalty to the patients, without which they couldn't accept the final responsibility.

The County was not genteel. The agony clashed with the smell of assorted pathology. To blood, sweat, toil and tears could be added pain, misery, piss and shit.

I saw Rush on rounds, and occasionally in the dining room, where he consumed pitchers of milk. After the first week I noticed that he walked slightly bent over and during rounds usually leaned against a bed, massaging his stomach lightly whenever he had a free hand.

"Wilkie. What's with the hand?"

29

"Nothing."

"What's with all the milk?"

"I like milk." But he was clearly uncomfortable. He had ulcers. "They never proved anything on X-ray beyond an irritable duodenal cap, but the doctor says I have an ulcer and it sure feels like one."

"Did you go through medical school holding your stomach?"

"No, but I was getting more rest, and able to take antacids more regularly. Here I don't even get a chance to piss. But it will be easier after I get off this service."

Wilkie was intent, sincere and reserved. He smiled a lot, possibly to cover his pain, and he worried constantly about his patients, which induced more pain.

Cushing was slightly gruff, because he thought that's what surgeons are supposed to be, but direct, honest and gentle. On a bad day when Wilkie was belching a lot Cushing would excuse him from duty and do the ward chores himself. The knowledge that he had this leeway made the service possible for Rush, and helped ease his pain. He swore undying fealty to Cushing. As a matter of fact, after about two weeks each of us would have done straight duty without sleep for as long as Cushing wanted. Rush and I talked it over at lunch one day, separated as always by a pitcher of milk. By this time we had become accustomed to fatigue and could gauge our reactions to it. We figured that we could probably do ninety-six hours straight without collapsing, and be fresh and on our feet again after twelve hours' sleep. Particularly if we were third assist in the OR, because we had already experienced the gaseous mesmeric experience of falling asleep on our feet during surgery, and had been amazed at how refreshing the cat naps had been. Cushing would nudge us when he saw it happen, because if Shaver noticed first he rapped our knuckles with whatever instrument he had in hand.

Interns were lowest rank at the operating table, certainly several rungs below the instrument nurse. They were consigned to hold the retractors, metal bars bent into the shape of an "L," that were designed to retract the incised body wall to expose the area for surgical intervention. The intern was generally excluded from the cordon of white-robed Klan-like figures clustered about the wound, and relegated to a distance that for practical purposes could be no more than an arm's length away. Of course during simple surgery when he was one of two or three doctors who performed the operation, he stood over the incision and had a bird's-eye view. But in complex procedures, when the space about the draped unconscious patient was occupied by five or six doctors, a wall of backs and shoulders barred his view, and only his arm extended through the white phalanx to grip the retractor.

The idea was to apply precisely that degree of tension to the wound that the surgeon wanted. If you didn't pull enough, the wound was too narrow; if you pulled too hard, the other sides of the wound collapsed on the operating field. Mistakes were punished by a sharp rap on the knuckles, particularly by Shaver.

"A little retraction, Doctor." Rap.

"You're pulling too hard, Doctor." Rap.

Shaver played my knuckles like a xylophone. Once, when we had a patient under spinal anesthesia and he was trying to find a bleeder deep in the belly, he became frenzied. "Come on, dammit. Pull that goddamn retractor. I can't see what I'm doing here. Nononono. You're pulling too hard for Chrissake, you'll rupture his spleen. What kind of idiots are they sending me this year? I want doctors, not idiots, goddamn it."

The patient, fully awake, spoke to me from beneath the anesthetist's canopy. "Please, Doctor," he implored hoarsely, "please, why don't you do like Dr. Shaver wants?"

Although Wilkie was more compliant than I, less rebellious, and occasionally a little obsequious, our knuckles were equally bruised. When Shaver performed the schedule (the most complex cases were put aside for Shaver, who devoted one day of the week for surgery at The County), Wilkie fortified himself with medications before entering the theater; when it was my turn, I prayed that I wouldn't faint dead away. The heat, blood and tension were torment enough, but when combined with the frustration of not being able to respond to the endless series of insults with which Shaver persistently bullied me (although he called it hazing, a test of my will and discipline), my heart would pound in seemingly futile efforts to counteract some visceral force that tried to drain blood from my brain. The room would become cloudy, my vision darkened by the transformation of smooth images into dotted halftones, and I would let my knees go slack, breathe rapidly, stomp with my right foot on my left to stimulate enough vascular tone to stay vertical.

Although Shaver was an exquisite surgeon, his sideshow was distracting. Surgery with him was an adversary action instead of a team effort. We resented the insinuation that he didn't need us, that he could always scrape together some johns to hold the instruments for him while he performed. We resented the surplus of dexterity and talent that allowed him to perform these remarkable tasks without expending his entire prowess. He was like a weight lifter who presses several hundred pounds to a world record while munching a peanut butter sandwich. Bombast was part of his technique, but by belittling his assistants he demeaned his patient and the profession of surgery as well. As great as he was, he could have been greater.

Lapius and I maintained a formal relationship circumscribed by the boundaries of The County. Outside we were friends.

"Well, Harry, how goes it in the world of medicine, or should I say surgery?" Simon Quentin Lapius leaned back in his chair and plugged his thumbs into the small pockets of his yellow plaid vest. He peered at me through the gold-rimmed spectacles that perched at the bulbous end of his nose. The crystal-clear lenses magnified his eyes to owl proportions. He lifted the glass of Chianti in silent salute, then sipped and set it down.

"It's hard work," I said.

"Do you like it?"

"I guess I do." I was yawning.

"Harry, I will interpret the yawn as a manifestation of fatigue, not boredom. But to be a doctor you must be more enthusiastic. It is not enough to like medicine. Medicine must be your passion. You must live medicine night and day; permit her to intrude into your dreams, and, in quiet moments, court her. You must awaken each morning yearning for her challenge, exhilarated by your successes, stimulated by the insoluble cases and frustrated by your failures. I say 'she,' Harry, because medicine will be your constant mistress."

Lapius paused for breath before pronging some curried chicken into his mouth with adroitly manipulated chopsticks. This was the only Chinese restaurant in town that served Chianti, and only to S. Q. Lapius and his guests because he had prevailed on Wong to keep a bottle for him in the pantry.

Once a week, on Monday, Spinelli's across the street delivered a quart of the stuff. It came over in milk bottles. The silver carafe in which it was served was a gift to Wong from Lapius, as were the ivory chopsticks Lapius used. "The wooden ones are washed after each meal, Harry. I'm not sure wood can be properly cleaned."

It must have been the combination of wine and fatigue, or perhaps just the fatigue alone. Suddenly the meal became lost in the fugue of sleep, which was terminated by a rap on the knuckles. "You sonofabitch," I said under my breath. "If you ever do that again, I'll kick you right in the balls."

Suddenly my shoulders were grasped in a vise grip and I was being shaken back and forth. I opened my eyes expecting to confront an opened abdomen ringed with steel and rubber-gloved hands, but the only flash of light I saw was reflected from the silver decanter and the unused knives and spoons on the table. "Wake up, Harry, what's wrong? Wake up." It was Lapius, standing, leaning across the table and shaking me.

"Sorry, Simon, I dozed off. When you rapped my knuckles with those damned chopsticks of yours, I thought it was Shaver banging me in the operating room. Someday, if he pulls that crap any more, I swear I'll clout him."

"Calm yourself, my boy. At least pretend to eat something. Not to eat would constitute an insult to Wong from which he would derive centuries of despair. You wouldn't want that on your conscience, would you?"

"Perish forbid," I said, digging into some delicacy that failed to arouse a shimmer of pleasure from my dormant taste buds.

Lapius was chuckling. "Shaver perpetuates the timeworn surgical pecking order."

"I don't know what it is with that guy. He's a sadistic sonofabitch. We can operate all week with Cushing and it's a pleasure, but Shaver comes in and the place congeals with tension. He has these idiot assistants of his who follow him around all the time—Farkas and Kiyler. As soon as we are lined up at the scrub sinks, Shaver starts off with a lecture on the proper procedure for scrubbing. First, soap the hands under warm water, till the nails become softened. Then take an orange stick and clean the dirt from under the nails. This must be done before the scrub, which will carry away bits of debris that we miss. Then three minutes on the back of the hand and three minutes on the palms, then up the forearms halfway to the elbows. Then throw the brush away, take a new one, and thirty seconds between each finger. Look at my hands, chapped, raw. Another month of this and I'll need a skin graft.

"Then while this is going on he starts humming snatches from operas and symphonies, except he sings unrecognizably. 'All right, Farkas. What was that I was humming?' Everyone takes a stab at it. If someone gets it, he goes to another tune. If we miss it, he lectures us on our ignorance, and extols the virtue of culture. He keeps talking while we go to the operating room, drape the patient and perform the surgery. I used to think he was crucifying Farkas and Kiyler, but actually he was teaching them, because when Shaver is out and either of them takes his place we go through the same nonsense."

"But he is a good surgeon," Lapius prodded.

"Fantastic—he could operate with his eyes closed. If he could shut his mouth as well, he'd be better."

"I'm glad you've had that experience, Harry. Shaver is an example of a school of surgeons trained by example to dominate and domineer. They will die out, hopefully to be replaced by the Cushings, quiet, confident, competent. But right now surgeons are a breed apart. They are tense, brusque, gruff. Shaver was always sweating, and always willing to work. Just think of the tension of their jobs, Harry. Day after day on their feet for eight-hour stretches, knowing that one false move could invite catastrophe. Men like Shaver assume that they are irreplaceable, that all depends on their presence, and so force themselves beyond endurance. They become bombastic bullies to mask their fears. Actually, when he's telling you to be alert, he's reminding himself to be alert. Shaver himself was subjected to a worse hazing than he inflicts on you. One time when he was operating with a particular surgeon, humiliated by verbal and physical abuse, he lost control. When the surgeon asked for a hemostat to stanch bleeding deep in the belly, Shaver hung the clamp on the surgeon's finger and locked it. The surgeon squealed in anguish, and cursed Shaver. Shaver said, 'I'm sorry, sir, but you had me so unnerved I misjudged the distance between your finger and the artery.' That surgeon was out of commission for four months, and no one bothered Shaver much after that.

"But finally he overstepped the bounds. His arrogance became unlimited as he rose through the ranks. Once, as a young chief, he was scheduled to do a breast biopsy. The patient had small breasts and the mass was large, so he figured he would do a simple mastectomy, and if the lesion was malignant go ahead and do a radical. But the pathologist was late. Shaver was fuming. The patient was under anesthesia. He and his assistants were forced to wait with their hands folded on the surgical drapes. When finally the pathologist sauntered into the OR, Shaver exploded. He grabbed the breast from the pan and flung it at the pathologist, struck him right in the face. That caused a flap. Cost Shaver his privileges at that hospital."

"Lucky he didn't get shot."

"In his written report of the incident the pathologist said that it only went to prove that surgeons had no respect for tissues, and passed it off finally as a titillating experience."

We had long since finished the meal, the Chianti, and Lapius had emptied the teapot. We were ready to leave. Wong approached the table and smiled. Lapius smiled back, and we departed. No bill was presented, no money changed hands.

"Is anyone expected to pay for this meal?" I asked.

"Oh," Lapius assured me, "I already paid him."

"With what?"

"With a smile."

Nurse Agnes Gibson dominated the emergency ward. That is somewhat inaccurate. The ward was dominated by disease, trauma, hemorrhage and death, but Gibson dominated the traffic flow. She moved continually. New patients off the ambulances were routed into receiving wards, as soon as a bed was available. Until then they lay on stretchers in the hall, and Gibson would march past, talking briefly to those who were conscious, starting intravenous glucose and water on the comatose or shocky patients to ensure a patent vein. She directed interns to the neediest. It was worst come first served. The receiving ward accepted patients in every specialty. Interns rotating through different services found their charts on wall bins labeled "Medicine," "Surgery," "Gynecology," "Neurosurgery," and worked individually on their patients in a common ward. Family and friends of the ill sat long hours on wooden benches waiting for word.

Admitting during the day wasn't too bad because there was a

lot of help. But in the evening we were suddenly alone, under yellow lights that brightened the blood. Shadows danced on the walls, and unused corners receded into darkness. By then our starched whites were moist and chafed the crotch with each of the endless steps, as we paraded from patient to patient until morning. Each patient required a written history and physical examination, and then, since there were no technicians, the intern did a white-cell count, a red-cell count and hemoglobin in the musty closet of a laboratory that smelled of piss and chemicals. Wooden workbenches were mottled by coalescent stains, relics that measured the age of The County. A Bunsen burner was attached to a gas cock by rotting tubing from which sweet-smelling gas escaped. Urine was boiled gently over the caress of the flame to search for the cloud that denoted protein. Test tubes cracked in the heat. Half asleep, the intern would pour more urine into another tube and start again to heat the tube oh so slowly to prevent another accident. Exhaustion bade him hurry. A centrifuge spun on uncertain bearings to force some urinary sediment to the bottom of the tube for microscopic examination. The intern's back was aching because all that day and half the night he had been, for most of his working moments, half-bent over a bed, a stretcher, a lab bench, suspended by muscles becoming spastic in rebellion. Daily under stresses we couldn't have imagined and really don't care to recall, we learned that the limits of our endurance had not yet been defined.

If preliminary examinations and tests failed to demonstrate a satisfactory working diagnosis for those in shock or coma, Gibson would set out the instrument trays, ready at bedside, to which we would return to do a spinal tap. Male orderlies would gather, turn the patient on his side and bend him double, knees to head, while we would scrub the skin at the puncture site and paint it with colored antiseptics, drape the patient with sterile cloths to frame the small foramen through which we would plunge the spinal needle. The small window of skin would be painted again and the long tubular dagger inserted, hopefully into the minute box canyon formed by articulating bony arches of the vertebral column.

For some reason fatigue never intervened during such a procedure, perhaps because we performed it sitting down, or perhaps because of the excitement of the search and the challenge to our dexterity. The needle, when misdirected, would scrape sickeningly on the bone, the gritty vibration transmitted to the rubbergloved hand. Then the needle would be withdrawn to just beneath the surface of the skin and redirected. The misleading dimensionalism of a jackknifed patient skewered our aim, and at first we worried lest we plunge too deeply in quest of the hidden space and pierce a vital organ. Eventually we were rewarded by that pulpy feeling when the needle has been thrust its proper length, and would withdraw the stylette slowly to permit the escape of a single drop of cerebrospinal fluid. Then the manometer was attached, pressures measured, and extra fluid collected in three tubes for microscopic, chemical and bacteriological examination. At four o'clock of any morning the true prize was a collection of the clearest, most sparkling watery fluid that can be imagined, because then we knew that meningitis could be ruled out, and that we could not have been contaminated by some infected spittle.

The thread of life is spun of timing and coincidence. One morning, early, I had a fractured hip to work up. Jack Doyle in the adjacent bed, his head swathed in bandages, watched intently, and asked a host of questions. I responded rudely in monosyllables to discourage the interruptions and put an end to the distractions, but he persisted. I called Gibson for a temporary traction, and pointing over my shoulder asked, "Is that character mine too?"

"No. Head injury. He's for the neurosurgeons."

"Where the hell are they?"

"They're coming."

Gradually, as I labored over the Thomas splint trying to recall the twists and turns of the hitch round the ankle to apply the proper traction, I realized that Jack Doyle was still talking, but his voice was weak, his mind wandered, he left sentences incomplete. I turned and saw a spreading stain, blood seeping through the bandages in the region of the left temple.

I stopped what I was doing, disregarding my patient, who groaned as soon as his heavy thigh muscles contracted into the spasm of injury, and grabbed a sphygmomanometer. Balancing it precariously on the bed, I took a blood pressure from the now clammy arm of Jack Doyle, who was quickly turning yellow white. His heart was racing, his pressure almost inaudible. I cut the bandages from his head, shouting for help. An orderly rolled up an emergency cart. As the last blood-drenched gauze was removed, thin jets of bright blood shot across the room from the jagged edges of a torn temporal artery. It was no trick to grab the bleeder with a hemostat, and turn the crisis back to an emergency. I don't remember whether he had to be transfused or not. But I do know that, had he not been in the very next bed, he would have slowly slithered into bloodless coma and died.

Of course not all nights were jammed. Occasionally somewhere between 2 and 5 A.M. there would be time to walk the chafing length of lonely corridors to a small room with four undesignated cots, and, fully clothed, fall onto one of them. A physiological redistribution of body fluids occurs during sleep, which causes sweat to flow. Normally the moisture dries, but the abrupt reveilles we suffered after an hour or perhaps two of drugged sleep caused us to waken chilled by the damp sweat that clung to our skin. We often stayed awake to avoid the discomfort of aborted slumber.

The hospital census was always high, and after crannies in the halls were filled with beds, the patient load backed up to the emergency room, which then became a holding area as well.

One night I had five patients there. One a fracture, another in the Trendelenberg position and morphinized in the hope that a strangulated hernia would be able to slip back through the compressing rings of body wall early enough to avoid surgery. A third was a hot belly, waiting for a possible trip to the OR; another a sprained wrist waiting for X-rays; and, finally, Carney with a crushed hand. He had been on his way to fetch his wife a loaf of bread when his car was struck amidships and rolled over on its side. Carney would have been unhurt except for his habit of driving with his left elbow on the window sill, his hand caressing the drain on the car roof. When the car fell on its side, it crushed Carney's hand.

I called Cushing. He came down quickly. He would become punitive if you delayed calling him for a case that required his attention.

"Always give the patient the benefit of doubt," he would say, "which means the benefit of my presence. Right?"

"Right."

Cushing lifted the vaseline dressings carefully and shook his head. We took Carney to the OR and with one blow sheared the hand from index finger to the opposite side of his palm. The bloody remnant fell into a pail. We had been clever. We had saved his apposition. He would still be able to hold things in that hand, with thumb and forefinger, the only digits he had left.

A Carney today would have reparative surgery by residents and their chiefs, dealing laboriously with the problem of hooking up appropriate tendon fragments and anastamosing minute arteries and veins. Powerful microscopes would help them suture millimeter fragments of blood vessels with threads too fine to visualize with the naked eye. But Carney took that drive just fifteen years too soon.

Miller, the surveyor, was another case in point. One morning at dawn he was working a lonely city street, peering through his transit, measuring angles and estimating planes. So intense was his concentration that Miller failed to see or even hear a lumbering oil truck backing toward him. Suddenly he was lying on the ground injured.

At the hospital he was labeled a crush injury. He was alert, quite wide-awake when I saw him. "I didn't even hear it, Doc," he said. He was free of pain, and thus I was ill-prepared for the shambles that greeted me when I lifted the blankets and sheets that covered his lower half. The pelvis was crushed, the abdominal wall exploded by pressure, the bladder hung over the pelvic brim, the bowel was disgorged, ruptured, feces spread through the wound, and his penis lay athwart his thigh.

The priest arrived. "Are you a Catholic, Mr. Miller?"

"No Father, I'm not." The priest left.

We applied a blood-pressure cuff to Miller's arm. An intravenous was started and morphine administered. He continued talking about the mystery of the accident, unaware of the extent of his morbid wounds. He lost blood slowly and inexorably from seepage, and we didn't bother to replace it because none of us at that time was prepared mentally, or by equipment, or by precedent, to put him back together again. He fell asleep and died in calm repose.

Scarcely ten years later a small boy in Sandusky, Ohio, was crushed by a boulder that rolled off a hill to pin him in a gulley. He was flown by helicopter to a nearby hospital and rushed to the operating room, with blood and plasma expanders coursing into all his veins. He was positioned in such a way as to relieve pressure on important arteries and veins going to his legs. Plastic tubes of various diameters were used to connect fragmented channels, such as ureters and urethras. Vessels were spliced by sure-handed surgeons educated to refined techniques which but a few years before had been the province of only a few of the great surgical centers. The little boy recovered after fourteen months of hospitalization. He was reconstructed month after month, system by system, by urologists, neurosurgeons, orthopods, plastic surgeons and general surgeons. In contrast my internship was a cave, I a caveman.

Miller died at noon. I tried to conjure images, a summer day, snowcapped mountains, redolent pines, the call of wild birds, to substitute for the sights, smells, sounds and other memory traces of Miller. I sought a scouring fantasy to shear the cottony threads that bound me to compassion.

Lunch seemed irrelevant. The priest joined me. He spoke loudly enough to be heard above the clatter and hubbub of the dining hall.

"He was a Catholic, that man. It said so on the admission sheet."

"I guess he wasn't a practicing Catholic."

"Even so, I should have given him last rites."

"But he said he wasn't a Catholic. Maybe they made a mistake."

"No. A Catholic wouldn't take chances like that. Something's wrong."

"Incidentally, Father, we haven't really met." I introduced myself. "Call me Harry," I said.

"My name is Delgado."

"Any special order?"

"Jesuit."

"What's your first name, Father?"

"Jesus."

"Great name for a Jesuit."

"Isn't it?" he agreed. "Call me Hesu; it avoids confusion."

After dinner I went back to emergency. Miller's wife was there waiting to speak with me, a spare woman with pale cheeks, moist from tears. "Did he suffer?" she asked.

"No, he didn't." I reassured her that Miller had felt no pain and erased the image of gore by telling her he died of internal injuries. "He didn't even know he was dying. The priest came over and wanted to give him last rites, but your husband said he wasn't a Catholic."

"He wasn't."

"But he wore a medal."

"He wore it for me. I'm Catholic."

The days fused, not into the checkerboard of nights and days that young lovers, intoxicated with the existentialism of Omar, quote to each other, but as a wrinkled gray surface of continuing labor.

Kummerman came in blowing foam all over the place, obvious pulmonary edema. I was busy as hell.

"Gibson. What's this guy doing on surgery? He's a medical case."

"History of head injury," she called back, reading her memory. "The medical resident says that takes precedence over his medical condition. He's yours."

"How about the neurosurgeon?"

"They're busy. Besides, it's really medical. You know that." I ordered a phlebotomy set and some positive pressure.

Kummerman was thin, gaunt, elderly and, at the moment, his skin was as gray as his hair. His blood pressure was way up, 240/160, and there was a small unimportant gash on the side of his head. Apparently he had fallen. But if we didn't take care of the acute pulmonary edema, neither the scalp problem nor the concussion, if indeed he had one, would require investigation.

He lay propped in the orthopneic position, that is, sitting in bed, the back half of which had been cranked up to about eighty degrees. His hair, the sheets that partially covered him, and the wrinkled, wet hospital gown with the torn tie cords had the disheveled look of catastrophe. He puffed rapidly, unable to satisfy his air hunger. His heart was racing. Gibson moved to bedside with the needle and vacuum bottle as I started to probe for one of the sliding bulging veins on his thin arm. The oxygen tank with positive pressure bag was rolled to the head of the bed by an orderly. I found the vein, and Gibson connected the vacuum bottle, which sucked a steady stream of his blood through the tubing, thus relieving the damned blood that engorged the veins of his lung.

Suddenly Father Delgado wedged himself in at bedside with his Bible and beads and other Catholic accouterments.

"What the hell are you doing, Father? You're in my way."

"Administering last rites."

"He's a Jew. His name is Kummerman."

"I'll administer first and ask afterward. I've been fooled before."

"Listen, Hesu! If we don't work fast, there won't be anyone to administer last rites to. Why don't you help out? We're short-handed. Then after we're finished, you can administer last rites—I promise."

"What do you want me to do?"

"Squeeze the pressure bag attached to the oxygen mask. Every time he draws a breath, squeeze the bag. Not too hard. The idea is that hopefully the pressure you provide will help force the fluid in his lungs back to the blood stream."

"Okay." He couldn't reach, so he jumped on the bed, muttering prayers and imprecations at the same time, and started to squeeze the bag. Meanwhile Gibson had given Kummerman one-quarter grain morphine intravenously. Nurses weren't supposed to do that, but Gibson had had plenty of practice doing things she wasn't supposed to do, which is why the emergency room at The County was so efficient.

I listened to Kummerman's chest with a stethoscope—still bubbly but improving. His respiratory rate had dropped from about forty-five a minute to thirty-six. The vacuum bottle was filled with a pint of blood, the morphine was taking effect, and Father Delgado was still crouched on the bed pumping the bag. He was as short of breath as Kummerman. Suddenly the crisis was over. The chest was almost dry except for moisture at the bases, and Kummerman, drowsy, murmured, "I feel better."

"Okay, Father, you can get down now," I said. Delgado crawled backward to the edge of the bed and let himself down, then started fumbling with his beads.

Kummerman, seeing collar and cloth for the first time, said, "What's he doing here?"

"Nothing now. He's a doctor, too. He helped save your life. Now he'd like to save your soul."

Kummerman appeared relieved. "I thought he was the malech-hamovess."

"What's that?" Delgado asked.

"The angel of death, Hesu, the angel of death."

Hesu started to walk away. "He doesn't want last rites."

"More important, Hesu, thanks in part to you, he doesn't need last rites."

"We all need them, Harry. But promise me one thing, will you? Next time I go first. You owe me one."

"Where are you going now?"

"To find me a Catholic." Delgado started walking from bed to bed.

I called Gibson. "Kummerman is okay now. Transfer him to medicine."

The man in the next bed had abdominal cramps. He had tenesmus, that dreadful sensation characterized by a continuing desire to defecate. I worked him up quickly, while trying to keep an eye on Kummerman. Finally I did a rectal examination, an earthy maneuver, performed by inserting a finger, dressed completely, we hoped, in a finger cot of rubber, as deeply into the rectum of the patient as possible. I encountered a stony, hard, nodular mass. There was blood on the cot when I withdrew my finger.

"I think it's bad," the patient said. "Oh, Doctor, I am frightened."

I sought Delgado. "I have a patient who is scared," I said.

"Is he Catholic?" Delgado asked.

"What difference does it make? Comfort him."

Delgado returned fifteen minutes later. "You found me a Catholic," he said triumphantly.

"See what you can discover through a rectal examination," I said. Delgado laughed, then frowned.

I was drinking coffee in the laboratory when Gibson ferreted me out. "Hilbert won't take Kummerman on medicine," she said curtly.

Hilbert was chief resident of the male medical service.

"What do you mean, he won't take him? Kummerman is not a surgical case."

43

"It doesn't matter, we're sending him up to the surgical ward."

"To hell with that noise. I'm not cluttering the ward with the Kummermans of the world. He'll be there for weeks, taking a good surgical bed. I'm going to call Hilbert."

"I wouldn't," Gibson said.

"Why not?"

"Interns speak only to interns and residents speak only to residents. Hilbert speaks only to Pier, but he might listen to Cushing."

"Christ, I'm not going to wake Cushing for this. He needs his sleep."

"If you want him to sleep, you better not call Hilbert either, because if you fuss with him, he'll call Cushing to complain. I'm sending him up to surgery."

The next morning on rounds I explained to Cushing how Kummerman got to the ward.

"He came in an emergency, and frankly I didn't take time to find the medical intern. He was blowing bubbles. I thought he would go out on us." Then I told him about Hilbert, and said, "Maybe if you spoke to him?"

Cushing nodded, and bent over almost double to talk to Kummerman, who was bright-eyed but still weak. "How do you feel this morning?"

"How should I feel?"

"A little short of breath."

"Why not? Look what I been through." Cushing nodded, and percussed his chest, listened to the lung bases through the stethoscope, estimated heart size by palpation, and probed for an enlarged liver and spleen. "Get me a finger cot." I passed one from the instrument cart, and he rolled the miniature condom onto his forefinger and did a rectal examination. Satisfied, he discarded the cot and examined the peripheral pulses, checked out the reflexes.

"Let's keep him here," Cushing said. "You'll be all right," he told Kummerman.

Kummerman, more fastidious with each succeeding level of consciousness, when fully alert became elegant. His nose curved prominently. His face was etched with the wisdom of the prophets. He spoke slowly, commandingly, even when he answered searching questions posed by doctors on rounds. His voice

44

was deep and resonant, his words accentuated by broad sweeps of his arms. He offered suggestions about the possibility of increasing the comfort of sick patients adjacent to him. When we asked him how he felt each morning, he paused for a moment as he searched his sensory registers, and then answered directly, with perception. He listed the categories of things that had improved and those that hadn't.

Then one morning, when we put the question to him, he said, simply, "Fine." He had fully recovered. We started to ambulate him slowly.

He spent the next several days out of bed. He had managed to find a shirt, and wore it tucked into his pajama bottoms beneath his robe. The collar was secured with a black shoestring bow tie. He wore an elegant smoking jacket as he helped with the trays, or to make a bed, or to assist another patient to walk. The day we discharged him, he said good-bye to each of us gently and with feeling. His eyes were moist. We were sorry to see him go. He lent a touch of class to the place.

He was dressed in threadbare splendor, his seedy clothes pressed and clean. But ten minutes after he had left us he was back.

"What's the trouble, Kummerman?"

"It's raining out."

"So take a taxi."

"I can't."

"Why not?"

"I don't have any money."

We decided to keep him for another day, and resolved that, rain or shine, Kummerman would ride home in the style to which he should have been accustomed. Nurses, doctors, orderlies contributed coins from the meager dole of hospital salaries, until ten dollars had been collected, enough for taxi fare and subsistence for a day or two.

The next morning, another round of emotional good-byes. We gave Kummerman the money and he again departed. Ten minutes later he was back up.

"What happened this time?" we asked.

"It's raining again."

"So take a taxi."

"I can't."

"Why not?"

"I have no money."

"What happened to the money we gave you?"

"Oh, that," said Kummerman, with an elegant sweep of his arm, "I used it to tip the nurses."

A hasty conference, a few more dollars. This time Rush and I escorted Kummerman to a cab and gave the fare directly to the driver.

"Good-bye, Kummerman," we called after him.

He waved as the cab pulled away.

Hilbert had been waiting for Cushing to transfer Kummerman to medicine. When it failed to happen, Hilbert broached the subject at lunch. "What's the matter with surgery? Not enough cases? Have to steal stuff from medicine?"

"I thought you had turned him down," Cushing retorted.

"Only till you guys checked out his scalp wound. It would have been proper for you to transfer him to our service after that," he said primly.

"Sorry, Hilbert. No offense," Cushing said blandly. "Just a misunderstanding. We handle a lot of medical problems on the surgical service. One more doesn't inconvenience us."

"We call you for consultation on our surgical cases."

"You have no choice, surgery is out of your domain."

Hilbert walked away, miffed.

"Next time, the bastard won't be so lazy," Cushing said. Delgado joined us.

"Understand you're specializing in pulmonary edema, Hesu," Cushing said, smiling.

"I think I am in general practice down there. Last night I helped to deliver a baby," said Delgado, cutting into the hamburger.

"That's convenient, Hesu. Once they have the cord tied and the baby bundled up you can baptize it," I said.

"Sure. With the Lysol from the ring stand basin, Harry," he said winking.

Rush came over and sat down. We moved the bread basket and grape clusters that they served for dessert to make room for the pitcher of milk that Rush was carrying.

"I don't see why you bother with the emergency room, Hesu,"

Cushing said. "There's no time there for religious matters. Things are too crucial."

"You're a Catholic, Paul. I thought you would understand."

"Of course I understand, but time is precious down there. No doctor is going to step aside to make way for a church service. On the wards it's different. We know who is dying well in advance, and we always give you a list. You have plenty of time then to meet the patient and prepare him."

"You know how bad you feel when you lose a patient? Well, that's how bad I feel when I lose a soul."

"Come on, Hesu. That's silly," I said. "You can't see a soul."

"I see the soul, Harry. I see those that are blessed, and in grace, and those that are not. We are all going to die, but not all of us will die in a state of grace."

"I understand what you are saying, Father," Rush said, "but at least we know what life is, and I think we are duty-bound to preserve it. It is God-given, after all. And no one really knows about life after death."

"Ah, but I do, Wilkie."

"And you mean to tell me that it doesn't matter if a person dies, as long as he dies properly?"

"That's correct."

"So left to your devices, you could do without doctors?"

"That's correct," Hesu said.

"Well, for my part we could do without the Church, Father, with all due respect," Wilkie said, testily.

"That's why we have both medicine and the clergy, to compromise the issue," Cushing said. He faced Delgado. "You're a little young to be a Jesuit, Hesu."

"I'm not a Jesuit, yet. I'm an ordained priest, but am working here under the auspices of the Jesuits until I enter my scholastic years."

"What are the scholastic years?" I asked.

"About nine years of study, theology, philosophy, science, and then missionary work, which for all I know might be an assignment back to The County. Lord knows it needs it."

"What actually is a Jesuit?" Rush asked. Delgado drew a deep breath, but Cushing interrupted him. "A Jesuit is a member of the Society of Jesus, started by Ignatius Loyola in the sixteenth century. The brotherhood is bound by vows to poverty and

47

chastity. Jesuits were the Christian militants. They were very influential in Europe, becoming confessors to many of the rulers. They grew so powerful that they incurred the enmity of the intelligentsia, the universities and the politicians, who felt they exercised undue influence and accused them of intrigue. In fact, Pope Clement XIV was persuaded to suppress them in 1773, saying, 'Sometimes we must cut down a mast to save a ship.' In short, they were as much a pain in the ass to eighteenth-century Europe as Delgado is to you fellows. I just bring this up to show you how tough these Jesuits are, Wilkie. Don't mess with them."

Rush kept needling. "You must be committed, Father, if you take vows of poverty and chastity. Poverty I can see, but chastity never. Don't you have the urge, Hesu?"

"You kidding? I got as much urge as you. But to fulfill my mission I have to suppress this urge. It's only hard to do this for the first fifty years. After that, they tell me, it becomes easier."

"How do you suppress it, Hesu? Forget about women?" Rush asked between sips of milk. The very thought of abjuring women gave him stomach pain.

"You should do our laundry, then you see if we forget about women."

"You mean you sin in the night by yourselves? You fulfill your emission instead of your mission?"

"Only in our sleep."

"Is that why they call it a semenary?"

Even Delgado laughed. "Rush, someday I hope your ulcer ruptures, you sonofabitch." Then he crossed himself twice.

At the time, Cardinal Cushing was head of the Boston Diocese, and we used to keep recalcitrant patients in line by kidding them that Cushing was the Cardinal's son. Even the Catholics enjoyed the irreverence when they saw how the other patients, not willing to bet that there wasn't some relationship, corrected their behavior and modified their language. Cushing nodded almost imperceptibly when they asked him if he really was the son of Cardinal Cushing. Anything to keep the peace.

The hospital was crowded. We jammed an overload of nine beds ticktacktoe fashion into the center of the ward, and wedged enough bedside stands into the square to service each bed. Robert Maitland Scott Cornell, a bedfast patient who at the time required the least care, was in the center bed. He couldn't get out, and only an acrobat could reach him. Born a Scotch Presbyterian, diabetic by inheritance, he migrated to these shores as a radical socialist after nearly starving in Scotland. Sclerosis had hardened the arteries of his legs, cutting the blood supply to a light drizzle. His feet were white and cold, and three steps caused exquisite pains to cramp the muscles of his calves. Only an amputation would stop the rapid ascension of a gangrenous infection that had started under the nail of his left big toe. He refused surgery, and prepared himself for the impossible chore of recovery. "All I need is a bit of rest," he would say. "Stay away from me with your butcher knives. And keep that little squirt away with his lamentations, he depresses me."

The "little squirt" was Hesu Delgado, whose clerical rounds brought him daily to the surgery wards. Cornell shuddered at the sight of the priest. "I'm sick enough," he proclaimed, "without having to listen to Vatican prattle all day long. Get him out of here."

Delgado would go about his business, but the patients in the ward were stirred to silent resentment. Cornell argued incessantly from his pillows, loudly trying to convert the other patients to a unanimous denial of the existence of God. When poor Crump, in the adjacent bed, received visits from Delgado and prayed with him, Cornell interrupted the prayerful intimacy with cutting remarks. Afterward he assailed Crump with searing comments about the futility of religion, and recited a liturgy of Catholic crimes against humanity culled from his schooldays in Scotland. "It is a fair question," he would say, "whether a Catholic is even human."

Therefore, one morning before dawn, when Crump started banging Cornell on the head with his urinal, the other patients listened with interest, but none came to his defense. Cornell tried to shield himself with his arms, shouting in his most resounding soapbox baritone, "It's here for all to see. The Papist bastard is trying to kill me."

"Piss in my drinking water, will you?" shouted Crump, again and again, banging away with the urinal.

It was a hell of a fight, and by the time Cushing and I got there both Crump and Cornell were exhausted.

"What's got into you, Crump?" Cushing asked.

49

"He pissed in my drinking water, he did," yelled Crump.

"The hell I did," said Cornell. "I wouldn't waste my piss on a Catholic. I pissed in my urinal is all."

But Cornell, confused in the dark, had indeed pissed in Crump's water pitcher. And when Crump awakened parched and took a long draught from the pitcher, the fight began.

Cornell was a huge-framed man whose muscles had atrophied, to leave skin-draped skeletalized landmarks. The arteries in his legs had become clay pipes, and the atheromatous process extended insidiously along the aorta to encroach on the ostia of the renal arteries. Once they closed, and the kidneys were deprived of blood, a terminal kidney shutdown would abort his life, if no other catastrophe intervened.

This bluff, hearty, vigorous man tried to maintain a tough arrogance to obscure his fatal disease. As his body withered, it was only by the words he spoke, the hale ring to his voice, the tart comments, the raging political polemic he'd employed all his life in his struggles as a radical socialist, that he maintained contact with himself. He had refused ever in his life to admit defeat, and only by contact with his raspy personality could he deny the inevitable truth presented to him daily, by his wasting body, that he had nowhere to go but to the grave.

The pain in his legs and feet he surmounted only by holding firmly with once powerful arms and hands to the iron rail below the mattress of his bed and setting his face in a granite pose that denied the intrusion of agony. We morphinized him lightly to allow him to relax his grip and watched as slowly he died.

Cushing spoke to him on rounds. "How are you today, Robert?"

"How do you expect me to be, Doctor? You keep me imprisoned here."

"Father Delgado would like to talk to you."

"Don't bring that imp of a Papist to my bedside. It's bad enough he's corrupting the souls of those around me. He's an agent of Christ, and all the other fantasies dredged up by those frizzled Church minds. I'll have none of it."

Delgado came around. "Can I help you, Robert?"

"Keep the hell away from me, that's how you can help me. Your God has created nothing but misery in this world. Misery I've spent a lifetime fighting. If there's a God, He's one sweet sonofabitch, Delgado. Are you going to spend your life in that Halloween outfit? Get out in the world and do something significant, instead of wasting your breath on the dying. It's the living you ought to be helping."

"You're frightened and upset. Maybe I can help you."

"Frightened and upset, am I?" He reached behind the night table and came up brandishing his cane over Delgado's head. "Beat it before I bash you. Foist your scummy playgrounds of God and virgin births, saints, and martyrs, limbos and heavens, devils and hells on someone else. I can do without them. What am I to do? Pray and thank God for putting me into such a mess as this?"

Cornell's daughter visited every day, and must have smuggled him a vial of barbiturates, because one evening the nurse found Cornell deep in coma, the empty bottle by his side beneath the covers. She called me and I irrigated his stomach, started oxygen and intravenous fluids. Finally he responded and lay safe but in a drugged sleep until the morning.

He was awake for rounds. "A great bunch of heroes you are," he said to Cushing. "You couldn't let an old man die in dignity, could you? You had to practice your malign machinations, to see if the textbooks were right and you could bring an old man back from death. You must take great pride in your accomplishment. Here I am, to go through another day of agony. You're fools, idiots, the lot of you. What do you call yourselves? Doctors? Didn't anyone in medical school ever teach you how useless life could be?"

"Let Father Delgado help you, Robert," Cushing urged sadly. "He can help you."

Cornell roared. "I came here to be cured, not converted, and all I've been subjected to is proselytizing by the goddamn mackerel snappers. Jesus help me," he cried, "save me from you minions."

Later that day a thrombus closed off the circulation below the calf of his right leg. His foot turned white, pulseless, and Cornell screamed in agony. Morphine in double doses scarcely caused the pain to abate. We prepared him for the operating room.

"Ye'll not mutilate me," he screamed, and shouted, "No, no, I won't let you."

We amputated at mid-thigh over his protestations, under the legal umbrella of permissions he had signed when he entered the hospital.

51

A small room next to the nurses' station had become vacant, and we put Cornell in there to afford him privacy, hopefully closer surveillance, and to remove his disruptive influence from the ward. But his moans could be heard throughout the halls, and somehow we saw him less often than normally we would have. One day Cushing walked in to find Cornell lying in puddles of shit—his stump, its dressing green with putrefaction, poking out from beneath the covers, his body athwart the bed, his pillow on the floor. Cushing was enraged. "Get in there and help me clean this man up. Don't ever let anyone go like this on my service. I don't care if you have to put someone in the room twenty-four hours a day. He has a right to his dignity. We've wronged this man enough."

We finally got his stump clean and starting to heal. Cornell wouldn't eat. His kidney function was falling off. His once magnificent baritone voice that had projected his radical litany in resounding chords was a hoarse whisper.

Then one day he said to Cushing, "I'm ready now, call Father Delgado."

Father Delgado, the Jesuit, provided the spiritual continuity that bridged the worlds of uncertainty in which the sick and dying dwell. He came to the dying Presbyterian and comforted him.

The surgeon occupies a small pulpit of power in a minor parish where he presides over a religious pecking order. His assistants are disciples who voluntarily assume the colors of his cloth. When Shaver appeared once a week on grand rounds, he was trailed by Farkas and Kiyler, who smiled when Shaver chuckled, frowned when he was angry and, in general, silently mimed his moods. They had permitted his power to pulverize their personalities into a dust as fine as the powder on a surgeon's glove.

We could not appear on these rounds bedraggled from a sleepless night in the admitting ward, our own skins yellowed by the mine-shaft lights of the dim-lit corridors. We could not display the fatigue that seemed to multiply the gravitational forces causing us to slump or lean against the beds. "Clean up. Cold shower. Make yourself look like a man, then you'll feel like one," Shaver would admonish. And if we failed to pass his meticulous inspection, he would remember the infraction from week to week. When, on the first rounds we made with him, Rush walked in like an unmade bed, having worked until the very last moment, Shaver ordered him to go back, shower and change. "We'll wait for you."

One day Shaver appeared for rounds with a red poppy in his lapel. Farkas and Kiyler wore them too, albeit slightly smaller ones. Cushing, Farkas and Kiyler stood at one side of a patient's bed. Shaver, alone on the other side, faced a semicircle of students standing like marble pillars in a stonecutter's yard. Rush and I flanked them. Cushing summarized the patient's history, but Shaver paid no attention. Instead, he singled out Arthur Fricht, a student who was eying the poppy.

"Do you recognize this, my boy?"

Fricht straightened and squared himself. "Yes sir."

"What is it?"

"It's a poppy."

"What does a poppy make you think of, Fricht?"

"Opium."

"True, Fricht, but don't let your mind get trapped entirely by medical things. Allow it to range. There's an entire world of culture waiting for you out there, if you want to take advantage of it."

Fricht was a nervous, agitated sort who felt that there was something ominous about Shaver's singling him out like this, by name no less. Although Shaver would ignore students in the hallways, and in general pay them no heed, he knew their names, and could recognize all of them from the admission photographs. But Fricht didn't know this, which made him meek. "Yes sir."

"Yes sir, what?" asked Shaver, having lost the thread of the conversation.

Fricht paused, puzzled. Then he said, "Yes sir, Sir."

Suddenly Shaver cocked his head toward the ceiling and sparkling highlights danced on his shimmering lenses. Then in a mellow voice, as if scanning Holy Writ, he recited:

In Flanders Field the poppies blow
Between the crosses, row on row. . . .

"That's what a poppy is supposed to remind you of. Who wrote that, Fricht?"

"John McCrae, sir."

"Who?" Shaver was incredulous.

"I thought it was John McCrae."

"Well, you're wrong, Fricht. You look that up. When's our next session with these boys, Kiyler? Next week? Ah, yes. All right, Fricht. I'll expect the correct answer when next we meet. This will count in your grades. That's an assignment. Understood?"

"Yes sir, I understand."

The remainder of the rounds was anticlimactic.

Later, Fricht joined Rush and me for lunch. Extern medical students usually didn't consort with interns, but we made an exception for Fricht because he was frightened.

"What am I going to do? I'll flunk out of here. That guy is crazy."

"What's the big deal, Fricht? Just find out who wrote the god-damn thing and tell him on Thursday."

"I can't, you don't understand."

"What he's trying to tell us," Rush interjected, "is that John McCrae wrote 'In Flanders Fields,' isn't that right, Fricht?"

"Yes, that's right. McCrae wrote it. That's a fact. And if Shaver thinks someone else wrote it, I'm dead."

"Why?" I said. "Just bring the book to class and show it to him."

"And embarrass him in front of all those people? He'd decapitate me. I'd fail surgery. It's too risky."

"Then write him a note and hand it to him privately."

"And sign my name to it? That would be worse."

"What are you going to do?"

"I don't really know. But I know one thing. I have six days to find out who he thinks wrote the goddamned maudlin rhyme."

Fricht left. We wished him good luck. "Hey," I asked Wilkie, "how do you know that McCrae wrote that poem?"

"Christ, Harry, everybody except you and Shaver knows that McCrae wrote it. That bastard Shaver—you ought to hear the combinations of tunes he sings to Kiyler and Farkas and asks them to identify. He mixes Schubert with Mozart, Brahms with Beethoven. He's a cultural Malaprop. He's no fucking good, and someday I'm going to fix his wagon," Wilkie said, grimacing and downing some more milk.

54

"What do you mean, Wilkie? You gonna hit him on the head? What are you going to do?"

"You wait and see. When I get done with him, he won't throw that culture shit around any more, not while I'm in his presence."

That night I called Lapius and related the incident.

"That's amusing, Harry" was all that Lapius would say.

The following week at grand rounds we assembled, feckless, speckless and starched. Shaver marched in with his retinue and as soon as the semicircle was formed he zeroed in. "Fricht? All right. Who wrote 'In Flanders Field'?"

There was a long pause.

"Fricht, Fricht?" Shaver called. He turned to Cushing. "Is he here?" Fricht was there. While all this was going on he detached himself from the group, walked to the foot of the bed and said, "Joyce Kilmer, sir."

Kiyler smiled, Farkas smiled and Shaver beamed. "That's right, boy. Let that be an example to you. Open your mind, boy, it will refresh you. Don't let it become stodgy with medical matters only." He clapped Fricht on the shoulder and we moved to the next bed.

The patient in the bed we had just deserted beckoned to me. I walked over quietly and bent my ear to his mouth. "They finished with me already, Doc?" he asked.

"I'm afraid so," I whispered.

"What da fuck did that have to do with my operation?" he wanted to know.

"They were talking about your operation, Catlip." I told him.

"Bullshit. I understood every word they said. If they were talking about my case, I woodna understood anything they said."

"It may be just as well," I consoled him.

At lunch that day Rush and I congratulated Fricht. "Gee Arthur, you sure pulled that one out of the hat. How did you know?"

"Funny thing," Fricht said. "I was having a cup of coffee at the snack bar and Dr. Lapius came over and asked if he could join me. And I sort of told him the story. Lapius laughed. Said Shaver hadn't changed. That he wouldn't know an iamb from a dithyramb."

"So."

"So he told me that Shaver believes Kilmer wrote 'In Flanders Fields.' Wasn't that a bit of good luck?"

A big day in the OR. Shaver to do an extensive visceral sympathectomy. Our schedules were cleared so that we could attend, to watch, learn and assist. Shaver was the surgeon. Farkas would be first to assist, Cushing second assist, and Rush and I third and fourth. Kiyler was to cover Shaver at other hospitals, starting early, and then rush to The County to be on hand if needed.

The patient was a man called Mielish. I didn't know him. He had been transferred to surgery for a sympathectomy from medical service, where he had been treated unsuccessfully for intractable hypertension. Sympathectomy, a surgical interruption of the small preganglionic fibers emanating from the thoracic and lumbar cords, was then in its experimental stages. If successful, it would cause relaxation of the arteriolar vasculature, and thus relieve the tensions that increased the diastolic blood pressure. Mielish already showed evidence of the flea-bite kidney changes caused by his soaring blood pressure. The damage to the kidneys induced chemical changes, which in turn further increased his blood pressure. Mielish was caught in a vicious upward spiral of cause and effect that, untreated, could end only in his death. The sympathectomy was an attempt to interrupt this malign sequence. The operation was exacting and tedious. Shaver hadn't performed too many of them. However, none of us doubted that with his technical mastery the surgical intervention would be flawless. Whether the desired medical results would accrue was another matter, but after comprehensive conferencing of the case, both medical and surgical departments, without dissent, had concluded that no alternatives remained for Mielish.

Cushing, with Rush at his side, explained the situation to Mielish. Rush loaded himself with a double dose of milk at breakfast, and we walked from the interns' quarters through the brisk dawning morning toward the hospital.

"That bastard should have to talk to Mielish himself. Don't you think that a patient should have the right to meet the man to whom he might be entrusting the last moments of his life?"

"I gather, Wilkie, you have reservations about Shaver."

"Oh! You've noticed?"

(Later, Lapius offered a defense of Shaver. "Shaver, after all, has reached the stage in his career when all he gets are the tough hopeless cases—cancer cases, or patients like your friend Mielish. Surgery with the happy ending eludes him. Shaver's patients, by the time they reach him, have paraded their illnesses through the ranks of lesser doctors, and are financially and emotionally drained. Shaver is their last resort, and is under no illusions that he has much to offer. If he allowed himself to recognize that death was the stalking horse of his practice, he would be in perpetual mourning.")

"So, how did Cushing handle it?" I asked. "Was Mielish amenable?"

"Paul was great," Rush enthused. "He pulled a chair to the bedside, and patiently reviewed the problem and the medical measures that had been tried unsuccessfully. He told Mielish that the decision to operate wasn't automatic and impersonal, but had been agreed upon after intensive study of the case at staff conferences. He assured Mielish that nothing would, or indeed could, be done without Mielish's express approval. 'It's our recommendation but, in the last analysis, your decision,' he told him. He outlined the odds, discussed the outlook and finally got Mielish to depersonalize it and discuss it as some sort of intellectual exercise, while at the same time leaving no doubt that, although the hard facts were unpleasant, the doctors involved had a deep interest in his welfare, and would spare no personal effort in his behalf.

"Mielish became a participant in his own case. He told Cushing that he understood the situation but wanted to think about it. He had a long talk with Delgado. Later he called for Cushing, and told him that he thought he would go through with the operation. Cushing considered the answer carefully, all the while keeping that sober steady gaze on Mielish, as if looking for any lack of resolve. Then he put his hand on Mielish's shoulder and said, 'I think you've made the right decision.' That was beautiful, because Mielish knew then and there that he wasn't being conned.

"Of course. Mielish is Cushing's patient, not Shaver's."

"Well, I think it would have been nice for Shaver to be there too," Rush said, his attitude softening a little.

57

At the scrub sinks Shaver started his humming. "What's that from, Farkas?"

"The 1812 Symphony, sir."

"Right you are. Now try this one. Cushing, do you recognize it?"

"No, I've got a tin ear, Dr. Shaver," Cushing said, ducking the question and keeping his eyes on the brush with which he was scrubbing his left forearm.

I thought it broke the tension and was glad for the interlude, but Rush was chafing.

We strutted single file into the operating room, forearms bent upward, hands pointed to the ceiling, and water dripping to the floor from our elbows. We dried with sterile towels, and one by one each of us was gowned, the gowns secured by the circulating nurse, who tied the bows silently behind our backs. Then we took our positions at the table. The humming stopped, and no sounds issued except for terse orders, the clicking of the hemostats, and the snipping sounds as sutures were severed at the knots. Cushing wanted Rush to be as far away from Shaver as possible, so he had assigned him to fourth assist.

In no time the deft Shaver had exposed the field and thrust the retractors at Rush and myself, having positioned them first. Strangely enough, despite the strain of the contorted imbalance of our posture in order to maintain traction on the distant wound, the time during surgery always went quickly. Perhaps it would be more accurate to say that time was a succession of procedural steps by which we measured progress. Kiyler arrived, but there was nothing for him to do. He remained standing against the wall.

Hours later it was over. Rush and I were relieved of our retractors, and rested our clasped hands on the sterile drapes while Farkas and Cushing closed the muscle layers under the watchful eye of Shaver. As they started to suture the long skin wound, the infernal humming started again.

"Recognize that—what's your name, fourth assist? I can't tell with the mask on."

"That's Dr. Rush, sir."

"Recognize that, Dr. Rush?"

"The second movement of Mendelssohn's violin concerto."

"Right! I heard Tygorski conduct that last night. Magnificent.

One of the great young conductors around. He creates a magnificent rapport with his orchestra, makes them all reach for the highest level of attainment." Shaver continued, enraptured by his own words, "He endows his music with a transcendental mystique that permeates his entire orchestra. He unites each member of the ensemble by the concentrated energy of his genius so that what would in ordinary hands be a babel of instruments, in his becomes a union of spiritual effort that is transmitted directly to the music." He paused to let the effect sink in.

Suddenly I heard Rush's voice, clear, resonant, definitive, breaking the rule of silence imposed traditionally on surgical interns. "Tygorski is a musical boor. He is incapable of creating any musical effect with an orchestra, and will soon return to his seat among the second violins. The only reason he conducts is because his wealthy aunt is a patron of the orchestra. He couldn't conduct the tambourine chorus of the Salvation Army."

Farkas and Cushing had stopped suturing the skin. Kiyler stepped closer to hear what was going on. Shaver turned slowly toward Rush and, peering through the top lens of his bifocals, searched for the source of the statement. The rest of us kept our eyes glued to the half-closed incision.

"What did you say?" Shaver asked incredulously.

Rush repeated his intemperate critique.

"What would you know of these matters, Doctor?" Shaver asked menacingly. "What are your credentials?"

"I played second violin for Tygorski before I decided to go into medicine." Shaver was stunned to silence. Cushing said, "Cut here." Farkas clipped a skin suture and they continued working.

"And furthermore," Rush added, " 'In Flanders Fields' was written by John McCrae."

The phone rang at 7 A.M. It was Rush.

"Harry, over to the ward stat. We need you."

"OR has been canceled. I'm sleeping." I hung up.

The phone jangled again. "Harry, Cushing wants you here pronto." I hung up again, but this time struggled out of bed. Rush had said "Cushing," and that was the magic word. If Cushing asked me to meet him under the ice cover of a frozen lake, I'd have done so. He was my leader. He was my teacher. I'll do anything he wants, I thought, as I fell back into a deep slumber on the bed. The phone rang. "Harry? Are you awake?" Rush again.

"Sure, I'm awake, I've been awake for twenty-four hours. What makes you think I'm not awake? You just called me a minute ago, didn't you?"

"Harry, that was thirty minutes ago. Scram over here."

The half-hour must have been beneficial, because this time I made it to the door. I grabbed coffee from the urn at the entrance to the dining room. It was weak. I would have to depend on the cold air to finish waking me.

When I reached surgery, Rush was at the door, and drew me in. There Farkas stood, draped in sterile robes, his hands folded neatly over his belly. Rush, two medical students and Cushing were in scrub suits.

"Enjoyed your sleep, I suppose," Farkas greeted me.

I was considering a devastating rejoinder when Cushing interjected, "Come on, Harry. Hurry and get scrubbed. We're going to operate."

"But the schedule was canceled. That's why I went to sleep. What are we doing here? Who we going to operate on?" I looked around for a patient.

"On me," said Cushing, hopping on the table. "Okay, fellows. Let's get going. Harry, you're the anesthetist." He let his head fall back and closed his eyes.

Perhaps because of the oft-repeated canard about Cushing being the Cardinal's son, we had always assumed that he was wedded to the ecclesiastical altars and sworn to celibacy, but it was to the marriage altar he was headed and he wanted to arrive in good shape. He was suffering from recurrent posthitis and phimosis, an embarrassing condition for a prospective groom, resulting from intermittent inflammation of the foreskin which tightens around the glans penis. The condition is painful enough to discourage erection, even if it doesn't always prevent it. Cushing thought it would be indelicate to expose this problem to the OR nurses. As he said later, he didn't want to make them jealous, which explained why we solemnly gathered in the privacy of the treatment room.

Farkas was no mohel, and I was a lousy anesthetist, but here we were acting out the charade of a major operating theater, ready to operate on one of our own. It was minor surgery, of little medical consequence, a simple procedure that Farkas took time off to perform, as a favor to Cushing. It was encore surgery, the little bagatelle the virtuoso might schedule last, after a morning of onerous performances that demanded every iota of concentration.

Farkas carefully placed the sterile drapes, creating a tiny aperture with towel clips, which permitted the tender part to protrude. I placed a tourniquet around Paul's arm, prior to injecting a measured amount of barbiturate slowly into his vein.

"Ready, Paul?"

"Okay, Harry. Shoot!"

"Start counting." Paul started to count, and I injected slowly until his voice faded into sleep. I nodded to Farkas, who grasped the foreskin tenderly with an Allis clamp and waited for a reaction. Nothing happened. He became bolder, and soon he and Rush were trimming tissue. Farkas stepping back occasionally like an artist, measuring angles. "There now, Rush. We must shape it to be a perfect instrument."

"From whom do you derive such criteria?" Rush asked.

"You're right, Rush. It's not for us to judge. We should have asked one of the nurses."

Suddenly Cushing stiffened. I looked down. His face was ashen. Farkas shouted, "He stopped bleeding. What happened?" I tried for a pulse. There was none. Farkas grabbed a laryngoscope from the tray, hyperextended Cushing's head and introduced the instrument. Rush pounded on Cushing's chest. "Suction, quickly," Farkas ordered. He introduced the suction tube. "Oxygen." I grabbed the mask, and as soon as Farkas had withdrawn the instruments put the mask over Cushing's mouth and pressed on the bag. Suddenly Paul sucked in and expelled a large jet of air which sounded as if it were passing through the compressed nipple of a balloon. His face was less dusky. Blood started to ooze from the partially repaired penis. The entire episode took less than a minute. We monitored him as his breathing became regular, his pulse stronger. Farkas strode to the table, and with a few adroit moves quickly finished the surgical procedure.

"Vaseline gauze," he commanded. A medical student opened the package and held the opened end toward him. "Okay, Rush. Let's just put a pressure dressing on. Keep the oxygen going, Harry."

We watched Cushing for thirty minutes. "What the hell happened?" Rush asked Farkas.

"Laryngeal spasm, I guess. I sucked out a blob of mucus."

"But he stopped bleeding."

"Must have had a momentary cardiac standstill. But he seems all right now."

Cushing stirred, and slowly emerged from layers of sleep that seemed to drop away from him like blankets kicked off in restless slumber.

"How'd it go?" That was Cushing's voice, hoarse, croaking.

"Fine, Paul. But we're keeping you on the ward overnight."

"Will I be able to piss?"

"Yes," Farkas laughed. "But hold it near the base."

The cardiograms checked out, but the stay on the ward cut into his plans, and the marriage had to be postponed a few days, which was just as well, since healing was slow and Cushing had overestimated his recuperative powers. He was still tender when he left the hospital a week later.

"You could probably do all right with some of the older nurses around here, but I don't think it's strong enough yet for breaking and entering," Farkas told him.

Cushing married, took a week for the honeymoon, and returned wearing the silly grin of a kid who had just made a pleasurable discovery. Two years after he left The County he dropped dead of a heart attack. Maybe that's what the cardiac standstill was trying to tell us.

Most of the surgery at The County was done under open-drip ether, administered by nurses. The nurse held an ether can over a gauze-filled mask and allowed the volatile material to drip onto the gauze, so that its vapors would concentrate over the mouth and nose of the patient, allowing him no alternative but to inhale the noxious substance and go to sleep.

The nurse, seated on a stainless-steel kick stool, would guide the patient carefully through the stages of anesthesia until the proper phase of the third stage was reached, and then say to the surgeon, "Doctor, your patient is ready." Ether was unpredictable, and after induction, when in the second or excitement stage, the unconscious patient often became obstreperous, agitated and struggled violently against his restraints, apparently to escape.

But the patient was unaware of all that was transpiring. The surgeon and his assistants might lean on the patient to quiet his movements. "He's too light, he's bucking. More anesthesia, for Christ's sake," the surgeon would shout, and the nurse would apply more anesthetic until the violence ceased and the patient, entirely relaxed, was ready for the knife. But there was a catch. In trying to rush through the second stage, an overdose of ether would sometimes be given, which could carry the patient into the fourth stage of anesthesia, or death.

There were many cases, the traumas, or the ruptured viscera, the bleeding ulcers, where chance for life was slim indeed even under ideal anesthesia. But as long as there were nurse-anesthetists at The County, there were no surgical deaths. Only anesthetic deaths. No matter how shorn the body, how infected the peritoneum, how drained of blood or deprived of essential conditions for life, when one of those patients died, the visiting surgeons invariably, at the moment of passing, threw their instruments to the floor in disgust, and turned to the quivering anesthetist and said menacingly, "He's dead. What did you do to him for God's sake?"

No surgeon today would challenge his anesthetist in such manner, for it wouldn't be a vulnerable nurse he would be bullying, but a physician, expertly schooled in the complex physiological processes that interact during anesthesia, a specialist, who would brook no interference in his domain, who would know and record from his monitoring instruments the precise sequence of events leading to death. At The County, the nurse anesthetist could only retreat to her room and cry.

The night of the near-debacle with Cushing, I was so shaken that I stayed with Lapius, who provided medicinal liquors to calm and warm me. He padded about the house in his sheepskin booties.

"Here, Harry," he said, emerging from a closet with a flasklike apparatus from which a hollowed wooden tube protruded. "This is a copy of the apparatus William Thomas Green Morton used at the Massachusetts General Hospital when he introduced ether anesthesia into surgery in 1846. Here it is one hundred years later, and we still administer ether just as crudely. Of course, during that one hundred years physicians learned to prescribe preoperative medications to counter some of the unpleasant and

63

dangerous effects of anesthesia, and although you and Rush and Farkas, to say nothing of Cushing himself, are all familiar with these, it is my guess that Cushing received none prior to submitting to the anesthesia that you so boldly and foolishly administered."

"I didn't think even to ask."

"And why not, Harry? You were the anesthetist. Yet you and the others entered into that serious business frivolously, as if it were a game. You lost control of the procedure before you had even begun."

"I'm just an intern. They were chiding me for being late. The whole thing seemed to have been set up on the spur of the moment. What the hell was I to do, walk in and take over from my resident and Farkas, an attending physician?"

"Yes."

"You must be kidding. I haven't the status to do a thing like that. Farkas would have made mincemeat out of me."

"Had Cushing died, Farkas would have made mincemeat out of you also. You would have borne the responsibility for having caused an anesthetic death."

I had never seen Lapius angered, but now he turned for an instant positively cold. "Never, as long as you practice your calling as a physician, should you accept responsibility without the commensurate authority."

He went on quietly. "You see, Harry, by oversight, by carelessness, through fear and timidity, you almost killed a man today. The anesthetist is in command until his patient is properly prepared. If Cushing wouldn't submit to preanesthetic medication, if Farkas wouldn't postpone the procedure until the patient had been properly prepared, if you were powerless to have this carried out, unable to assume command, you should have excused yourself. Never be a pawn for another man's folly. All of you, Cushing included, trifled with the most serious medical responsibility, the life of a patient, and, in so doing, debased the solemn work of generations of doctors and scientists that preceded you.

"Before anesthesia patients were bound to the operating table, held there by strong men who tried to quell their violent thrashing. Cheselden could remove a gallstone in fifty-four seconds and Liston could amputate a leg in thirty seconds."

Lapius rose and lumbered to his bookshelves. "Here, let me read you a patient's account of his operation without anesthesia:

> During the operation in spite of the pain my senses were preternaturally acute. I watched all that the surgeon did with a fascinating intensity. I still recall with unwelcome vividness the spreading out of the instruments, the twisting of the tourniquet, the first incision, the fingering of the sawed bone, the sponge pressed on the flap, the tying of the blood vessels, the stitching of the skin, and the bloody dismembered limb lying on the floor. These are not pleasant remembrances. For a long time they haunted me and though they cannot bring back the suffering, they can occasion a disquiet which favors neither mental nor bodily health."

Lapius stopped suddenly. "I've been carried away, Harry. Almost anesthetized both of us with the gaseousness of my own verbosity. But here, I have a surprise for you."

He took Morton's primitive apparatus and disappeared into the kitchen. When he returned, a colorless liquid sloshed in the flask.

"You know, Harry, before Morton's demonstration, students knew full well the power of ether, having demonstrated it at ether parties. For some reason none had the perspicacity to realize its full potential. But try a few whiffs. Put the wooden tube into your mouth and inhale deeply. After all, we doctors should experience that which we inflict on our patients."

I placed the tube between my lips and, as Lapius had instructed, inhaled the irritating sweet ether vapor deeply. My sensorium clouded. When the evening ended, I was giggling uncontrollably.

5

"OBSTETRICS" COMES FROM the Latin *"obstare,"* "to stand before." On the obstetrical service at The County, I spent three months standing before woman. Literally, I stood before their pudenda, their legs arched over the padded obstetrical stirrups, waiting for either caput or buttocks of the baby to present at the distending vaginal entroitus. Until that moment, we busied ourselves with antiseptic preparation of the pudendum, the simple hygienic measures that had been advocated by Oliver Wendell Holmes (and for which the Hungarian Semmelweis was persecuted), that saved so many women from oft fatal childbirth fever; then we injected through long needles to the pudendal nerves a modest amount of local anesthesia. Hopefully, this would provide enough nerve block so that the episiotomy, an incision through the labia and part of the vaginal vault to prevent indiscriminate laceration when the newborn forced its way through the female passages, could be performed painlessly.

We worked at night in the obstetrical pavilion, which was seen from afar as a lighted platform suspended in air over one wing of the darkened hospital. Interns performed all deliveries, and for that reason general anesthesia was barred to protect the mother and newborn child from the additional risk of chloroform inexpertly administered.

In obstetrics, poverty conferred on prospective mothers the privilege of lying awake during childbirth. The wealthier women on the private service of experienced practitioners paid large sums for painless childbirth, for the assurance that they would be put to sleep and wouldn't feel a thing. So following their scopolaminic twilight sleep and general anesthesia their only memories included commencing labor with a full belly, and emerging, hours later, with an empty belly, after which someone showed them a baby and assured them it was theirs.

Our mothers were spared the amnesia of monitored childbirth. They consciously experienced each pang, the quickening of the uterine muscle as the frequency of pains increased to a crescendo of activity until a final titanic contraction provided the torque of childbirth, to propel the baby, head firmly ensconced in the gloved hands of the intern, shoulders twisting through the roomy arch of the pubis, into the outer world. The mother, at this moment of pain and triumph, could peer directly through the V of her abducted thighs and see the ankle-clutched baby dangling upside down, then watch, after the last cordal residue of physiological dependence was tied and severed, as the baby was tucked into his first bindle. Our mothers were witness to the power and glory of childbirth, alert and awake so that later they could fondle the memory of each of the pains of their labor.

We were privileged as interns to participate in the wonder of childbirth, to watch the concommitant eruption of child and excreta, as the head of the babe squeegeed the rectum clean of its content during the final, momentous bearing down. After the baby emerged we cleansed the parts tenderly. Then, while awaiting the spontaneous extrusion of the placenta, sutured carefully, starting at its apex, the vaginal wound we had created to encourage free egress. We learned to sew with the precision of tailors to avoid distortional errors that might crimp the vagina and alter the marital relationship. We learned to expect the screaming response of the infant to the single drop of one percent silver nitrate instilled into each eye to prevent gonococcal ophthalmia, in case the mother harbored the infection at the moment of birth. Then we looked from betwixt blood-smeared thighs and vulva to the sweat-stained body of the mother so recently released from her agonies.

Under the stark lights, the mother, often fat and toothless, eyes closed, rested with the solemn sighs of early sleep, her features magically composed into the beautiful expression of someone recently gifted, blessed by the beatitude of a miraculous process that only a woman can comprehend. In the act of childbirth, these wretched wrens fell into calm and satisfied repose. No matter how ungainly, distorted or unkempt, at that moment each had the placid, certain, all-knowing face of an angel.

Each birth is a replication of the species, the newborn formed from sequential derivatives of the genetic storehouse of chemical information, which lies dormant and incomplete until the complemental portions of sperm and ovum join to form the zygote. From that moment of union the biologic history of the new being to be formed is foreordained and immutable. Its height, sex, body build, coloration, muscle mass, organ efficiency, intellectual profile and even predilection for disease, in short its biological future, are encoded in the particular manner in which atoms of carbon, hydrogen, oxygen and nitrogen are arranged. This chemical information then releases biological energy which, with the measured pace of disciplined command, builds the body of the future animal.

It is awesome to observe the newborn, delivered from the succoring waters of the womb, suddenly drawing its first breath, the result an instant replay of a process which consumed millennia before the first water-beings crawled from the murky depths to spawn finally a landed gentry.

Father Delgado prowled the halls of the obstetrical wing. I would meet him frequently when I walked from the delivery room, stripping the gauze mask from my face. "It was successful, Harry?" he would ask.

"Sure. It almost always is. But what brings you to these hallowed halls at two in the morning?"

"The miracle of life."

"Bullshit. I have to fill out the birth certificate and write up the chart now. And there's another one in labor. The miracle of life has been transformed into a clerical nightmare."

"But you feel it, Harry. I know you do. How can you not?"

"I'm too tired to rhapsodize on the subject, Hesu. Incidentally, when the hell do you sleep?"

"Oh, I sleep in snatches," he said diffidently.

"Bite your tongue, Hesu," I said, laughing. "Remember your vows."

"Why? What did I say?"

"Nothing, Father, nothing." I sat down at the desk in the hall and started on the paper work.

"What are you doing now, Harry?"

"I'm making a miracle of my own, Hesu."

"How so?"

"I'm creating a child out of the alphabet for the files at City Hall."

Childbirth could be tumultuous. Once with a behemoth of a woman who was gravida three para two, I sat facing the roomy pelvis and pendulous vulva, impatient and fatigued. I finished the pudendal block and the nurse pushed up the instrument tray for the episiotomy. I waved her away. "Christ, she's built like the Lincoln Tunnel. A small car could drive through that hole without touching the walls. She don't need an episiotomy." The caput suddenly appeared, and I placed my hand against the crown of the head to slow its descent. But the gigantic mother was just as impatient as I, and with a heaving motion that brought her buttocks off the table, she bore down mightily, barreled the baby into my midriff like a cannon shell and almost blasted me off the stool with the accompanying gargantuan fart. I had all I could do to catch the baby, no less stop it. Sprays of liquid and tracers of blood shot across my uniform, my face, into my eyes. I cuffed at the sticky liquid until I could see, then tied the cord. In a few minutes she bore down again and the pulpy placenta slithered into my lap. By the time I had handed the baby to the horrified nurse and disposed of the placenta I looked like a hemorrhage, and the blood was still coming. I examined the vagina and found a third-degree laceration that extended through the rectum. An hour later I was still placing silk sutures as carefully as possible between tattered flaps of skin, trying to recreate the original

69

alignment. Luckily the rectal sphincter was intact. Otherwise, she would have been out of control, and I would have been out of a job.

I was worried about my eyes. They were full of her blood and secretions. "Any Argyrol?" I asked.

"No. I'll run down to the pharmacy and get some," one of the aides replied.

"The hell with that. Here, give me some of the stuff you put in the baby's eye."

I sat down on the slippery stool, leaned back, and they put one drop of one percent silver nitrate into each of my eyes. Suddenly my eyes felt as if they had been lanced by sharp needles. Yellow lights exploded in my head. My lids clamped shut, and when the spasm abated, no amount of blinking could produce tears enough to wash away the searing pain. I staggered into the hall, into the waiting arms of Delgado.

"Something is wrong, Harry?" he asked alarmed.

"You're fucking well informed something is wrong, Father. I'm going blind. I've just scarred my corneas for life. They must have put the wrong stuff in my eyes."

"Come with me, Harry." Delgado led me down to the accident room, where he explained to Gibson what had happened while I staggered around raging like the blind Lear in the wilderness. Gibson got some local anesthetic and put a drop into each eye. The pain left, and my muscles relaxed. I charged back through the dark halls to the delivery room, Delgado at my heels.

"Where the hell is that bottle, the stuff you put in my eyes?" I screamed. The nurse handed it to me. I read the label: "1% Silver Nitrate."

"Is this the stuff you put in the babies' eyes?" I asked, incredulously.

She smiled demurely and nodded.

"Christ, Hesu, no wonder they scream when they are born. I always thought it was because someone slapped them on the ass. It's that fucking silver nitrate. What a lousy welcome to a cold world."

Fred Manning was resident on obstetrics and gynecology. He was the backup. I turned to him for problems beyond my ken and experience. Like the lady with the slow ooze. I couldn't stop the post-partum bleeding. Minor rivulets of blood drained from the vagina. Not a hemorrhagic storm, but rather a persistent trickle of the life substance. But it kept coming. I sponged the vagina again and again, inserted specula, and examined under the brightest lights available, but couldn't find the source of the bleeding. Something perhaps deep in the fornix, or at the cervix. Whatever it was, there was no way I could stop it because I couldn't place the origin. "Call Dr. Manning," I instructed the nurse.

After half an hour Manning hadn't shown. I went to the phone myself.

"Dr. Manning, I have a post partum. She delivered about half an hour ago. But she's bleeding. Oozing continually."

"What time is it?" Manning was yawning into the phone.

"Midnight." What the hell was he doing asleep at midnight?

"Okay, Harry, tamponade it with sponges, and if it doesn't stop call me back."

I made a pack of four-by-four gauze sponges and shoved them into her vagina. She was capacious, having just delivered. I packed her tightly, but the gauzes soon began to show telltale pink as the blood slowly seeped through them. It wouldn't stop. I was getting nowhere. She was restless. She had been in stirrups for several hours. Her legs were cramping. She moaned. I called Manning.

"What is it this time, Harry?"

"Same thing. Still bleeding."

"In danger?"

"Not immediately. But if it keeps up, she won't have any blood left by morning."

"What time is it?" Why was he always worried about the time? "One o'clock."

"Call me in a half-hour."

At one-thirty I called him and told him she was in shock. He said he would be right down. He was annoyed. She wasn't in shock.

"Don't you know the medical signs of shock, Doctor?" he asked tartly.

"I guess I misjudged. But now that you are here maybe you can stop the bleeding."

He positioned himself between her legs and expertly spun the speculum around to disclose a small cervical laceration. "Triple-

71

ought sutures." The nurse handed the filamentous gut to him, and within minutes the bleeding had stopped. We took her down and sent her to the post-partum ward.

"You should have been able to spot that, Harry."

"Next time. That was the first one I ever saw. You did a swell job. I learned something."

"Glad you did, Harry. Keep up the good work." Manning went back to bed. He was exceptionally competent, but seemed addicted to sleep. He never showed up with his hair mussed, and I suspected that half the waiting time that I put in at the crotches of the emergencies, waiting for Manning to arrive, was due to his fastidious habit of never appearing unless decorously attired, hair combed straight back on either side of a remarkably straight part, as if etched with the aid of a ruler. His light brown hair glistened, and the smell of pomade diluted the pungent odors of the delivery room. His face glistened, although I doubted he applied any oily substances. Manning strode through the residency in effortless style. The County was just a way station on the path to the greater glories of the gynecologic suburbia to which he was headed. He was great during the day, but at night he guarded his sleep more than his patients. It was painful to call him, because it meant repeated calls that kept you up half the night.

Luckily Rush had bombed out with his stomach pains and was hospitalized; otherwise his ulcer would have perforated for sure.

The trouble with any obstetrical service is that everybody expects a happy ending. Even the ponderous bitches popping their seventh or twelfth baby with the ease of a hound pissing against a tree, swearing during the lonely and painful hours of labor that they wouldn't let that fucker husband of theirs touch them ever again, softened to dreamy-eyed insouciance after the delivery, and became forgiving, compliant and even wanton.

That's why when something went wrong, it had the emotional crunch of a bomb blast at a birthday party. Suddenly the expected happiness and fulfillment became a grotesque charade of evil intents, as if a curse had been malevolently cast.

Heather Wormley was one of those macabre cases.

Heather was forty, in her eighth month and having abdominal pains. It was clear from the moment she came on the ward that something unique was transpiring.

Her swollen belly was the site of an anguish that transcended the normal pains of labor. Combined with this was the inconstant quality of the heartbeat of the baby that could be heard through the stethoscope placed on the abdominal wall. It raced, it slowed, it seemed louder one time, then faded. Heather was tortured by lancinating pains that made her wince, and they had none of the normal rhythmicity of labor. Her blood pressure kept falling. I called Manning.

"Watch her and call me back."

"She's in trouble. You better come down."

"What time is it?"

"Eleven o'clock."

"Okay. I'll be down." Manning probably figured he'd wind up the problem in time to assure himself six hours' sleep. Heather wasn't doing well at all. She was clearly in crisis, or so it seemed to me. Manning arrived, crisp and in ambassadorial control of himself. He examined Heather carefully, ignoring the obvious quality of her distress, and then checked the urine specimen under the microscope.

"Aha!" he said. "Here's the problem. Look at this, Harry."

I peered through the lenses of the microscope at the fragile cellular elements swimming in the urine pool, and then looked at Manning blankly.

"Don't you see it?"

"See what?"

"The leucocytes. She has a pyelonephritis. That's why she has pain in the back, that's why she's sweating. Give her some sulfa drugs and let's get her to bed. She'll be all right in the morning. If her condition persists, we'll precipitate the delivery."

He left the floor. There are doctors who are precise in taking a medical history and exacting in performing a physical examination, who extract the necessary information, but who are unable to fit the material into correct diagnostic patterns. Manning was one of these.

I stayed with Heather, having nothing better to do. No sense going to bed. Interns don't sleep on obstetrics. Her blood pressure kept falling. The fetal heart sounds were irregular. I told the nurses that I thought something terrible was happening.

One of them smiled and turned to the other saying, "All these new interns are so anxious." This put my mind at ease. Manning must be right. The nurses see this day in and day out. They aren't worried. The blood pressure dropped some more. Heather was sweating.

I called Manning. "She doesn't look well," I said.

"Go to sleep. I made the diagnosis." As if that were the conclusive act in the medical drama. Forget the patient. Ignore her distress, the signs of ruptured uterus, the dying baby. It can all be explained because of a few leucocytes seen in the urine. I looked again at the nurses. They were smiling at me complacently.

An hour later I called Manning again. "You better come down."

"Get the hell off my back, Harry. I've seen the patient. I've written my note on the chart. She's okay, I tell you. For Christ's sake I've seen hundreds of these."

"Please come down."

"Go to bed."

An hour later the situation was deteriorating. Even the nurses were concerned. I called Manning again.

He exploded. "If you call me once more, I'm going to have you kicked off the goddamn service. Now leave me alone."

I didn't know what to do. I was paralyzed. No matter what happened to Heather Wormley, I was in no position to save her. I must be wrong. As desperate as the situation looked, as low and floundering as her blood pressure seemed to be, as shocky as her body was, glistening in the frost of quick-drying sweat, as pale as was her skin, who was I to argue with an experienced resident?

"Maybe I should call McCrae?" I wondered aloud to the nurses. They looked at me as if I were some crazed hysteric. "You can't call him. If you are wrong, that's the end of your career. You can't go over the head of the resident."

Heather said, "Help me, Doctor."

Manning had ordered narcotics. Heather was slipping into a stupor. That was why she was clammy and the blood pressure was dropping. That's why the pain was abating. Of course I was hyperexcitable. Of course I was wrong. I had done my job. I went to bed.

Gubiner was McCrae's assistant. He prowled the obstetrical service at The County at dawn hours because McCrae had ordered him to do so. He resented the imposition, but no assistant to McCrae could afford disobedience. The pious chief demanded

74

fealty, discipline and an orderly patrol of his domain. Gubiner was forced to rise an hour earlier than his own practice demanded, often after a semisleepless night delivering babies for his own patients, to satisfy the requirement that an attending physician visit the obstetrical ward at The County at least once a day. Gubiner's rounds were invariably hurried. But he had an instinct for the treacherous nature of childbearing, and although he flew around in the dim light of dawn, often without removing his overcoat, there was something about the pallor, or the smell, or the stillness of Heather that affected him. He marched over and felt her belly. His hand came away moist with her sweat.

"Who the hell has been farting around with this case?" he bellowed. Nurses leaped to their feet. By the time they arrived at Heather's bedside, Gubiner had already removed his coat and let it drop to the floor. He called for a stretcher. I struggled out of bed at his first shout.

Heather was unconscious and in shock. I helped force her onto a stretcher. Two orderlies appeared from nowhere and rolled her to the operating suite. Her respirations were shallow.

Gubiner didn't bother to change. As soon as Heather was transferred to the operating table, a surgical tray was pushed up beside him. The anesthetist had been called. Without waiting, without scrubbing, with rolled sleeves and naught but a pair of sterile gloves, Gubiner stroked cleanly with the scalpel and split Heather's belly wide-open. A masked, clean-scented scrub nurse appeared opposite him at the table. The inevitable retractors were shoved into my hands. Gubiner took giant clamps and thrust them into the belly, grabbing blindly for the uterine arteries. The baby was floating free in the abdominal cavity and blood welled from the rent uterus. The adept nurse anesthetist arrived. Her services for the relief of pain not required for the nearly dead Heather, she started an intravenous and blood soon was coursing into Heather's veins. Gubiner extracted the tortured uterus and sutured the entire abdominal wall together crudely with heavy wire. He told me to start another pint of blood in the other arm. The bleeding had stopped. Heather stopped getting whiter. The nurse anesthetist now administered oxygen to the stricken patient. After a while a tint of color seemed to suffuse her cheeks, and the blood pressure stabilized. Heather, still half in shock, still too obtunded to feel the pain of her stripped belly, was removed to a stretcher and rolled to the recovery room. When Heather recovered, she thanked her doctors, unaware of their contribution to the calamitous series of events that had robbed her both of her baby and of her ability to bear another one.

The case was discussed at the weekly staff conference. McCrae, chain and watch fob glittering gold over a blue vest, sat at the head of the table. His neat fringe of grayed hair shone like a silver halo. Manning laboriously read from the patient's chart, pointedly observing that when he saw the patient she evidenced none of the distressful signs that Gubiner observed the following morning.

"Why did Harry call you?" Gubiner asked.

"He was anxious. I thought he had overdiagnosed the case."

"Maybe he did, maybe he didn't," Gubiner observed. "It seems a peculiar coincidence that he would consider that the patient had a ruptured uterus, which you say she didn't have, and that she would then develop one. Maybe a lousy diagnosis, but a great prediction." Gubiner said acerbically.

"Now, now, gentlemen," McCrae observed. "Medicine is difficult. Here we have one of the great tragedies that occur from time to time in obstetrics. Mrs. Wormley will never again be able to have a baby. But on the other hand, these things happen, and we can congratulate ourselves on the fact that she is alive and well, no doubt due to the efficiency of our staff. I think as a matter of professional courtesy we must accept Dr. Manning's account of the matter. According to his findings I believe his initial conclusions were justified. It's unfortunate that the manifestations of her rupturing uterus were hidden by the kidney infection. But then, gentlemen, if medicine were that clear-cut, there would be no need for doctors."

The conference closed on that note. On the way out Gubiner clutched at McCrae's sleeve.

"I think it was an open-and-shut case from the start. Even the stupid intern made the diagnosis."

"That will be all, Gubiner," McCrae admonished gently. "I am sure there is a lesson here for all of us."

Before Gubiner left the floor I collared him. "What would you have done if I had called you last night?"

"If you were wrong, I'd have kicked your ass off the goddamn service," he said.

When Rush got out of the hospital, we alternated on obstetrics and gynecology. When he was in clinic, I was in the delivery room and vice versa. We rarely saw each other, and I knew of his presence only by the milk containers sitting on the window sill during the colder months.

I heard about him, however. He chafed at the unwritten laws that prevented us from referring patients to birth-control clinics (of which only one existed in the city, a sort of experimental defiance, by a famous and rebellious woman, of the mores of the times), or even to advise patients about birth-control devices, or even to hint that there were ways other than abstinence of preventing pregnancy. True, Andrew McCrae was chief of the service, but even had there been a Shinto extremist running the place, birth-control education would have been forbidden. The clinic was firmly guided by diocesan will, so that none of the impoverished multiparous women, some of whom had given birth to ten or twelve babies out of twenty pregnancies, could be fitted for a diaphragm.

Rush, not a Catholic, bought some diaphragms, which he proceeded to fit to the patients who demanded an end to the servitude of continual pregnancy. The young nurse assigned to him reported him to Manning. Finally, McCrae forced Rush, under threat of expulsion, to desist. The next time Rush encountered the nurse he tore the gold cross pendant from her neck. "You're out of uniform," he said.

The number of milk containers on the window sill multiplied during the crisis in almost direct proportion to the number of new pregnancies that showed up in OB clinic.

One miraculous night when there was no one in labor I went back to the room to sleep. I turned on the lights to illuminate Rush squirming in bed, holding his stomach.

"Hi, Harry."

"Pain?"

"I'm always in pain. What do you think of that sonofabitch threatening me because I want to offer some birth control down at that clinic?"

"He's a sonofabitch," I said, agreeably.

"He's not only a sonofabitch. He's a Catholic sonofabitch."

The door opened and Delgado stepped in. "Hello, fellas. I saw your light. What's new?"

"Christ," said Rush. Delgado nodded modestly. "Another fucking mackerel snapper. I'm surrounded by them. You can't excommunicate me, Delgado, I'm Protestant."

"I didn't come to excommunicate you." Delgado was bewildered.

"What then, burn me at the stake?"

"What's with Rush?" Delgado asked me. "Delirious?"

"No, Hesu. Just a touch of paranoia. They won't let him teach birth control at gynie clinic."

"Oh!"

"So he sees Catholics under the bed. He's filled up to here with it," I said, indicating my throat.

"What the hell have they got you goddamn friars running around this place for? To proselytize the helpless patients? Where the hell are the rabbis and ministers? The Church keeps them out, that's what."

"You're wrong, Wilkie," Delgado said softly. The Church doesn't keep them out."

"Of course not. I didn't mean that," Rush said as if apologizing. "It's the goddamn hospital that keeps them out because the Church tells them to."

"That's not true either, Wilkie. I'm here, it is true, because the Church, the Jesuits, have assigned me here. No rabbis or ministers are assigned to the hospital. As a matter of fact I could use a little help. I do not feel at home ministering to the sick of other faiths. I do what I can to help, but sometimes I feel I am imposing."

"You sound like a reasonable man, Delgado," Rush said. "Don't you think that birth control should be taught in the clinics? Look at those poor women, a dozen children, broke, hungry, no money to feed another mouth. How can they raise another kid properly without depriving those already there? Each additional baby increases their level of poverty and the depths of their misery. How can you push a system like that? Seriously, Delgado, in good conscience, how can you?"

"To the Church it is immoral to deny the miracle of life, or to prevent it."

"Bullshit. You just want to flood the world with Catholics."

"We believe it is wrong for anyone to practice birth control, whatever their religion."

"But not everyone in the clinic believes as you do. Where does the Church get the right to impose its views on all these people in a hospital run on municipal funds, paid for in fact through taxes collected from everybody in the city, not just the Catholics?" Rush rose and struggled to the window, groping for a container of milk.

"What's the sense of getting yourself upset, Wilkie?" Delgado said. "You're making yourself sick."

A long draught of milk seemed to perk Rush up. He faced Delgado full of fight. "Making myself sick?" he yelped. "You are making me sick. You and all the other heathen Catholics around this place. Where's your milk of human kindness, where's your understanding, where's your compassion for these poor women forced to become enchained in perpetuity to the yoke of a full belly and squalling hungry children? How can you tell me after all you've seen here that birth shouldn't be controlled?"

"To deprive any potential being of a chance at life is a mortal sin. You see, Wilkie, to us, being alive isn't a finite moment from the first breath to the last, and it doesn't matter the degree of suffering on earth. It is the entire continuity of the cosmic process of life that interests us. The heavenly rewards for which we live, and which cannot be obtained without life on earth. To deprive an individual of the right to be born deprives him of the right to the hereafter."

Rush turned to me, laughing. "This poor bastard is talking voodoo. What was it Cornell said, Harry: a Catholic isn't a Christian." Rush enjoyed his own sarcasm, and pushed his advantage while Delgado was pondering the last remark.

"Tell me, O Solomon of the cloth, how would you solve this problem? I had a dame in clinic today who had a double uterus and septum dividing the vagina. Understand?"

Delgado nodded. Rush continued, enjoying himself immensely. "Well, a couple of years ago she had a tubal pregnancy on the left side and they had to operate. When they went in, they took out the left uterine horn. Now she has one uterus on the right, with its own cervix, a septum dividing the vagina from the left side which has no uterus."

"So?" Delgado was wary.

"So, you poor schnook. Her old man is screwing her. If he veers to the left she cannot be pregnant. He is Catholic and knows about the choices. If he goes to the left purposely, is he committing a mortal sin?"

Delgado was puzzled. "That's a difficult problem, Wilkie. It is one that I suspect only his conscience could answer."

"You know what, Delgado, you're pussyfooting."

Hesu looked puzzled as Rush rolled back on his bed, howling.

"You're doing great, Wilkie," I said. "First Shaver, then Mc-Crae. You're bowling them over one by one."

Gubiner was competent, but on obstetrical service he deferred to McCrae every time a pregnancy had to be interrupted. Steeped in medical lore is the proscription against abortion. Hippocrates said, "I will not give to a woman an instrument to produce abortion."

The practice was taken over by mangy women in back rooms, cellars and attics, who for a fee would introduce knitting needles and other implements, as well as infection, into the wombs of vulnerable women. Many died.

It wasn't this that caused Gubiner to defer to McCrae, but the additional burden of Church dogma, which, stated simply, insisted that if the birth of the baby endangered the mother, doctors would do everything in their power to save both, but in no instance could they kill the fetus to save the mother. If the mother died during delivery or late pregnancy, it was the will of God.

Since McCrae was a studious, devout Catholic layman, well versed in the religious ethic as well as clerical law, Gubiner preferred him to make the decisions in all such cases.

Although he never performed the abortion himself, McCrae often decided in their favor as long as Gubiner would do them. However, he agonized over them like a warden the night of an execution. It was a moment during which his religion and profession clashed, and there was no way other than by accepting the feelings of guilt that he could resolve the conflict.

McCrae was a striking man, large-framed, with precise, prominent features. His nose had the clean lines of a ship's prow, and set the standard for the precise elegance of his brows.

When he was operating, his baldness hidden by the scrub cap, one could picture how patrician his appearance might have been with hair, fine as a calligrapher's brush, combed obliquely to form a mantle of silver. He was a privileged individual whose commanding presence permitted him to speak slowly, with long breaks between words and sentences, without fear of interruption. Equally, he never interrupted, but listened quietly to lengthy discourse, or questions addressed to him, then paused to digest the information before issuing a reply. At times he would merely nod or shake his head. He was a man whose very presence epitomized the even pace of pregnancy between its initial and final spasms of passion. His life was a harmonic resonance between his God and his work, his angels and his women.

This composure was seriously disrupted when Praline Pender was admitted one night to the obstetrical service. She had ten children, was in her eighth month of pregnancy and was seriously ill.

The stars were out the night I brought Praline to the hospital. Gibson called me from admitting. "An OB case called in. Bucky's going to pick her up in the bus. Maybe you better go along." I agreed. It was only a ten-minute ride. I figured the fresh air would do me good. Bucky drove there quickly and didn't bother with the siren.

"We're just providing transportation. No emergency," he said.

Praline lived with her family in a meager two-room apartment. A small double electric burner sat on a table near a dilapidated icebox in what passed for a kitchenette, but which was really an alcove in the main room. Mr. Pender, in the dusty mismatched clothes of poverty, sat on a crate. Praline rocked slowly back and forth in a straight-backed rocker, her hands clasped around her big belly. As my eyes became accustomed to the dark shadows, forms and faces of her children seemed to appear out of nowhere, even the weanling girl tucked in the half-opened drawer of an old cabinet. I realized suddenly that one of the problems blacks would have as actors in movies and plays would be the lighting. Their forms and faces were obscured in the gray blanket of semidarkness.

81

Praline struggled to her feet, turned to her torpid husband and said, "I'm going, Sam."

He looked up at her and said, "So long," as Bucky and I assisted Praline to the door so that she could go to the hospital and wrestle with the problems imposed by the imminent arrival of her eleventh child.

The problem soon proved to be anything but simple. Praline was a diabetic and the initial urine samples curdled the copper sulfate solutions to a deep orange flocculant, indicating large quantities of sugar in her urine. She was in partial acidosis, and her huge belly was regarded ominously by those of us who knew that diabetics often gave birth to abnormally large babies.

I had originally ascribed her huffing and puffing to the gravid load she was carrying, but when she was put to bed her breathing became labored and it was apparent that she couldn't get enough air when supine. The bed was cranked to a sitting position. "I been sleeping sittin' up in that ole rocker for three weeks now," she told us.

Black skin confers more than the obvious disadvantages. Cyanosis is hard to see, unless one visualizes the nail beds in daylight; neck veins that pulsate abnormally, and fail to empty when the patient is in the sitting position, are not as clearly delineated in blacks as in whites. Praline had these signs and more. Her legs were water-filled. Her blood pressure was elevated to 220/130 mm. of mercury. Her milk-filled breasts heaved with each of the rapid beats of her heart. A palpable thrill could be felt over the precordium, and blowing murmurs assailed the stethoscopes placed against her chest.

Manning checked her over shortly after I did, and said, "Shit."

I knew he was referring to her medical condition, but Praline didn't and looked at him reproachfully. He walked out of the room and I followed.

"What a fucking mess," he said.

"You gonna call Gubiner?"

"He's on vacation."

"McCrae?"

"Shit, no. I'll handle it."

"What are you going to do? She's awfully sick."

"A section is out of the question. She would never survive surgery. I'll induce labor and hope for the best."

The fetal heart was strong and the baby was deep in the pelvis. We started an intravenous, and each drop carried small amounts of the powerful Pituitrin, a posterior pituitary hormone that would, we hoped, induce the uterus to strong rhythmic contractions. Within an hour Praline was well into labor. Manning looked at his watch and increased the rate of drip. "Christ, the way she's going I'll be up all night."

The contractions became more violent and Praline's moans became short shrieks with each contraction as they mounted in a crescendo of uterine violence. We moved her into the delivery room. Suddenly the uterus went into a tetanic contraction, the cervix dilated and the arm of the baby protruded from the vaginal entroitus. Manning moved to the foot of the table, and introduced his gloved hand. "Okay, let's get this over with." A look of consternation creased his brow. The uterine tetany let up. "Slow the intravenous," he shouted. "Check the fetal heart, Harry."

"It's okay. Can you deliver the baby?"

"I'm trying." He worked for a few more minutes. Father Delgado, capped and gowned, appeared at the side of the table.

"Trouble?" he asked quietly.

Manning quit. "Watch her, Harry." Sweat beaded his forehead. "I'm going to call McCrae."

I didn't want any more contractions while Manning was gone, so I clamped off the intravenous. Delgado took Praline's hand in both of his. "You'll be all right," he reassured her. Until now, she had had no inkling that she wouldn't be, so the reassurance scared her. The fetal heart, which had raced under the stress of the sustained uterine contraction evoked by the Pituitrin, slowed somewhat. The dusky color of the baby's arm returned to the café-au-lait complexion of newborn blacks whose pigmental scar has yet to be mobilized.

We held the tableau for almost half an hour. During this time Praline developed moisture at the bases of her lungs. Manning would pop his head in from time to time. "How's everything going?" he would ask.

If she died, Manning wouldn't be there to see it, I thought. "She has moist rales. Don't you think we should give her some Mercuhydrin?"

"Sure, sure. Whatever you think best," he said.

83

I remembered my medical school experiences, and gave Praline digitalis and Mercuhydrin, injected slowly into the muscle of her arm, from separate syringes. It would help her within a few hours. If McCrae decided to operate, she would be stronger for the stress than she was now. But for the next hour little would help. We started to give her oxygen. I was anxious for McCrae to arrive. The feeling of helplessness, my inability to take decisive action, was nerve-racking. I cursed my ignorance. I wanted to join Manning in the hallway.

By the time McCrae entered the delivery room my heart was thumping as hard as Praline's poor heart, and I was almost as breathless as she. McCrae was in his scrub suit. Manning followed him into the room sketching the history of the past few hours in a low voice. "She went into premature labor," he said, "and I can't budge the baby. I think she has a dystocia."

I didn't see how he could get away with a lie like that, but he was going to give it a good try, because while McCrae was starting his examination Manning busied himself with quietly removing the bottle of Pituitrin and replacing it with a bottle of glucose and water.

After McCrae fumbled in the vagina for a while he turned and said quietly to Manning, "You are right, Doctor. The baby can't deliver from below."

"What's the matter?" Delgado asked me in a whisper.

"The baby's shoulders are larger than the widest diameter of the mother's pelvis."

"What are they going to do?"

"I don't know."

"Will you do a section, sir?" Manning asked. It was the only way they'd get the baby out alive.

"The mother won't survive a section." McCrae called to the nurse, "Chloroform anesthesia. Keep it light and be very careful," he instructed. A nurse stepped to the head of the table with the mask. Praline went through a violent excitement stage. "Deeper, deeper," called McCrae. As soon as the bucking stopped he told the nurse to remove the mask. "Just keep her at this level. No deeper." Then he called to the remaining nurse, "Rongeur, please."

"We don't have one. I'll have to get one from the OR."

"Hurry then."

A hush had fallen over the room as the implication of the order sank in. We stood like statues. Delgado broke the silence.

"What are you about to do, Dr. McCrae?"

"I'm going to get the baby out of there."

"Alive?"

"Impossible."

"You can't do that, Dr. McCrae. You can't kill that baby."

"If I operate to extract a live baby, I'll kill the mother."

"But the mother will be sanctified if she dies in childbirth. The baby must be given a chance. You can't knowingly deprive the baby of a chance to grow up and know God."

"If I do nothing, both will die. I have to make a choice. I can't willfully make the choice that will save the baby and kill the mother. She has ten other children to care for. I can't take their mother."

"God knows the mother and will honor her. His will is that the baby shall live."

"His will, Father, is that the baby shall die and the mother shall live."

"That is your will, not His."

"It's His." I never saw McCrae ruffled before, but now his face was deep red. "He has seen fit to give the choice to me. He has forced me to make a choice. He has endowed me with free will. I will under no circumstances sacrifice the mother. If I do what my conscience insists I do, Father, then God's will be done."

"Please, Doctor," Delgado said in desperation, knowing he was pushing McCrae to the limits of his patience. "The mother is known to God. The baby, were it to die now, would be lost in limbo."

The nurse entered the room slowly and handed the rongeur on a sterile towel reluctantly to McCrae. He accepted it gingerly, then turned to Delgado. "The baby is still alive. The arm is protruding. Baptize the baby."

"I can't. I need the whole baby. I need the head of the baby."

"Any part of the living baby is acceptable under these circumstances."

"No, the Church says—"

"Goddamn it, I know what the Church says. Stop pressing me. Just do what you have to do."

"I'll give it last rites at the same time," Delgado said cuttingly.

"That won't be necessary, Father. The baby is innocent, free of sin. Baptize, quickly. Then leave the room, please."

Delgado started to leave. "Come back here. Do what I tell you."

"I was going to get holy water."

"Any water will do. Hurry, before the baby dies."

Delgado took a cupful of water from the sink and poured it over the arm of the baby. The sacrament was over. Delgado left.

McCrae changed his gown and donned sterile gloves. "Dr. Manning. Step up here, please. You will assist me."

Manning cowered at the sound of his name and struggled, hesitantly, to the foot of the table. McCrae extracted the baby's arm full length, and with the other hand groped deeply into the womb, finally extracting the pulsing umbilical cord. He cut it.

"Tell me when the fetal heart has stopped, Harry."

I monitored the waning thrusts of the wee heart until no sounds could be heard. "I think it has stopped, sir."

McCrae used a scalpel to cut deeply to the hidden shoulder joint. Then, holding the arm extended, he reached for the rongeur with his free hand and held it out to Manning. "Take this, Doctor, and cut the arm free."

Manning was shaking. "Quickly, Doctor," McCrae said in a strained voice. Manning inserted the instrument and soon there was a crunching sound muffled by the soft encircling tissues. McCrae withdrew the useless limb. Then he reached in, found the other arm and pulled it toward him and extracted the mutilated child. He cradled it in his arms and waited patiently while Manning delivered the placenta. Then he handed the torn corpse to Manning and said, "Here is your patient, Doctor."

He paused, as if to say something else, then strode from the room.

Praline Pender recovered slowly, incompletely and without lament.

Before she was discharged, I told her, "You know, Praline, there was a point there where we had a choice. We could have saved the baby but you would have died for sure."

She pondered that. "Someone else is always gonna make another baby, Doctor, but no one else is gonna make another woman for my ten kids."

"You are Catholic, aren't you?"

"Yeah, but I didn't do the choosin'."

I was always welcome at Lapius's house whatever the hour. I couldn't sleep. It was late when I let myself in. Lapius was reading. A curtain of lute music in the background damped the street noises. Lapius poured me a cordial. "Rough night?" he asked.

"I can't handle the message," I told him. "I could never do what McCrae had to do tonight."

"Of course you could. The key word is 'had.' Once you know that McCrae *had* to do it, you would have done the same in his place. It's more difficult to wait for someone else to make a decision. You are helpless, powerless—"

"He made the only decision I could live with."

"Nonsense. You will have to live with all the decisions made by your chiefs. People live or die because of them. That, Harry, is the process of learning in medicine. You can't hide from it."

"It's expensive."

"Everything is expensive. Disease is expensive. You never grow up in this business. The best you can hope for is to keep growing."

Although gynecology emergency was sometimes rewardingly dramatic, the gynecology clinic was a vaginal cesspool. Gubiner could never conceal his contempt for these classless people from the pit of society, whores, vagrants, runaways. To the older motherly types with menopausal problems, or the postmenopausal signals that might mean cancer, Gubiner was kind and deferential.

But to the others, he was rough. "C'mon, spread your twikky. Hurry up. I can't be here all day. Relax for Christ's sake. Goddamn it, spread your legs. You'll break my glasses. Jesus Christ, where did you get that dose?"

Then he would call out, "Manning, Harry, get over here. Look at these condyloma. Okay, Harry, what are they, syphilitic or intertriginous?"

I would peer at the warty clusters. Sometimes the harmless

warts clustered like pointed pine trees among the more insidious flat excrescences that denoted lues. "Probably syphilis."

"Good. Take a blood for serology. Have her back in a week."

That was a redundant order, because all the women had Wassermann tests performed routinely as they entered the clinic.

Manning, on the other hand, was polite and deferential to all patients. He was remote as he busied himself with their intimate pudendal parts. Refined clinical distinctions didn't interest him, and all patients with positive blood tests were treated automatically. As a result some were treated needlessly because of false positive results.

"What difference does it make?" he said. "The penicillin will cure them."

"But they are stigmatized."

"So they're stigmatized. So what? They're cured, aren't they?"

In my view the patients didn't have much to choose from, but those who returned time and again asked for Gubiner.

"Dr. Gubiner isn't here today. Dr. Manning will see you," I said to one of them.

"I'll come back some other time."

"That's silly," I said. "They are both good doctors."

"That Manning. He insult me. I don't want him to touch me."

"I never heard Dr. Manning insult anybody," I told her.

"That's just it," she said. "He never talks to me at all. Just tells things to the nurse and the other doctors. Like I was a piece of baggage. Like he was reading things off a menu. Gubiner talks to me. He doesn't always talk nice, but he treats me like a person when he examines me. I know that whether he likes me or not, or whether he likes what I'm doing or not, he'll take good care of me. That Manning, when he examine you, you hardly feel it. Gubiner hurts you, and I know he's goin' deep and won't miss anything. Shit, Manning ain't gonna break anything if he goes deep. He just fusses around like you're dirty or somethin'. That Gubiner, he ain't afraid of a little pus."

"Doesn't McCrae ever come to clinic?" I asked Gubiner.

"He's busy. It offends him. Besides, I like it. These dames come in looking like garbage cans and I send them out with pretty pussies. Only I wish they would use them for something other than to make money with."

"Doesn't it bother you that the same ones come back again and again?"

Gubiner rolled down his shirtsleeves. "That's their business, Harry. Mine is to fix them up. That's what makes it tough on McCrae. It offends his morality. But me, I don't care."

"And Manning?"

"Manning is going to practice in the suburbs and make money. He'll do the hysterectomies, the repairs, the tumors. You can do them by the book. But this work is different. These dames not only have venereal disease, but on top of it have fecal organisms contaminating the vagina, yeast infections, strep, staph, you name it. It's not enough to clear up the VD. What about the rest of it? Are they diabetic? Is that why they have yeast? Are they having frequent urinary infections which can never be cleared entirely because they are reinfecting from a contaminated vagina? Do they know how to wipe their asses so they don't pull shit into their pussies? I teach them all these things. How to douche, how to take care of themselves. My God, and the men!"

"The men?"

"How can a man introduce his pecker into that kind of slime? Christ, the sex urges are powerful. No one in his right mind would touch that without gloves, yet after a few drinks these dames find guys who will be undeterred by the stench and filth and screw 'em without rubbers. I may talk rough to them and tease them. I don't hide my disdain, but by God after I get done with them they've had a course in gynecological hygiene, and they damn well know they've been taken care of."

He was right. But the "stench and slime," as Gubiner put it, were getting to me.

Under the best circumstances the most that can be said for the female genitalia is that they are unique. There has been no universal acclaim of their aesthetic qualities.

Whereas women in the delivery room were sublime and reconfirmed my awe of motherhood, gynecology clinic was quite the opposite. Whereas obstetrics assured me of the pudendal power of the female, gynecology turned me pudent. Although many of the women attended clinic because of tumescent changes of their internal organs, or for dysfunctional uterine bleeding, the great majority presented themselves with one or another venereal disease, or a reasonable facsimile. Whereas the genitalia of the

89

fastidious female, when exposed by the coaxing of the gloved examining fingers, have the delicacy of butterfly wings, the interiors pink, lubricated with the pearly milkiness of the mucoid discharge, the genitalia of the disease-ridden women were inevitably thickened, inflamed, encrusted. Weeping sores defaced the vault, which was covered by purulent matter. The inner membranes would be raging red in color.

I vowed never again to touch a woman, a vainglorious vow because in retrospect I don't believe that at that time I had ever meaningfully touched one.

I clung to my resolve for about a week. Then Elspeth taught me to believe that it was brash and imprudent for one so young to bind oneself irrevocably to celibacy.

6

ELSPETH. A nurse, chameleon-like, moving effortlessly in the shadows of daily turmoil. I took no notice of her until she handed me a slip of paper that read: "Call me later."

Elspeth guided me gently through a primer of love. Under her quiet tutelage my dormant instincts came alive again, and fired all the senses of which a body is capable. She cleansed with beguiling fragrance and the perfume of desire my memory of rot, stench and pus of the gynie clinic.

Elspeth, beautifully formed, was perhaps more alluring because naked she still wore earrings and a jade pendant that swung gently from a chain of fine-spun gold between her quivering breasts. I was captivated. We lay in each other's arms. Suddenly she peered at the dawn bleaching the black of night and said, "I think you had better go now."

"When will I see you again?" I asked tenderly.

Elspeth stiffened, turned away and paused as if digesting the question. Then in the cold, distant voice of a woman discouraging a rejected suitor, she said, "How can I answer that now? Call me one day." I searched in vain for a wistful note in her reply. Elspeth, who had saved me from the fear, nay an inculcated abhorrence, of physical contact, was to introduce me to the emotional mutilation of love and passion.

I called Elspeth as she had suggested.

"Sorry, I'm busy," she said as to a stranger.

"Do you know who this is?" I asked, sure that she had mistaken the voice.

"Yes, Harry. Good night." Click.

A week later she met me in the hall. "Will I see you tonight?" she asked.

"Sure, if you like," I said, but she had retreated so quickly I doubted that she heard my answer. I ran after her. "Look, Elspeth, I'd like to come over, but I don't like to be treated like a stranger afterward."

"But you are a stranger, Harry dear," she said sweetly.

My second lesson was total immersion. I rose from the bed of Venus enraptured, captured, enslaved. "Are we still strangers?" I asked, sure from her impassioned responses to my ardent and competent love-making that I held the upper hand.

"Of course we are, Harry. I hardly know you."

Lola Perez, sixteen years old, single, in her eighth month of pregnancy, was brought to the hospital by her mother because of abdominal pain. She didn't want to be in the hospital. She fussed when the nurses helped undress her, and again when they cajoled her into donning a hospital gown.

"Iss nawthin'," she kept insisting, and answered most of my questions with an indifferent shrug of her shoulders. She was perky and, in contrast to her mother, not in the least upset about the prospects of motherhood out of wedlock.

"Jus' a leetle pain," she said over and over again. "Iss nawthin'. Will go away."

She was wrong. She had generalized abdominal tenderness, which increased even while I examined her. She winced when I palpated the lower quadrants. The baby moved from time to time. Initially the fetal heart was strong. There was no cause for alarm, but the abdominal distress was disconcerting. I worked her up and sent studies to the laboratory. They came back normal. Her blood pressure was adequate, her pulse strong. Remembering the fetish Manning had about white cells in the urine, I scrutinized the specimen carefully, but found no abnormalities. Manning wouldn't be able to call this one pyelonephritis, I told myself. Since we had catheterized her for the initial urine, I decided to leave an indwelling Foley in place to be certain when Manning checked the urine there would be no contamination by vaginal secretions. I called Manning and told him of the case.

"Is she sick?"

"She's here. Something must be wrong."

"Call me later and keep me informed," he said, like a recording. I vowed I would. We placed a blood pressure cuff on her arm and I monitored her carefully throughout the afternoon. I was puzzled. Certainly, appendicitis can occur in a pregnant woman, diverticulitis, intussusception, volvulus of bowel, and even, in deference to Manning, disorders of the urinary system. Lola showed no true signs of any of these, yet her abdomen was becoming increasingly tender.

Lola's mother arrived with Luis Peralta, the father-to-be. The way he carried on no one could doubt that he was in love with Lola, and wanted to marry her and have more children.

"How is Luis?" he asked me.

"You mean Lola," I said.

"No, Luis."

"Who is Luis?"

"My baby."

"So far so good."

"How's my baby?" Lola's mother asked.

"You mean Luis?"

"No, Lola."

"So far so good."

Shortly after nine in the evening, about six hours after Lola was admitted, Manning strolled onto the ward. He half-listened to my presentation of the case. He checked Lola's abdomen carefully, then her groin. She was much more tender and no longer dissembled about the pain. "Eet's getting worse, hey, Doctor? I gonna have babee soon?" The pain was steady and uncompromising, with none of the periodicity of labor. Manning said nothing, left the room and went to the nurses' desk to write up the chart. I checked the fetal heart again and finally concluded that it wasn't quite as strong as it had been before.

I apprised Manning of this. "Of course not, Harry. She has more abdominal rigidity than before and that would damp the fetal heart sounds." Sounded reasonable. I let the matter drop.

"What do you think?" I asked Manning when he had finished.

"Hernia. Not an obstetrical problem."

"I didn't feel a hernia."

"Try again." He checked his watch. "I have to go out for an hour. Call the surgeons and have them watch her."

Lola's pains were increasing. I checked her groin carefully. Indeed, there was a small, painless, nontender bulge on the right inguinal area, but I couldn't see how that was connected with the case.

Manning waved to me as he left. "Don't be long," I called after him. "Something's going on here that I don't understand."

"Call Cushing if you get into any trouble."

Cushing was snoozing when I got to his room. I prodded him. "Oh, hello, Harry." He was bleary-eyed.

"Hate to bother you, but there's a case in obstetrics I'd like you to see."

"What's the problem?"

"I'm not sure, but I think it's trouble." I sketched the details as he struggled from bed.

"Go down and get another blood count. I'll follow as soon as I splash some cold water on my face."

Cushing came down shortly and Lola submitted once again to a physical examination. Cushing, though, started with her eyes and worked his way down.

"What did the internal examination show, Harry?"

"To tell you the truth, I didn't do one."

"Oh?"

"Well, I hated to put the kid through too many, and I expected Manning to do it when he saw her."

"Manning didn't do it either?"

"I guess once he decided that it was a surgical problem there was no need for one."

"What's the matter with you, Harry? You're forgetting all the thoroughness you learned on surgery."

"I guess so."

Lola's belly was becoming distended.

"Did you order another count?"

I nodded. Cushing was becoming impatient. "I think this is an obstetrical problem, Harry. I can't find a hernia."

"How about that bulge?"

"Whatever that is, it's not causing her any trouble. Let's get her into the examining room."

We put Lola up in stirrups, and Cushing introduced a speculum gently into the vagina. "Easy, girl," he said to the tense Lola, "I won't hurt you."

He peered into the entroitus for an extended period of time, longer, I thought, than was necessary to inspect the cervix.

"Here, Harry, take a look." I peered over his shoulder. "No, Doctor, not that way. Take hold of the speculum and do it properly." We changed places. I grabbed the handle of the speculum and followed the light beam along the metal tongue of the instrument. "What do you see, Harry?" Cushing asked.

"Nothing unusual."

"How does the cervix look to you?"

"I can't see the cervix."

"That's the point. Why the hell can't we see the cervix?"

An hour or more must have passed because Manning was back. He walked jauntily into the examining room. "Well, Paul," he said formally, "will you operate?"

"Operate? On what?"

"The hernia."

"I don't think she has a hernia. Incidentally, Manning, what did you find on your internal examination?"

Manning was flustered. For a gynecologist to omit a pelvic exam was like Billy the Kid marching to a shootout without guns. "As a matter of fact, I intended to do it in the OR when she was relaxed, under anesthesia."

"Take a look now, Manning, and tell us what you think. Us surgeons can't do a pelvic examination as well as you fellows."

Manning strode to the foot of the table. "Hold it," Cushing said. "Maybe you ought to wash up and put some gloves on."

"I intended to, Paul, don't worry." He turned to the sink and soon was back at the table holding the speculum. He fiddled with it for a while, rotated it, then withdrew it and did a bimanual examination.

We waited expectantly. "Everything seems normal," he said.

"Did you see the cervix?" Cushing asked.

"No, but I felt it."

"Why can't we see it?"

"Distortion of the vagina by the baby," Manning said briskly.

"It's strange, don't you think? I've never lost a cervix before," Cushing said.

"You don't do obstetrics for a living," Manning replied.

"I think it's an obstetrical case, Manning."

"I think it's surgical."

A nurse walked in with the lab slips. Lola's hemoglobin was down to ten grams. I checked the fetal heart again and motioned to Cushing. He checked it and invited Manning to do the same. "Whatever it is, we better take her up to the OR right away," Cushing said.

"I still think it's your case, Paul," Manning said, fidgeting. He was anxious to go somewhere, and Cushing wasn't about to let him. "We'll scrub together, Manning. If it turns out to be surgical, I'll take over; if it's obstetrical, I'll assist you. How's that for a compromise?"

Manning couldn't get out of it. We moved Lola to the OR. I sought her seething relatives and tried to explain that Lola was in more trouble than we had originally anticipated.

The OR shone like polar ice in the moonlight, a white island in the sea of darkened corridors and rooms. I blinked several times to adjust my eyes to the light. The towels, the masks, the caps, the gowns, the stretcher, the nurses, the sweet bulging softness of the drowsy nubile Lola, and the tray of sharpened steel with which to cut her. I suppressed with a shrug the chill at the nape of my neck.

There were no sounds. Cushing waited patiently until Lola was asleep. The anesthetist peered over her mask. "She's ready now, Doctor."

Cushing pressed the point of the scalpel into Lola's fleshy belly, which quivered. "Deeper anesthesia, please," he said quietly. No histrionics. After a while he tried again. The breathing was slow and measured. Manning was restless.

"Let's go, I've got—"

"Be patient, Doctor, we may be here for a while yet," Cushing said courteously. He drew a fine line with the scalpel. Lola lay perfectly still. Pinpoint droplets of blood coalesced in the wound to form a red streak, like an aftereffect. More blood welled into rivulets as the muscles were incised, and soon the crisp tympani of snapping steel was heard as we applied hemostats to the bleeders. The peritoneum bulged like a purple jellyfish. Cushing incised it quickly. The baby was floating free in the abdominal cavity.

"It's your case, Doctor," he said to Manning, stepping back from the table. Manning moved over and Cushing took his place as first assist. Blood welled up from the belly.

"My God, a ruptured uterus," Manning exclaimed. He scooped the baby from the abdominal cavity and handed it to a nurse.

"Hemostats, the largest you have, quickly," he shouted. He laid his palm flat out, waiting for the instruments to be slapped into his gloved hand. One at a time he plunged them into the pelvis and clamped them tight.

"I've got the uterine arteries," he said to Cushing. "That should stop the bleeding. Scissors, please." Feeling his way deep beneath the sea of blood, he extended the scissors, guiding them with his free hand, and snipped once on either side of the uterus.

"Suction."

The suction tip was introduced. Currant jelly clots clogged the tube. Manning freed it and scooped them out with his hand. Cushing and I were busy sponging. The placenta was lying athwart several coils of intestines. Manning paused. "Everything seems under control now," he said victoriously. Cushing poked his finger under the placenta and tried to nudge it away from the bowel.

"How's the baby?" Manning called to the nurse.

"Expired. Dead on delivery."

"That's too bad," he murmured. "Well, we'll save the mother anyway. Okay, let's get the uterus out."

"What for? It was an abdominal pregnancy," Cushing said.

"What are you talking about? It was a ruptured uterus—" Manning felt deep into the pelvis and blanched. "I'm committed," he said. "I've got to take it out now. I've cut the uterine arteries."

Cushing helped him complete the hysterectomy. When we had finished, Cushing and I went for coffee. We left Manning to dictate the case.

Lola did well. The next morning the beehive of relatives was still in the halls. Manning entered and extricated her father and mother from the throng.

"It was a close call," he told them. "We're heartbroken about the baby, but at least Lola is all right." They patted him on the back and broke into the sickly smiles bred by the sudden release of anxiety.

Afterward I asked Manning, "Aren't you going to tell them that Lola can't have any more children?"

"That's privileged information," he told me. "That's between Lola and her doctor. I'll tell her when I see fit. If I told her now, it might impede her recovery."

He never did tell her. It was a long time before she realized that she would never be able to have a baby.

The case came up again many years later. We were in Lapius's apartment. Lapius was angry. His voice was booming. Manning slunk deep in the upholstered wing chair while Lapius hurled charges at him. "You lied to her. You told her that she would never have any more periods but that it would not affect her ability to conceive. In a moment of misjudgment or possibly panic you had excised her uterus. Then you covered up your error. You filed a false operative report, omitting mention of the hysterectomy. What did you do with the uterus? It never arrived at the pathology laboratory. You were in the clear, except that Lola came back to the clinic to find out why she couldn't conceive. We dug out her old records, and the sordid business came to light. By all rights I should submit these records to the medical society, or even to the district attorney. Or to a lawyer," Lapius added as an afterthought. "But I think we can settle it right here, Dr. Manning. You will pay Lola Perez ten thousand dollars a year for ten years from the lucrative proceeds of your suburban practice in obstetrics and gynecology."

Manning straightened suddenly. "That's blackmail!" he exclaimed.

"I'm trying to be kind to you, Doctor," Lapius said, having difficulty enunciating the word "Doctor" without having it sound sarcastic. "After all, a good malpractice lawyer could easily extract at least as much in open court. I have the necessary documents here for you to sign."

Manning signed quickly and left.

The room was quiet now.

"There was something else," I muttered. "I remember Cushing

98

saying that he'd never forgive himself. But I can't remember what it was about."

"Yes, the absence of the cervix," Lapius said. "As soon as the operation was over, Cushing realized the significance of the fact that none of you could see the cervix on the internal examination, yet you could feel it."

"What was the significance of that?" I asked.

"The baby's head was in the cul-de-sac compressing the posterior vaginal wall against the anterior vaginal wall. The speculum wasn't long enough to penetrate. But on manual examination you could feel it. That was the clue to the fact that the baby was completely outside the uterus, that there was an abdominal pregnancy. Cushing said he could never forgive himself for not having figured that out in advance. He could have saved her uterus."

Suddenly a memory jogged me. A shiver ran through my body. The shivering increased until I trembled violently. I was soaked. The night drench of fatigue that bathed me whenever I wakened prematurely penetrated my clothing. Cloying moisture beaded my lip. The image of Lapius vanished as I opened my eyes, and the memory of Cushing brought tears to my eyes. But that bastard Manning, there was to be no punishment for him worse than the retribution of the court of my dreams.

In contrast to the gangrene of surgery and the aseptic acrid odors of obstetrics, or the purulence of the GYN service, the flavor of the medical service was death, the smell urea. It was also a less immediate service, a protracted cause where patients often remained for "the duration." It was a service of tenacious clinging to a thread of life, of sustaining measures often effective, and thus cruel in their sustenance.

The medical wards were quiet and solemn compared to surgery, where a fervor of immediacy prevailed, where the stricken were usually the victims of acute assault that had not yet robbed the spirit. Surgery was the knight entering combat, medicine the ministry of the dying.

On medicine doctors could do little else than hone their diagnostic tools, so that with stethoscope, percussion note and probing fingers, they could discover faults for which there were no cures, delineate the hampered heart valves that would do no more than foretell the fate of the damaged organ. For most diseases we could do little but make an ally of time.

Medicine was the service where Christine Connolly died after months during which her belly swelled with the fluids dammed by the vascular shunts of a damaged liver. How many times we performed paracenteses, puncturing her abdominal wall with giant cannulae to drain the several gallons of fluid that threatened to strangle her by intense pressure, could be counted by the small crosshatched scars on her belly. And each time we removed the ascitic fluid, ounces of precious protein drained irretrievably away. She lay sallow-cheeked for weeks on the cruel pallet of a bed uncomplaining, large blue and wondering eyes set in sockets that daily seemed to become deeper to form the orbital crevices of a human skull, while her lips drew back from her browning teeth in a sepulchral smile. Yet Christine remained soft, gentle. Perhaps these qualities were conferred on her by the languor of the disease, and I have often wondered whether good health would have transformed her into a vigorous shrew. She seemed most remote of all the patients, yet most loving, like a helpless fawn between the sights of a gun. Delgado saw her frequently. They talked quietly and smiled at each other often. He described so often the journey to another place that it became familiar to her. Christine talked to me about her family, her childhood, her God. I listened. There was no other way I could help her.

When I left for a week of vacation, she waved a cheery good-bye. I returned quite late one night and, before bedding down, decided to check the ward. Christine's bed was at the entrance; she was asleep but restless. I leaned down and whispered her name.

Her eyes opened wide and she thrust herself up in bed and threw her arms around me. She cried on my shoulder, and shed the only tears I had ever seen upon her cheeks. "Oh, I'm glad you're back," she sobbed. "I was afraid I would never see you again."

"Good night, princess," I said, tucking her in and fluffing her pillow. Her cheeks were waxen in the glow of the night lights. "I was gone only a week. Sleep now. I'll see you in the morning."

The morning was bright, but within the hospital the bleak gray ceilings and dirty walls surrounded us like a sullen overcast. I passed a body in the hall, covered entirely by sheets. I hoped it wasn't Christine. Foreman, chief resident on female medicine, was waiting for me, center ward, a pocket watch in his hand, dramatically demonstrating that I was late. "Five minutes this time, Harry," he said.

We made rounds quickly. Foreman did little other than count the patients. "Who died?" I asked, after we were finished.

"Mafkovsky," he said, slurring the word, as if it didn't really matter who it was. We walked from the ward. Hummil, the nurse in charge, who had followed us during the rounds dutifully noting suggestions and comments about the patients, accompanied us to the hall. I looked at the stiff body under the sheets, when suddenly the portion covering her head billowed upward.

"Is that Mafkovsky?" I asked Hummil, in a whisper.

"Yes."

"Who pronounced her?"

"Foreman. I'm waiting for an orderly to take her to the morgue." A body was still a gender until it got to the morgue, after which it became an "it."

"Before she goes it might be a good idea to check her pulse," I suggested. Hummil walked to the stretcher and extended a hand beneath the sheets. She turned to me in wide-eyed wonder. "I feel a pulse," she muttered.

"I think she's breathing too. I just saw her sigh," I told her.

Foreman was halfway down the hall, and I decided it might be best not to disturb his equanimity, which always made him more unpleasant than usual.

We uncovered Mafkovsky and rolled her back to the ward. On the way I noticed that Christine had an unnatural pallor, grayish superimposed on the usual yellow, and her head was turned to the pillow.

Mafkovsky was awakening as we transferred her from the stretcher to the bed.

"You changed your mind?" she asked.

"What do you mean?" I said.

"You were taking me someplace?"

"We changed our minds. We thought you might need an X-ray, but we changed our minds," I said.

I went over to Christine, who was now dead, and we transferred her to the stretcher vacated by Mafkovsky. We bound Christine with the shroud sheets, and when Foreman returned later to the ward, little had changed, and there was still a body in the hall.

"Get this thing down to the morgue, for Chrissake," Foreman yelled. "It's depressing."

"Soon as we can," I reassured him.

Mafkovsky had hypertension, at the moment in medical history when the disease was treated by the Kempner rice diet, effective, mainly, because it was free of salt. In addition, when served in the limited quantities that seemed second nature to the County kitchen, it was a diet low in calories. Mafkovsky had lost considerable weight, and flesh hung loosely on her body. She hated the diet.

"I'm so weak from not eating," she said, "maybe you shouldn't give such a strong sleeping pill. I thought I was in a coma. When I woke up, I must have been crazy," she said. "I pulled the sheets up over my head. I never do that usually, you know."

I pulled her chart and reduced the dose of her bedtime soporific.

Every morning on rounds, Mafkovsky had the same complaint.

"I need more to eat. I'm wasting away. What am I, a pigeon, you are feeding me rice all the time?"

Her blood pressure had dropped precipitously. We had her up and around in a week or so, and ready for discharge. "Get her the hell out of here," Foreman urged. "We need the beds."

Mafkovsky was comfortable on the ward now. We put her on a regular diet low in salt, and she no longer complained of being a bird fed daily rations of rice. But she wouldn't go home.

"I like it here. I can help out."

"But we need the bed," I explained to her.

She drew herself up to her full fifty-nine inches height. "I'm not going, and you can't make me go," she said firmly. "I will help here. I will help with making beds, and getting things for patients."

"You've got to leave," I told her. "You are not sick. You don't have to be in a hospital."

"But you can't make me leave," she said firmly.

"Why not?"

"Because it's a poorhouse and I am poor. So I can stay as long as I like."

102

"Ridiculous," stormed Foreman. "I need the beds. Get her the hell out of here. Discharge her."

"I did." I showed him the chart.

"Then get her dressed and bring her to emergency and call a cab to take her home."

I told Hummil to get Mafkovsky dressed. Then I called Social Service, who assured me Mafkovsky had a place to live. We put her, protesting, into a wheelchair, and I had an orderly push the chair to admitting, with orders to get her into a cab.

An hour later the orderly brought her back to the ward. "And Dr. Lapius wants to see you in his office," he told me.

The secretary, behind an immense desk, showed me in.

"Sit down, Harry." Lapius indicated a chair. "There seems to be some confusion. Mrs. Mafkovsky tells me you are trying to force her to leave the hospital."

"She had recovered. We are short of beds. Dr. Foreman told me to have her brought to admitting and to get her into a cab."

"What did Mrs. Mafkovsky say?"

"She said that she could stay here as long as she liked. No one could make her leave."

"I'm afraid she's right, Harry. The County is chartered as an almshouse. The charter is derivative of the English Poor Law of 1647, after which many of the original hospitals in the colonies were established."

"You mean she can stay here forever?"

"No. But in order to remove her we must follow legal procedures." Lapius leaned back and chuckled. "You've heard about jailhouse lawyers," he asked. "Well, there is an entire population of hospital lawyers who know their rights. Mrs. Mafkovsky will earn herself another several months here before we get this straightened out."

"I'm sorry, I didn't know—"

"No harm done," he said, his eyes twinkling. "But in the future, tread gently."

"But we need the beds."

"The County is elastic. We can always find an extra bed," Lapius said.

I brought the news to Foreman.

"What kind of shit is that?" he exploded. He used the term so frequently that his breath was developing a fecal odor.

103

"Goddamn it, we got to get her out of here." He was becoming obsessional. "Put her back on the fucking rice diet. We'll starve her out."

The next morning Mrs. Mafkovsky was complaining again. "What am I, a pigeon, you feeding me rice?"

Meanwhile she kept busy all day, rustling bedpans, helping patients to ambulate, emptying baskets, tidying the beds. She was like an extra nurse, but Foreman couldn't see that.

"Why don't you leave her be?" I asked. "She's becoming invaluable around here."

"But she's still taking a fucking bed. Now even the interns are telling me how to run the ward." He complained to no one in particular.

William Pier, the Chief of Medicine, made grand rounds. Foreman explained to Pier the problem with Mafkovsky, and Pier was sympathetic. "Why don't you have the psychiatrists see her? She's obviously senile. Let her sit with the other old ladies in the psychiatric hospital." Foreman was beaming.

"Put in a psychiatric consult," he said to me.

"What the hell good will that do?" I asked him after rounds. "They turned down our last four requests, first the manic-depressive, second the alcoholic with Korsakoff's syndrome, then the paranoid, then the catatonic."

"Just do what I tell you," Foreman ordered brusquely.

I made out the psychiatric consult, and a week later Adams, the psychiatrist, interviewed Mrs. Mafkovsky. She was accepted to the psychiatric service.

I accosted Adams as he was leaving the floor.

"You are taking her?" I asked astounded.

"Of course. She's looney."

"Well, Dr. Adams, I must say that your decision to accept Mrs. Mafkovsky was unusually perceptive. After all, she's outwardly sane."

"But that's the whole point in psychiatry, Doctor. We have learned to look beneath the surface, and I say she is clearly insane, out of touch with her senses."

"But how were you able to perceive that in so brief an interview?"

"Simply by listening to her, Doctor. She kept telling me she was a bird, and that men in white coats were feeding her rice every morning."

William Pier didn't walk, he flowed, his tall, angular figure hunched slightly forward, as if to anticipate his rapid pace, as he stalked disease. His retinue of white-coated figures trailed him like the tail of a kite. His face was carved like planes of cliffside granite from which jutted a finely honed and delicate nose. His jaw, his posture, his gestures, the momentum of his demeanor thrust forward. Even when standing still, his darting eyes probed the place he next would be.

His mind was as ferreting, sharp and incisive as his body. His memory had gouged all the fructifying sod from the mossy annals of medicine and medical lore, so that to us, at least, he appeared the compleat physician. He was as one with medicine—the science, not the patient. During rounds, Foreman, Rush or I would recount the history and physical findings of each patient. Pier listened acutely, screening all but the salient facts from our often too florid presentations. He might step to the bedside and gently percuss the chest with tapered fingers that seemed to respond to the induced vibrations as delicately as high-pitched tuning forks. He would place his hand over the heart and feel for thrills, the result of altered hemodynamics that foretold of murmurs to be heard. More often than not, however, he stood at the foot of the bed, assimilating the surfeit of facts we proposed to him, and meticulously assembled them into a meaningful arrangement.

He simplified the complexity of differential diagnoses by teaching us that initially we must distinguish the curable from the incurable diseases. To spend time distinguishing two incurable entities from each other was wasteful and useless.

Dr. Lapius, who would join us on rounds from time to time, concurred with this, but gently pointed out that diseases thought to be incurable today might be subject to cure in the near future, so that our diagnostic efforts would not be in vain.

Pier always listened respectfully to Lapius. Foreman ascribed it to politics.

Jake Jarmon was a heavy-set, bulbous-nosed successful internist whose voice boomed like the hollow percussion notes he elicited from the chests of the skinniest patients. Jarmon had the perfect reflexes for percussion. He practiced continually. I once saw him percuss an elevator button. He could detail the fine differences between sounds like the tympanist of a symphony.

Rounds with Jarmon were demonstrative lectures, as if the patient were not there.

There were many young rheumatics on the ward. It was said that if you saw a kid with red hair, chances were he had rheumatic heart disease. Furthermore, many rosy-cheeked kids, whose mothers took pride in their fresh complexions, really had red cheeks because leaky heart valves prevented the blood from returning quickly enough to the heart.

Jarmon held forth in front of one such youngster.

"Gentlemen, stand back. All right, sonny, take off the top of your pajamas. Gentlemen, do you see the apical thrust? Way over to the axilla? Do you see the slight flutter in the chest at the base of the heart? Of course not. But if you put your hands there, you'll feel it. All right, gentlemen. Look at his neck. The veins are bulging."

Then to the scared kid: "Sonny, how long have you been sick?" Not intimately, personally or considerately, but demonstratively.

The kid whispered something to him.

"Six years you say? Can you sleep lying flat? No? You have to sleep sitting up, otherwise you can't breathe?"

Then to us: "Classical. Dyspnea, orthopnea, a heart barely compensated. A difficult case. Easy to diagnose, hard to treat."

The residents felt the heart, percussed its size and listened to the murmurs. The ritual was repeated by the interns. Then, as we drifted like a slow-moving cloud of white to the next bed, Jarmon grasped the sick boy's shoulder with a hand the size of a beef loin and said, "You'll be all right."

"Thank you, Doctor." And the youngster closed his eyes to continue the struggle for breath.

Jarmon caught one of the interns sitting on the bed of a patient. The temptation was great, since we were chronically fatigued. "For God's sake. What's the matter with you? Get the hell off that bed. How many times must I tell you idiots never to sit on the patient's bed? Christ, there are bedbugs all over the place, you'll be taking them home with you."

When Pier made rounds, he ignored Jarmon. He never appeared on Jarmon's rounds, but it was mandatory for Jarmon to attend Pier's rounds. Pier approached patients gracefully and quietly. He listened attentively to the history presented by an intern or resident. His percussion notes were silent personal affairs. He felt the vibrations in his fingers, and then enunciated his finding. He would encapsulate the details, come to a conclusion and turn to Jarmon: "Isn't that right, Doctor?" or "Wouldn't you agree?" Jarmon would nod assent. Pier overwhelmed him. Jarmon did not enjoy grand rounds with Pier, who pricked the bubbles of his usual effervescence.

The grand rounds were the stellar attraction of the week on medical service. They were headed by Pier, assisted by Jarmon, and attended by Foreman, Rush, myself, the medical students and quite frequently by Lapius, when he could substitute an hour of medical challenge for administrative duties.

Foreman couldn't stand it when Lapius showed up. "Pier has Lapius in spades," he said. "That old fart hasn't practiced medicine in years. He slows us up. Why don't he stay in his office where he belongs?"

Lapius was with us when the two jaundiced women were presented.

One was a thirty-three-year-old girl, her skin bronzed by the bile pigment, the sclera of her eyes ocher in color. The second, a clearly uncomfortable thin marasmic woman of eighty, was lemon yellow. The cases were presented in tandem. Pier assembled the data in an orderly manner, suggested certain laboratory tests and then, after we had walked from the bedside for a brief conference in the center of the ward, out of earshot of any patient, he said quietly, "Clearly, Miss Jennings has a stone," indicating the young girl, "and the elderly woman probably has cancer of the pancreas."

Dr. Lapius was still examining the patients. He was scrupulous and unorthodox. His hands roamed like spider legs, pressing, plucking, traveling gently over the yellow abdominal surfaces. He ambled over just as Pier was ending his pronouncement. "Wouldn't you agree?"

Lapius paused. "Yes, Dr. Pier, I agree, except for one thing."

"Yes, Dr. Lapius," Pier said impatiently.

"I agree with the diagnoses, except it's the other way around. The young one will die, the older one will be cured—if you operate, that is."

We hung back silently, waiting for Pier to pounce. But he

107

simply turned to Lapius and said, "Well, we'll see. You could be right." We moved on.

Pier included Lapius in the discussion of every case. In most instances they agreed.

Eventually the laboratory data and X-rays on the jaundiced women proved Lapius to be correct. The young one died. The old lady had her gall bladder removed and went home.

Later, I stopped Lapius at the elevator. We were alone.

"Dr. Lapius, how did you know that the young girl had the cancer? Certainly statistics, the age, everything would indicate the opposite."

"Just a feeling, Harry."

Later at lunch with the house staff and Pier that day I described my brief encounter with Lapius to one of the other interns. Pier was listening. "He couldn't tell why, he just felt that it was something different," I said. The other doctor said, "Maybe he was showboating. One of those doctors who takes the wild guess in front of a crowd in the hope that his one-in-a-thousand shot will pay off and make him a hero."

"There are doctors who do that," Pier interrupted. "They come up with some far-out diagnosis at each conference hoping that once they will be right. They're like broken clocks that for an infinitesimal moment of each day are exactly on time. But not Lapius.

It was the color of the jaundice. The young girl was brown, the older woman lighter yellow. I think that's what clewed him in. I had noted the difference too, but felt that the ages were more important. How many thirty-three-year-old girls have cancer of the pancreas? Lapius paid more attention to the memory of his instincts. That brown jaundice never appears with simple acute obstruction. I always listen to Lapius carefully."

The word "infarcation" comes from the Latin verb *"infarcia,"* meaning "to stuff." The perfect participle passive, is *"infartus,"* which has incorrectly been altered to *"infarctus,"* probably to avoid giggles in the classroom. But the puerile mirth of the student at the sound of these words lasts only until the concept graduates to reality, until he encounters his first case of myocardial infarction—a heart muscle, literally stuffed with inflammation, that has been turned to jelly by the sudden occlusion of

108

one of the coronary arteries, thus cutting the blood-born oxygen to that part of the heart.

When Hopkins was taken from the ambulance into the emergency room, it was clear that he was deathly sick. He vomited, contorted his relatively young face in pain and struggled for breath. His wife clutched at his hands and cried as she ran alongside the stretcher, then wrung her own hands as we pried her loose and led her to the waiting room.

The electrocardiogram proved what we had suspected. Hopkins was suffering the throes of a myocardial infarction, a word that suddenly evoked dread, not the laughter of the classroom.

I worked him up rapidly. As soon as the morphine took effect, and released the crushing pains that constricted his chest, as soon as the congesting fluids that filled the spongy surfaces of his lung receded, as soon as his blood pressure stabilized just above shock level, and fluid was flowing into his veins in an attempt to maintain the pressure, I called Rush and warned him to be ready to receive Hopkins on the ward.

Rush stayed on the ward all night. He monitored the fluid that kept collecting in the lungs, inserted needles, injected adrenalin, and once even pounded the chest when the heartbeat seemed to stop. He did this for a man he did not know, who had never spoken a word to him, whose face he had never seen, hidden as it was behind the heavy oxygen mask. Miraculously, Hopkins was alive in the morning. Rush was nearly dead of exhaustion.

Foreman started rounds, as usual with a snarl. He glanced over Hopkins' chart quickly. "How the fuck do you expect me to read any of these chicken scratches, for Chrissake?" he said. He walked into the room and placed his stethoscope to Hopkins' chest. He perused the cardiogram. Then he turned to Rush.

"You are a great hero," he snarled. "You know, Rush, because of heroes like you we don't have enough beds in the hospital."

Rush didn't catch on at first. He knew Foreman wouldn't crown him with a wreath of roses, but expected at the very least recognition for effort. Then the meaning of Foreman's words started to dawn on him.

"What's troubling you, Monty?" he asked.

"What's troubling me is filling the ward with a census of hopeless cases. Leave a guy like this downstairs. He's gonna die anyway. He's wasting oxygen."

"Maybe we can pull him through."

"Never. He's had a massive coronary. Let him go. We need the beds."

Rush clamped his mouth tight. We moved to the next case. By the time we reached Dillingham, Foreman was already tired of rounds. Dillingham was twenty-nine years old. His heart had been mutilated by rheumatic disease. Running out of cardiac reserve, he'd been kept alive by digitalis, oxygen and diuretics. He was bolstered upright in bed by a cushion of pillows, and gasped noisily into an oxygen mask, his face pale, his legs swollen, his chest heaving. He greeted us with his eyes only, while continuing his struggle for breath.

Foreman pressed his finger into Dillingham's leg, leaving a small rounded pit in the doughy flesh. "What are we gonna do with this guy? He's liable to be here for weeks yet."

Hopkins died while we were making rounds. "That's a break," Foreman said. The business of vacant beds had become an obsession with Foreman. He wanted the ward neat and clean. His manifest attitude was that the pressed linen on empty beds looked better than lumpy heaps of white-shrouded patients. The clean linen bespoke efficiency. Rapid turnover equaled successful therapy. Dillingham was a scar to Foreman, because he couldn't cure him, and he wouldn't die.

Later that week, on grand rounds, Foreman, vexed and frustrated, presented the case to Pier. He detailed the therapy: the mercurial injections daily to increase fluid excretion by the kidneys, and thus lessen the onerous columns of blood the weakened heart would have to propel through the vascular system; the digitalis that was supposed to strengthen the cardiac musculature; the oxygen to make up the deficits incurred by the sluggish circulation; lastly, the increasing deterioration of Mr. Dillingham.

"What else can we do, Dr. Pier? I've tried everything." That wasn't precisely a true statement, because it had been Rush and myself who had tried everything, but the pecking order was such that all positive values were supposed to have emanated from the chief resident, a role Foreman eschewed only when things were going poorly.

Pier turned away and strode down the hall. Foreman followed him out of the room. "There's no hope, is there, Dr. Pier?" he asked, fawning, seeking confirmation of an obvious fact.

Jarmon lagged behind with the medical students, again demonstrating his percussion notes and ausculatory techniques on the hapless Dillingham, who turned his head toward the window to catch the first yellow sun rays of morning.

"Yup," Jarmon said loudly, "it's a rheumatic heart all right, an almost classical presystolic bruit with snapping first sound. The systolic murmur can be heard clearly in the axilla." The students marched up one at a time and placed their stethoscopes at the point Jarmon indicated. "You'll be okay, son," Jarmon said to Dillingham when the last of the students had turned to follow Pier. "We have the diagnosis now. That's half the battle." At least he spoke to the patient, I thought.

We caught up with Pier in time to hear the tail end of a rumination about mercy-death and how this might be accomplished without detection. ". . . If fluid intake is diminished," he said in his stilted, reedy voice, "and normal doses of morphine are given, the net effect, to the dehydrated patient, is an overdose."

"What the hell is he talking about?" Jarmon asked me in a whisper. I shrugged my shoulders.

Within a week Dillingham was dead. He went to sleep quietly and his respirations simply became slower and slower, then ceased. Until then my posture toward Pier was obeisance born of reverence, but I was starting to feel the chill from the ice that encrusted his intellect.

Rush was agitated that night. Our room was large enough for two beds and a shared closet.

Rush turned down the radio.

"What do you think happened to Dillingham, Harry?"

"He died."

"Do you think Foreman killed him?"

"Come on, Rush, Dillingham had enough diseases to kill a regiment."

"They cut his fluid intake, Harry, you know that, don't you?"

"Sure, it's a reasonable thing to do with a guy who is edematous. What difference does that make?"

"Well, you remember Pier telling him about—"

"Sure I remember. Forget it, Rush. Dillingham was hopeless. Maybe it was a kind decision. Anyway, Foreman's the resident, the chief, so he can do what he likes."

"Not on my patients he can't." And he stalked out of the room.

That night Gibson was missing a thermometer. A patient who was admitted to the medicine ward didn't have a temperature marked on his chart. Gibson knew she had stuck the thermometer up his ass, and now wondered whether she hadn't plunged it too far. Anyway, he must have rolled over in bed and somehow someone forgot about it. Gibson asked me as a favor to find that thermometer.

I trotted the quarter-mile of corridor to get to the medical ward. The patient was husky, tattooed and in an alcoholic stupor. My rectal examination revived him a little, and sure enough I felt the tip of the thermometer. I rolled him over, and, with two orderlies holding tight to keep him from rolling off the bed, I passed a sigmoidoscope into his rectum. I saw a thermometer half covered with feces. I couldn't reach it at first with a biopsy clamp, and when I finally did, it slithered farther up. At least I knew where the thermometer was.

I pulled the scope out and told the orderlies to give him an enema, hoping he would pass the thermometer in the effluent. He was awake now, and positively garrulous.

"Wassamatta, Doc? Wassa trouble? Watcha poke me in the ass for? I ain't done nothin' to you."

"Take it easy, Rembrandt," I said, admiring his tattoos. "We're just trying to recover a thermometer you were trying to steal. Them things cost money."

When the orderly poked the enema tube into him, he bellowed and fought. We had to hold him.

"Wassamatter with you crazy guys? Leave me alone."

"Come on, be good. We're just trying to take your temperature."

"Oh, okay"—he became tractable—"go ahead. I just never had it took this way before, Doc."

He cooperated, and rewarded us with an explosion of gaseous vapors followed by a cataract of expelled water and the metallic sound of something hitting the bedpan.

Our patient plunged his hand into the foul contents and came up triumphantly with the thermometer, which he held high against the light, peering at it intently. Then he handed it to the dumfounded orderly, and proclaimed for all to hear, "It's one hundred degrees, Doc. Mark it down this time." Then he fell back on the bed and started to snore.

Mielish was transferred back to medicine from surgery. The sympathectomy had helped temporarily, but suddenly his blood pressure shot up, and his urine got bloody. The diagnosis was apparent. He had recurrent nephritis. He became uremic. We managed to control him for a while, but were losing ground daily. Rush spent a lot of time with him. He tried to balance Mielish's electrolytes, the mineral salts essential to acid base balance. He tried to keep him out of acidosis and control the blood pressure.

Mielish was possibly fifty. A loser. After his divorce he had led a derelict existence. The fight had been drained out of him long ago. He didn't want to die, but when he realized how soon it might happen, he concentrated on making it painless. That he would die comfortably became an act of faith to Rush.

"What are you going to do, give him morphine and cut his water?" I asked him one day.

"You sonofabitch. I'm a doctor, Harry, not a goon." Rush had suddenly matured.

Foreman pointedly skipped Mielish on rounds. "There's nothing we can do for him," he would say loudly. But Mielish was content. Rush helped him through each day. He assigned orderlies to feed Mielish baby foods, visited frequently, and they had serious talks. Some people, when cornered by death, make an accommodation. Eventually patients start to accept the small closet of life to which they have been reduced, with the door closing a little more each day, until finally it shuts out all the light.

But Rush kept his foot wedged in the door. In fact, he pushed it wider.

For Mielish, for any patient, hospital life has a barracks quality. The day is dominated by routine. Temperatures and vital signs four times, meals three times, bed making, sponge baths, ward rounds, special examinations, medications. Most time is accounted for. Mielish made his adjustments. The scope of his interests narrowed perceptibly as he grew more sickly. He became increasingly aware of his body, its parts, their manifestations. One day he passed his fingers over his forehead. It felt rough, and small white flakes, like camphor dust, adhered to his fingertips. When he rubbed his fingers together, the fine powder disappeared, melting like snowflakes. It was his first encounter with uremic frost. The concentration of urea in his body was so great due to failure of his kidneys that, as his urea-rich sweat evaporated, the urea crystallized on his skin.

He passed through various levels of consciousness during each day. Large patches of time disappeared unaccountably. His appetite was poor, and when people spoke to him, they averted their heads. He realized that he was physically disagreeable to them. But Rush faced him directly. Mielish imagined that his breath might be heavy and took to brushing his teeth several times during the day. He would try to hold his breath when people spoke with him. But to no avail. They kept their distance. His breath had the odor of urine.

"It's the smell of urea," Rush told him. "Some people find it unpleasant. Don't worry, it will disappear when we get the urea levels down again."

Foreman was quite succinct about it. "He's going downhill fast. Smells like pure piss now."

Mielish heard it of course. Then when people approached his bed, he would place his hand over his mouth so as to cut off the offensive urea-laden exhalations. He became increasingly involved with the minutiae of his body functions. His horizons, already limited by the physical enclosure of the ward, soon became confined to the boundaries of his bed, indeed to the small volume he occupied between the sheets. And when his sensorium dulled, he would be impaled on the bed by therapeutic impediments. A tangle of tubes emanated from the drawn dyspneic carcass; tubes from his nose, veins, urinary bladder became his umbilici to the world beyond, his final channels of contact. They were death lines. Because he had lost interest in even his closest neighbor, death had lost for him most of its terror. Having already been removed from a world of living things, the final event would merely separate him from himself. He had entered and returned from the coma of death so often, so easily, so pleasantly, that the point of no return became a matter of indifference.

But when the rubber conduits bringing salted carbonates to his veins, oxygen to his lungs and urine from his bladder had relieved the acidosis, lowered the urea and cleared his mind, a terror gripped him. For with clarity came hope. The reality of his plight became acute, and he half-wanted to live again. When this happened, we removed the tubes.

Mielish started to ambulate. Soon he was walking the length of

114

the corridor. We knew it was only temporary, but were overjoyed, and Mielish, with the passive gentleness of the enslaved, enjoyed the respite and momentary freedom. Foreman was annoyed. "That fucking Rush is playing God again. What does he hope to accomplish with that crock? Make an Olympic track star out of him?"

On grand rounds Foreman presented the case to Pier. "We've gone about as far as we can go with him. He's as good as he'll ever be. My thought is that we should let him go home now while he's as well as he is." Pier nodded to signal that he had heard, but Foreman accepted it as assent. That afternoon he discharged Mielish from the hospital.

Rush was furious. "He's my patient. I'll discharge him when I think he's ready."

"It's my ward. I'll discharge him when I can't do anything more for him."

"His brother is flying in from Europe. He'll be here in three or four days. I promised him we'd keep him alive till then. Now you want to kick him out."

"You promised what?"

"Please, Foreman. It means a lot to him. What else has he got to live for right now?"

"What the hell do you think we're running here, some kind of a goddamn sewing circle? It's a hospital, Rush. Someone else needs that bed. Nothing doing. Out he goes."

"He'll die."

"That's not my fault. He's going to die soon no matter where he is."

The next morning Mielish was worse. He was cold and sweaty. The orderlies dressed him, and Rush and I got him a wheelchair and rolled him to the elevator.

"Where's he going?" I asked Rush.

"He has a cold-water flat somewhere."

"Please, Dr. Rush, I'm too weak to go home. I'll die there."

"I'm sorry, Mielish," Rush said quietly. "There's nothing I can do."

"But you promised—"

"I know I promised. But I didn't expect this."

"Can't you go to Dr. Pier? He wouldn't allow this. He knows how sick I am."

"I would help you if I could, believe me. Look, Mielish. It's not that bad. Go home for a few days, and then have an ambulance bring you in again. We'll readmit you. We'll have to take you again."

Mielish looked at him, unbelieving.

At 4 P.M. of the day Mielish was discharged I was called to admitting. It was Mielish. In coma. They found him on the street. He had collapsed under a lamppost. He died that night.

Rush cursed himself. He was inconsolable. His professionalism had been betrayed; his sense of propriety had been tampered with; his sense of the balance between good and evil had become distorted. He tried to reach Foreman. Foreman was out.

Rush arrived for morning rounds early. When Foreman showed up, he followed him to the nurses' station.

"Mielish—the police found him unconscious under a lamppost yesterday afternoon. Brought him back here and he died."

"The poor bastard," Foreman said sardonically.

Rush whipped the back of his hand across Foreman's face. Before Foreman could recover, Rush pressed a strong, thin forearm into his neck, pinning him against the wall. Foreman got red and started turning blue. "If you ever do that to a patient of mine again, Foreman, I'll kill you." Then he let him go. Except for the fury of the attack, Rush hadn't lost his composure. The threat was uttered as a fact without dramatic intonations. Foreman sagged to his knees, recovered, wobbled to a chair. He rubbed at his neck. He was hoarse when he spoke. "You're finished here. I'm bringing charges against you."

That day Rush was suspended by the administration.

Rush was suspended because he had physically attacked Foreman. Nurses and orderlies, who had been milling about just before the incident, were witness only to the final event, Foreman pressed up against the wall with Rush issuing dire threats. Only the moment of violence attracted their attention.

I covered Rush's patients while he was off duty, and a medical student was impressed to help with admissions. Rush sat around the room most of the week, drinking milk, clutching his stomach, reading and occasionally going to the movies. He tossed in his sleep and awakened each morning exhausted.

"I'm finished here. Where will I get another internship or residency? This could finish my career in medicine."

116

"It's not that dire, Wilkie," I said, trying to console him. "They'll transfer you to another service. No one is out to get you."

"Foreman is."

"He won't push his luck. After all, look what you have on him. He probably murdered Dillingham, and he turned Mielish out of the hospital when he was too sick to walk. He doesn't want that to be brought out."

"Maybe you're right," Rush said, unconvinced.

That week he and I ate by ourselves in the dining room. Other doctors on the staff maintained a safe distance, waiting, watchful, curious, polite, uninvolved. "What the hell, patient care can't be quantitated," Jarmon put it succinctly. "The kid blew over something that most of us swallow. Who's to say he's wrong?"

Rush was to appear before a board composed of Pier, Shaver and Bernie Caspar, the pathologist. Prior to the hearing, although none of the other doctors so much as nodded to Rush during his week of Coventry, a group of residents headed by Cushing approached Pier and offered testimonials in behalf of Rush, his diligence, the conscientious manner in which he performed while on the other services. Pier was attentive and polite, but wouldn't budge.

"The issue, gentlemen," he said, "is not whether Dr. Rush is diligent, conscientious or possesses all of these excellent qualities. The question is whether he possesses additional qualities, which if given full reign would disrupt the entire medical service. He will be given a fair hearing, of that you can rest assured."

Cushing pleaded for arbitration, but Pier was adamant.

After the hearing, Rush sought me out on the ward to say good-bye. We walked back to the room together. I put my arm around his shoulder.

"What happened?"

"Not too much," he said. We walked slowly. He recounted the events so concisely that by the time we reached the room he had finished.

"It was all very informal. Pier, Shaver, Caspar and I sat around the conference table. Pier read from a paper the details of the charge that I had attacked Foreman. They asked me if I had anything to say in my defense, and I started to describe the relationship between Foreman and us. But how do you describe rudeness, badgering, irresponsibility?

117

"Instead, I told them about the Hopkins case, but halfway through, Pier waved me to silence and said that we weren't here to judge Foreman."

"What was Foreman doing while this was going on?"

"Foreman?" Rush looked at me like an owl. "Christ, he wasn't there. Oh, my God. I never realized till just now. Foreman wasn't even at the hearing.

"I then related the Mielish case. But Shaver said that the only issue was whether or not I had attacked Foreman, and been mutinous. I tried to point out that I had been trying to protect a human life. Then Shaver said everything that happened at the hospital involved human life and human judgments. There was no way I could illustrate the cruelty of Foreman and make it sound credible. On the medical chart it was just an assortment of clinical facts. Another set of values. Caspar agreed with Shaver that if everyone behaved as I had, the place might disintegrate. I finally got sore and told them that if everyone stuck to his principles the place might be better than it was. That, of course, was disastrous.

"Shaver became livid. 'Do you accuse me—any of us—of not adhering to the highest standards of medical practice, Doctor?'

"By the time they got done with me I was in tears."

"Did you mention Dillingham?"

"As a last resort. I knew it wouldn't do me any good, but I wanted them to have something stuck in their memories about the character of this guy the next time he steps out of line. So I told them I suspected that Dillingham's death was unnecessary, and that actually his final medical orders violated sound medical principles."

"How did they react to that?"

"That was easy for them. Pier said, 'Dr. Foreman is not on trial here. He is not accused by the administration. No one has brought charges against him. I can't permit this type of slur in his absence.' "

"Maybe instead of slugging Foreman you should have brought charges against him!"

"On what grounds? Sympathy for Mielish? I couldn't really prove a damn thing. I just don't like Foreman. He's dangerous, and dangerous to his patients. But legally it's me who is the danger. They almost have me convinced. A doctor must be cool

118

under all circumstances, suppress his feelings, not make waves. No, Harry, there's no other way I could have handled it. And the more I think about it, the more I realize that to turn something around, to change something, you have to make a personal sacrifice. I didn't set out to do it, but that's the way it turned out. I'm finished, but they will be watching Foreman from now on."

I did double duty on the ward, and occasionally when I seemed about to drop with fatigue another intern was rotated to help me out. The year was coming to an end.

Wilkie received a visit from Lapius, who informed him that although the unanimous opinion of the board was that Wilkie should be expelled, after a meeting, during which Lapius pointed out that it might ruin the career of a promising, albeit undisciplined young doctor, the board agreed to rescind its decision providing Wilkie Rush would proffer his resignation. Wilkie accepted this and penned a letter of resignation, which was accepted with regrets by Dr. Simon Quentin Lapius as Medical Director.

Jarmon was becoming his old irrepressible, almost unpalatable self. But for once I was glad to hear him, glad he couldn't speak softly, and that his confidential tones reverberated throughout the dining room so that all could hear. The gabled regularity of his features was spoiled only by coarseness of nose and lips. He spoke with an expletive emphasis that adorned each word with a pearlet of spittle, and from time to time used the back of his hand to wipe moisture from his chin.

". . . letting that kid go was a crime, a crime. This damn place is dying of administrative sclerosis. It has become such a tangle of rules and regulations that it's lost sight of its purpose, in fact the purpose of medicine. Look, here Harry . . ." He leaned closer, speaking conspiratorially into my ear. Something good was coming. To Jarmon anyone espousing ideals was suspect, so when his own idealism surfaced, he was clandestine, like a kid saying a dirty word.

"You know I like to make a buck out of medicine. Lord knows I have to, the way my wife spends, and those daughters of mine—but that doesn't mean I don't love medicine, and what it stands for." He was whispering now, afraid of getting caught. "I tell you, Harry, one Rush is worth a thousand Piers and maybe five thousand Jarmons. Sure Pier is the smartest doctor in the place, maybe in the city. But he's a smart-ass. When did you ever see him make a patient comfortable, tuck in a sheet, arrange a pillow, soothe, encourage? Sure he'll diagnose everything, separate the curables from the incurables, teach, pontificate. But that isn't medicine, Harry, that's pedantry. Sure we need him—for the one case in a hundred that the average doc can't figure out. For the other ninety-nine cases the diagnosis is clear, treatment is cut and dried. When all is said and done, the art of medicine is what counts in the long run. Good docs take the pain out of living and the fear out of sickness. That's what Rush was doing. For this they can him. A goddamn shame. Administrative sclerosis. They attend the rules, not the patients. They toady to hierarchies, rank, procedure in the belief that if the blueprints and flow sheets are followed the patients will thrive. That's bullshit.

"It's a funny thing, Harry. Until Pier threw Rush out I was in awe of him. But when he did that and let that crummy Foreman off the hook, I realized he was flawed, just another guy. Once I realized that he wasn't perfect I could deal with him as more or less an equal. Because after all, Harry"—Jarmon became confidential—"you know, I'm not perfect either."

Now that Jarmon's secret was out in the open, I excused myself.

"Stay around awhile," he said. "Where you rushing?"

"To confession."

Benny, the orderly, was a shakedown artist. Everything was for sale. Cigarettes were a nickel apiece when the entire package was eighteen cents at the corner drugstore. The towels of patients who couldn't or wouldn't pay up were somehow moist when they tried to use them. He frosted bedpans on the window sill, and gave them to the patients who wouldn't pay for protection. I tried to prove this, but couldn't uncover the secret hiding place. Yet in every culprit a noble instinct lurks. When Leffert, who, besides being sick with liver cancer, developed a deep depression and tried to hurl himself from the seventh floor of the tower on which the medical ward was situated, Benny happened to be standing by. He grabbed Leffert by the scruff of his pajamas, but Leffert's momentum carried Benny halfway over the sill of the opened window. He screamed for help. I had entered the ward with

Foreman just behind me. It took a second to understand the tableau, aided somewhat by the shouts of other patients and an assortment of arms waving toward the window of crisis. I ran to the window, wending my way between the beds. Benny cried, "Help me, willya? I can't hold the guy much longer."

I was within ten feet of them, ready to tackle Benny and anchor his legs, which were already halfway up the sill, drawn there by the weight of the dangling Leffert, when suddenly Foreman shouted, "Let him go."

Benny, never one to disobey a command from a superior, released his grip, and Leffert was preceded to the ground by his own piercing shriek. There was a dull thud and Leffert lay still on the setback.

"Jeez," said Benny, "I think I could have saved him."

"What for?" said Foreman. "He was gonna die anyway. No sense losing the two of you."

Dr. Lapius held a dinner for the medical staff at the end of the service term. Pier was out of town attending a meeting. Rush of course was gone, Jarmon was sick, so the evening was restricted to Foreman and myself. I didn't look forward to it.

Foreman and I showed up at almost the same time, to share a banquet of wines and cheeses, wheat wafers and a Caesar's salad that was demonstrable testimony to Lapius's efforts at weight reduction.

After a few goblets of a delicious red wine Lapius became informal, and Foreman addressed him as "S.Q."

"It must have been difficult for you in the war," said Lapius, drawing him out.

"Not at all, S.Q. Just another job."

"Where were you stationed?"

"I was at a field hospital in Europe."

"Upsetting, isn't it, to see all those young lives wasted?" Lapius murmured.

"It is if you let it bother you," Foreman said.

"Has either of you ever been seriously ill?" Lapius asked.

Foreman said no and I shook my head.

"Too bad," said Lapius. "It is an experience that is bound to generate humility in any doctor. You must learn to be gentle with your patients, gentlemen. You are all that they have."

121

Lapius was becoming maudlin. Next, I supposed, he would lecture us on the bedside manner.

"The bedside manner is now considered cliché," Lapius continued. The wine had made him dreamy. "But it is the way in which a physician inspires the confidence of a total stranger that you not only can help him, but also are totally committed to the effort."

Foreman placed his wine glass on the table. "That may be true in private practice, but at a city hospital like The County the patient doesn't seek a specific doctor. He is brought in and takes potluck."

"All the more reason for a bedside manner at The County."

"Ah—" Foreman said scowling, "who wants to get involved with every old crock, every smelly scabietic derelict that wanders in?"

"What do you think, Harry?" Lapius turned toward me.

"I tend to identify with them, with their helplessness and hopelessness—"

"That's the mistake, Harry," Foreman said. "You can't become part of the misery. Christ, there'll be nothing left of you. You have to walk away from them. Do your job, but leave the emotional trauma to the psychiatrists."

"But that's the trick," Lapius said. "And the glory of medicine. You must develop a kinship close enough to succor but not so close as to impair your objectivity or drain your emotions. You must identify with the wounded without feeling the pain, work with the wretched without becoming wretched, comfort the dying without dying a little yourself."

He filled our glasses without waiting for an answer.

"You must give the patient hope and reassurance."

"Suppose you know they won't get better. Do you lie to them?" Foreman asked cynically.

"Not always. But try to put things into proper perspective."

"How do you do that?"

"It depends on the individual, the case, the type of illness. When I was younger and in practice, I had a young patient with leukemia. Eleven years old. Young enough to place her complete trust in me and in what her parents told her; too young to discern the worry and anguish that the parents tried so hard, and not always successfully, to mask; yet old enough to know the sense of death, and its finite meaning, the ultimate separation from loved ones and the other things she loved. I lied to her. I told her she had an anemia, and on that basis rationalized every ache, every pain, every weakness, palpitation, indeed every symptom that she experienced during her trial. Finally she hemorrhaged slowly into her brain, and for the first time, as her vision blurred and scotomata developed, she started to lose faith in what I said. "What's happening to me?" she asked. I gave her enough morphine to put her to sleep and maintained the dosage continually until she died. She never awakened to know the fear that blindness and paralysis would have evoked. In the grownup unless given totally to self-delusion, men particularly will demand a diagnosis. People become insecure if they catch their doctor in an outright lie. But half-truths and deception may be desirable and acceptable. The idea is to reduce the duration of mental anguish, without eradicating entirely the prospect of death.

"One of the reasons doctors have trouble preparing their patients for death is that many haven't come to terms with it themselves. They are so busy fending it off that I suspect many develop some omnipotent sense—a delusion of immortality. Our frocked colleagues don't have this. They admit the reality of death or some transportation to another level of life, and, facing the reality in personal terms, they can talk about it and prepare the dying for the oncoming event. They don't get embarrassed about last rites. For a doctor to give last rites or something comparable would be an admission of failure.

"Osler, however, had no such scruples." Lapius rose and plucked a book from the shelves, leafing through the pages as he returned.

"Harvey Cushing's biography of Osler. Listen. A mother's account of Osler's approach to the death of her daughter." He read gravely:

> He visited our little Janet twice every day from the middle of October until her death, a month later, and these visits she looked forward to with pathetic eagerness and joy.—Instantly, the sick room was turned into a fairyland, and in fairy language he would talk about the flowers, the birds, and the dolls—In the course of this he would find out all he wanted to know about the little patient.
>
> The most exquisite moment came one cold, raw, November

morning, when the end was near, and he brought out from his pocket a beautiful red rose, carefully wrapped in paper, and told how he had watched this last rose of summer growing in his garden and how the rose had called out to him as he passed by, that she wished to go along with him to see his "little lassie." That evening we all had a fairy tea party at a tiny table by the bed, Sir William talking to the rose, his little lassie and her mother in a most exquisite way . . . and the little girl understood that neither fairies nor people could always have the color of a red rose in their cheeks, or stay as long as they wanted in one place, but that they nevertheless would be happy in another home and must not let the people they left behind, particularly their parents, feel badly about it; and the little girl understood and was not unhappy.

"You and I might feel guilty about not being able to stave off death, and so become reticent about broaching the subject to the dying, but Osler was free about this. Doctors too often deal with death as a stranger—odd, since they have so much experience with it.

"Finally, it is the job of the doctor to maintain the comfort of the patient, and without doubt must help, at all costs, to preserve his dignity as a human being. You look dubious, Dr. Foreman."

Foreman was staring dreamily at the ceiling, a little bored perhaps.

Lapius continued. "This boy Rush, who was just kicked out, he seemed to have the right idea."

Foreman no longer looked bored.

"That little jerk—I don't know what the hell was wrong with him. He tried to kill me. That's what happens when you lose your heart to a patient. Christ, it throws everything off balance."

"True, he didn't handle himself with restraint, but that quality of compassion, when he gets it under control, will make him a better doctor. Well," Lapius murmured, "I must be up early. What do you say to a few more drams of wine, then you'll be on your way. I have a special vintage from the Loire valley, we'll finish the bottle. It's a treat." Lapius went to the cupboard and returned with the three shimmering tulips of wine. Foreman downed his quickly. When we rose to say good night, he was a little shaky on his feet.

We decided to walk back to the hospital. "A nice guy," I ventured to Foreman.

"Shit, I got better things to do than to listen to that fat jerk lecture me on my responsibilities! Jesus Christ. What's he think he's running there, a nursery?"

Suddenly Foreman started wavering, and clutched a lamppost as I reached out to steady him. "You all right?" I asked.

Before he could answer, he thrust his head forward and started retching. I tried to hold my hand to his forehead, but he sank to the ground and lay there vomiting, in a limp heap. It was a warm spring night, and the stench had a cloying quality as it climbed the vines of the moist evening air. There were no cars at this late hour. The streets were still. I told Foreman to be quiet, I'd return to Lapius's house and get help.

Lapius answered the door in his bathrobe. "Yes, Harry. You have forgotten something?"

"Foreman collapsed under the lamppost about a block from here. Sick to his stomach, wretching all over the place."

"Oh, that's too bad," Lapius said.

"What should I do—maybe we should call an ambulance? I can't budge him."

"I'll call the police. They'll take him back to the hospital," Lapius said. Under a lamppost, you say. Like Mielish?"

I shot back to where Foreman was now sitting up, mopping his face with a handkerchief.

"Take it easy," I said. "The police will be here in a moment, and we'll get a lift back to the hospital."

"Every time I lift my head up I feel faint. Jesus Christ, Harry, I swear that old bastard poisoned me."

"Couldn't have happened to a nicer guy, Monty," I told him consolingly. And remembering the lessons Lapius had taught: "But don't worry. You aren't going to die."

The morgue at The County was a white-tiled place. Tiled floors with centrally located drains into which blood can be mopped. Tile tables for the stiffs awaiting dissection, six in all. As soon as one body is finished, the morgue attendants sew it up with shoemaker's needles and thin cord. They sponge down the body and hose the table. The body is moved to a waiting stretcher, deposited in the icebox, then another stiff is brought to the table. Some of the bodies come from the hospital, some from the street, the residue of shootings, auto accidents, suicides, heart attacks, strokes. They are the bodies of people who fail to show up at home that night, who leave worried relatives in empty rooms. I had a dear friend recently returned from the army. He lived in an apartment not far from The County. One night when we were out together, he seemed vaguely disturbed. The following day at work I found his body on one of the slabs and a medical examiner slicing his organs. "Suicide," he said noncommittally. The shock made me sick.

The morgue is depressing. Some of the bodies we autopsied were warm, others cold. The cold ones had been in the icebox and were rigid. The skin was stiff, the blood congealed. They didn't smell when they were opened. Bowel was not distended. The fat under the skin was compact, not greasy. The warmth of life had been removed. It made the autopsy more comfortable more remote, less real.

The warm bodies claimed immediacy. The flesh was resilient, the eyelids closed, the body in repose. The tactile qualities were those of life. It was like cutting someone who was sleeping. Particularly the children.

It is hard to get used to the morgue. I never felt comfortable during a post-mortem until the flap of chest skin was lifted and placed over the face.

The pathologist must never forget that he is examining a human being, that death is a continuation of the living process of disease, not a separated, disjointed event. The body on the cold enamel must be treated in its nakedness with all the respect accorded the living. Too often the autopsy is a bloody mess, with organs scattered about, the scales on which they are weighed dripping blood. Slime begrimes every working surface.

That is clearly wrong. The autopsy should be performed with the solemnity of surgery. The body, recently alive, is being consecrated to the living. When thought of in terms of the vast contribution the dead body has made to medical science, there is almost a beauty to the morgue dead, the pallor, or cyanosis, or the slack jaw, or the asymmetry of the eyes, one lid half open, the soil between the legs.

When the body is laid open by the traditional "Y"-shaped incision that starts from the armpits and meets at the xiphoid, and then extends to the pubis, and the sternum and portions of the ribs are removed, to expose the neat, glistening package of

126

organs, and the prosector inspects these carefully, studiously, and starts his precise dissection, the procedure suddenly becomes purposeful.

The science of medicine was built on the autopsy. Too often it is performed by indifferent pathologists, as a chore to satisfy the requirements of the Joint Committee for the Accreditation of Hospitals, which decrees that accreditation may be lost if at least 30 percent of the dead do not come to autopsy. But for the doctor who performs it properly, the autopsy becomes the visual instrument that forms the basis of medical practice. Each of the tissues excised is placed in Formalin or comparable fixatives, which mummify and preserve them so that they may be processed in wax, cut into sliver widths, placed on glass slides, and stained so that the microscopic distortions caused by disease can be inspected. The light microscope transports the viewer into a universe of microcosmic battlefields where the destiny of the deceased was decided. Those easily lulled into imaginative foraging can spend hours peering through the blackened tubes to become immersed in this Lilliputian world of critical dimension, and fantasize themselves at the frontier of conflict; hordes of bacteria, surrounded by defending leucoknights in shining reds and blues, enmeshed in fibrin tank-traps, paralyzed by the antagonistic guns of the complement system.

When death is the textbook, pathology is the great medical teacher. Working at his own pace, the pathologist painstakingly unfolds the fatal progress of disease as the body is disassembled organ by organ, and the blood vessels to and from each organ are laid open. The pathologist studies the structural alterations that correlate with clinical disease. He details both the gross and microscopic anatomical distortions that coincide with malfunction. After two months in pathology, daily hunched over corpses on slabs that seemed always too low to the ground, medicine to me became a rainbow of morgue tones: blood red, liver mahogany, fat yellow, splenic maroon, capsular gray. In the braille of disease my fingers learned to distinguish normal crepitus from hyperaeration, the doughy feel of necrosis, the liver-like solidity of lobar pneumonia, the golfball hardness of fibromyomata, the pitted surface of chronically infected kidneys, the fine irregularities of cirrhosis. Everything was measured and weighed, and all the data plus our observations were compiled in lengthy descriptive reports that detailed, with as much precision as we could muster, the visual appearance of things.

Bernie Caspar held daily his fabled organ recitals, jovially going over the organs of the day's cases, cutting additional blocks of tissue for microscopic examination whenever he thought it necessary, and adding or subtracting from our rough-typed protocols. When the slides finally came back from the histologist, we would describe the findings as revealed by the microscope, and again write detailed descriptions of what we thought we saw. Then to the conference room, where the slides were flashed on a screen, and the cases conferenced. An attempt was made to seek cause for every clinical manifestation. When something unique showed up, a smudging of blood vessel muscularis, a tumor of uncertain origin, an unexpected degenerative change that had no precedent in our files, the cases were set aside, more tissues cut, special stains applied.

Monthly we assembled in the gray auditorium of the pathology department, host to the entire staff for the traditional clinical-pathological conference, that hallowed medical exercise during which the clinical aspects of a case were carefully expounded, and staff members were supposed to assemble the known facts and come up with a pathological or final diagnosis. The conference was a trap for clinicians, and Bernie Caspar would sit back, elfin-like, smiling dreamily, waiting for the clinical exposition to end so he could flash his slides and illustrate clinical errors.

"Sorry Doctor, you were wrong. The abdominal pain was not due to gall bladder disease, but the result of basal pneumonia. That is why you found a normal gall bladder during the surgery that precipitated the death of the patient."

This endeared him to nobody. Of course it wasn't fair. Bernie knew the answers all the time. But he etched indelible lessons that never were to be forgotten.

Once, when cortisone was new and its effects on the adrenal gland poorly understood, Caspar presented a case of apparent Addison's disease, an entity characterized by weakness, sodium loss, circulatory collapse and death. "No adrenal tissues could be located," he told the assemblage.

"How can you tell that?" Pier asked.

"We did serial sections of the suprarenal fat," Caspar answered smugly.

128

"That's not the best way to search for atrophic adrenal tissue, Dr. Caspar," Pier answered, his patrician figure drawn to its lean six-foot height.

"Can you suggest a better way, Dr. Pier?"

"Certainly, sir. Follow the adrenal vein from the renal vein. It should lead you directly to the adrenal remnant if there is any. Your method is inexact and tedious. I suggest that you missed the adrenal. The adrenal fat pad is too large for serial sections. You would end up with ten thousand slides. I gather you just made an educated guess at where you thought the adrenal should be. Not good enough, sir, for the conclusions you have drawn." Pier sat down victoriously.

Caspar flushed. "Well, even if there were a few cells, they didn't amount to much. The diagnosis is still the same."

"That's not the point. If there were a few cells, we don't know what they looked like, or why they atrophied. But I think they were suppressed by the large amount of cortisone the patient received. The point is that to teach us our errors, the pathology department must be more precise."

The staff had found a champion. Bernie Caspar would be more gentle with them in the future.

I tried to forget that the body was really Jack Conroy, the guy with twinkling eyes and a broad Irish grin.

A small hole punctured the skull above each ear. The hole on the right was plugged with a single drop of glistening pus. The pus was from an abscess. Cultures would demonstrate that the bacteria were staphylococci.

I incised the dome of the scalp from ear to ear, dissected the flaps, pushed one forward so that it hung like a curtain over his eyes, and retracted the posterior flap to expose the skull. The electric saw made a grinding noise as it cut a circular groove around the skull, which would permit me to lift off the calvaria and expose the brain.

The air was filled with a smell of burning bone dust. I inserted a head chisel into the groove and cracked off the calvaria to uncover the meninges covering the brain, dulled and partly covered with a fibrinous exudate that gave the dura a sugar-coated appearance. I cut the cranial nerves and sliced across the tentorium on either side to free the cerebellum. I allowed the cerebral hemispheres to fall into my gloved hands, then cut across the spinal cord just below the medulla to free the brain. It lifted out easily, and I placed it in a bucket of formaldehyde, suspended from the delicate basilar artery by a string which I clamped beneath the lid of the fiberboard cask. A voice suddenly whispered in my ear: "Call me when it is ready to be dissected, Harry. This is an important case."

I spun around looking for ghosts in the eerie loneliness of the morgue, to come face to face with Dr. S. Q. Lapius.

"Yes sir, I will."

I turned back to the body, removed the pituitary and proceeded to eviscerate the body. When I glanced up again, Lapius was gone.

Five weeks earlier Jack Conroy had been seated in his car waiting for a traffic light to turn green. Another car came up too fast behind him and rammed the rear of his auto. Jack and the other driver exchanged names and numbers and insurance companies. A few days later Jack's neck started to hurt him and he consulted a doctor. This, it turned out, was a fatal error.

Later the day of the autopsy Lapius called me to his office. He was seated in front of a viewing box sorting X-rays, throwing them up in front of the light and examining them with minute care, making notes.

"Were you standing behind me in the morgue today," I asked innocently, "or was that my imagination?"

"Must have been your imagination," he murmured.

"I figured as much. I thought for a moment you were interested in the Conroy case."

"Should I be?"

"Not especially. Whose X-rays are you looking at?"

"A fellow named Conroy."

"What a coincidence."

"Isn't it?" said Lapius. He retreated to the shadows of the X-rays. Finally he looked up. "I called you in, Harry, to learn what if anything you found at autopsy."

"Nothing yet, but Conroy must have had a brain abscess. We'll know in a few days when the brain is fixed and I can section it."

"I fail to understand this case," Lapius said in a tone that betrayed exasperation. "How a simple whiplash injury can be converted to a death defies me. I've reviewed the records and each step of medical care seems logical, but taken in context the entire case is illogical. The man should never have been hospitalized. His doctor has been on the staff for only a short while, and I must confess that I don't know him. Yet he was well recommended. Burton Peck, M.D. Do you know him?"

"Yes."

"What do you know about him?"

"He's crazy."

If I hadn't known Lapius, or rather if he hadn't known me for so many years, I would have been hesitant to speak so freely. "He's crazy because he carries a gun, holds group sessions in hypnosis, and drives around in a car with a revolving police light on the roof."

"Eccentric, perhaps, but not crazy. Why do you insist that he's crazy?"

"Because he's psychotic."

Lapius said crisply, "What basis do you have for that accusation?"

"Because he does inappropriate things with an insistent logic."

"That's what troubles me about this case, Harry. All the steps follow logically, but there is a lack of proper context."

"Sounds like Burton Peck."

"Did you know Conroy?"

"Slightly."

"Anything in particular you can tell me about him?"

"No. Just a hell of a nice guy. Used to walk around in the hall with that metallic contraption on his head. At first I didn't pay too much attention. Figured it was another one of those orthopedic braces for a sprain. Then one day I passed him in the hall and kidded him about it. 'I like your chapeau,' I told him.

" 'That's more than a chapeau, Doc, that's my castle on my head.' "

Lapius drove his fingers under his own abundant graying locks, and scratched gently. "Why should he say a thing like that?"

"Oh, you can't read something into everything a man says. He was sort of a cocky, flippant guy."

"Perhaps."

"Anyway, I figured a castle is worth looking into, so I inspected it more carefully. He had a goddamn pair of ice tongs stuck into his skull just above the ears."

131

"Yes, Krutchfield tongs. For traction."

"Yeah, for traction when the neck is broken to keep the vertebrae from overriding and severing the spinal cord. But Conroy was walking around with the contraption. Then from time to time he would slip into bed and attach the traction."

"Incredible," murmured Lapius. "How can you stabilize a pair of tongs drilled into your head?"

"That's the genius of Peck. He worked out a set of aluminum tubes that inserted into a small metal saddle he had fashioned for each shoulder. Then he had a crossbar or two and suspended the tongs from them so they were immobile and weightless. It was a clever contraption. But only a crazy man would build one."

"Of course you're right, Harry. That's what I meant before when I said things were proper but disconnected. If there's an indication for the use of the tongs, the patient shouldn't be walking. But if for some reason the patient has to walk, then the superstructure is a reasonable device to enable him to quickly get back into traction. But why the traction in the first place, Harry?"

Lapius went on. "Interstate Insurance actually asked us if they could go over the records of the case. Mrs. Conroy was beneficiary of a hundred-thousand-dollar life policy. The insurance company wants to know why Conroy died of whiplash. I can't say I blame them; I'd like to know that myself."

That was an unexpected twist.

"But from the clinical record it was obviously a brain abscess."

"Yes," said Lapius. "Doesn't that strike you as unusual?"

"Brain abscesses occur. Why is that so unusual?"

"Because it was so obviously a brain abscess. There was no mistake in diagnosis. Think, Harry. Why didn't they operate? It was his only chance."

"Quackenbush wrote a note saying that he wouldn't operate until the abscess had localized." That jerk who called himself a neurosurgeon was aptly named.

"All right, Harry. I'll have to go over the details more thoroughly. Be good enough to write me a complete clinical summary of the case. Have it on my desk at the beginning of the week."

I decided to write the report at Elspeth's place. She made me sleep on the living room couch. Our affair was over, interrupted by some other interest she had developed. Each night when I arrived she dutifully had dinner prepared. She dressed inevitably in a form-fitting pink robe collared with Flemish lace, a white pedestal for her graceful neck and elegant head. Her blond hair swept down to her shoulders. I died five nights on the couch. I should have stood at home, as Joe Jacobs used to say every time one of his fighters was knocked out.

On my last night, I prepared drinks. We lounged on the couch together. I reached to caress her. She slapped my hand petulantly.

"Elspeth, for God's sake. Remember me? I'm Harry."

"I don't remember you. I don't know anything about you. Anyway, there's something bothering you. What is it, Harry?"

Having nothing better to do, I told her about the Conroy case, recounting all the details. "So the net result is that Conroy is dead. He started with a simple whiplash, they put him in neck traction. His jaw became painful and tender. The dentist was called and said that he had a mandibular arthritis and that some other form of traction should be used if, indeed, traction was necessary. Then Peck drilled two holes and applied the Krutchfield tongs. One of the holes pierced the inner table of the skull. Conroy developed an abscess and died. Peck is a nut. Quackenbush missed the boat. But Paris in orthopedics okayed the tongs, Weaver in X-ray failed to report that the X-rays showed one of the tongs had pierced the skull. They are competent men. Yet no one stopped the carnage. It doesn't make sense."

"There's collusion, Harry," Elspeth said quietly.

"What do you mean by that, Elspeth?"

"Oh, Harry, take me to bed." I lost interest in collusion and off we went. The damnedest thing how she got turned on when I started talking medicine to her. I should have been doing it all week instead of sulking and trying to seduce her in time-honored ways.

The brains were stored, wrapped in gauze, each labeled, in large crocks filled with formaldehyde. I donned rubber gloves and rummaged through them looking for Conroy. The vapors stung my eyes and caused them to tear. Then the tears became real. I couldn't find Conroy's brain. I was gripped by fear. "Where the hell is Conroy's brain, Mike?"

"I don't know. Look in the crocks."

I shot up to Caspar's office. He was looking at some tissues through his microscope and swiveled around when I burst in. "Sir, there's a brain missing from the morgue."

He held one hand up like a traffic cop. "Slow down, Harry. Is it Conroy's brain?"

"Yes."

"I have it under lock and key. When Lapius gets here, we'll dissect it together."

Lapius arrived. Caspar unlocked a small closet and indicated the crock. "Carry it down, Harry, we'll be along in a moment."

The dissection was simple. I took the long flat double-ended brain knife and made a series of parallel coronal slices, making certain that one passed through a small puncture abscess filled with pus, turned to a cheesy coagulum by ten days of fixation in Formalin. The lesion was walled off by granulation tissue. There was a spreading meningitis. Death was obviously due to the increased pressure produced by the abscess.

"I can't understand why they didn't decompress this," Caspar said, clucking with surprise.

"According to the notes," said Lapius, "Quackenbush refused to go in until there were localizing symptoms."

"But he had pus draining from the tract in which the tongs had been inserted," Caspar said. "I don't understand that. But more important, why were the tongs inserted in the first place?"

"Because there was collusion," I said.

"Collusion! What kind of nonsense is that, Harry?"

"Wait," said Lapius to Caspar. Then he turned to me. "Where did you get the information that there was collusion?"

"I didn't have information that there was collusion. Someone told me there was collusion."

"Who?"

"Someone who comprehends the illogical."

"We'll schedule the case for tissue committee," Caspar said, then excused himself. "I have another case to finish," he said.

Lapius asked me to accompany him to X-ray. Weaver, as usual, was defensive but tried to be jovial. "Well, Simon, what brings you from the high tower of administration to mingle with men from the ranks?"

"Business, Weaver. I wonder whether you can help me out?"

"No trouble, Simon. What can I do for you?"

"I want to see John Conroy's X-rays."

134

Weaver buzzed his secretary and gave her the instruction. She returned shortly with a large folder. Weaver started shuffling through the celluloid pictures and moving them on and off the viewing box. Lapius leafed through the typewritten reports. Then he examined each X-ray minutely and sorted the reports to correspond with each film.

"I'm most anxious to see the one with the Krutchfield tongs." Weaver probed the envelope and retrieved a lone film. He handed it to Lapius. On the viewing box the frontal view showed the projection of Jack Conroy's skull. The tongs were in place. A small point of steel was seen clearly extending beyond the inner table of the skull in the temporal area. Lapius examined it closely. Then, going to the corresponding report, he read slowly:

" 'The Krutchfield tongs are in place. The right prong penetrates to the inner table of the skull. *Diagnosis:* Krutchfield tongs in place.' "

"Weaver," Lapius intoned slowly, "there is a discrepancy between the report and the film."

"Where do you see that?" Weaver grabbed the report and read it slowly to himself. "Darn that secretary. Of course there is. It should have read 'through the inner table' instead of 'to the inner table.' That's not important. We can change that."

"You had better not, Dr. Weaver. A boy died for that error in transcription."

"Of course, that's what it was, an error in transcription."

"It seems curious that so important a diagnostic fact doesn't appear under '*Diagnosis.*' "

"Well, I couldn't be absolutely sure. I did have Peck in here and we went over the films together. I told him that I thought the tong had penetrated, but he told me it was just an error in parallax. It might be, you know."

"But you didn't take other shots to confirm, did you?"

"No," Weaver said lamely.

"Thank you, Dr. Weaver. You've been helpful." We left.

Lapius was tight-lipped. "Too many Weavers around. They should burn these fellows at their mistakes, crucify their cowardice, stamp them out of medicine." Lapius sighed.

"Initial X-rays of the cervical vertebrae were negative. Then Conroy was brought to the hospital and placed in neck traction. He developed some temperomandibular joint pain. The dentist

135

was called in and diagnosed temperomandibular arthritis, and the head traction was removed. Then the Krutchfield tongs were inserted."

"And he had his castle on his head," I finished.

"What does that mean?" Lapius glared at me.

"That's what he used to call the contraption."

Lapius ruminated about that for a while, then said, "Be in my office at 11 A.M."

When I arrived at his office, a pert brunette with Irish blue eyes was seated on a small leather chair to the right of his desk. Lapius introduced us, but it was redundant. Mrs. Conroy kept blotting at her eyes with a tissue. I knew who she was, having seen her many times when she was visiting her husband.

Lapius turned to her. "I realize how painful this must be for you, Mrs. Conroy, but we are concerned about the death of your husband. Did Dr. Peck explain to you why he put Jack in that traction?"

"He said traction was the treatment for whiplash."

"Tell me, Madam, have you ever heard the expression 'a castle on my head'?"

She burst into tears. "Oh, that's what Jack used to call the contraption. He always used figures of speech. 'My home is my castle,' he would say."

"Is there a connection between 'My home is a castle' and 'There's a castle on my head'?"

"Maybe he thought that he would collect enough insurance money from the accident to pay off the mortgage on the house. It would be like Jack to romanticize the contraption. Like he had to suffer for his gain."

"Thank you, Mrs. Conroy. You have been very helpful."

"I'm tired and sad," she said.

After she had left I looked at Lapius incredulously. "My God, all she has to do is put two and two together and sue Peck, and she'll include the hospital in the suit."

"Let her," said Lapius, unperturbed. "Possibly too few suits are entered against city hospitals. Imagine that sonofabitch Peck, using this place to pick up some commissions on insurance paid to injury cases. There's your collusion, Harry. Between Peck and Conroy to milk the insurance company. What an irony," he chuckled. "The wrong company is paying off, and now Peck doesn't get his cut."

Caspar as head of the tissue committee held an open meeting, inviting the chiefs of surgery and medicine, Shaver and Pier.

Peck showed up in blue-serge pants, tieless, with the open collar of his white shirt exposed over the neck of a gray woolen sweater. He carried a briefcase, partially opened. Caspar chaired the meeting. The rest of us filled the front rows of the solid amphitheater seats. Caspar was in the well. Lapius sat to the rear. Caspar briefly reviewed the clinical events which led finally to Conroy's death. I was called to give the autopsy findings, and did so briefly, describing the abscess, its location and extent. Caspar, speaking loudly enough for all to hear, addressed all his remarks to Peck. "Briefly, Dr. Peck, we have a simple case of whiplash, brought into the hospital, placed in a simple neck traction by a brace sling under the mandible leading to weights strung over the back of the bed. The patient complained that this hurt his temperomandibular joint, and Dr. Colin, of the dental department, was called in consultation. He suggested that the sling be removed to avoid further joint damage. The sling was removed and replaced by the Krutchfield tongs. Why this drastic form of treatment?"

"It isn't drastic," Peck snapped. "It's just another form of traction. How else could you apply traction if the head sling was hurting him?"

"But was additional traction necessary?"

"Of course. Otherwise, I wouldn't have done it. Traction is indicated for all severe whiplash injuries."

"What constitutes a severe whiplash injury? That is, how do you gauge the severity of it?"

"By the degree of pain."

"Wouldn't some analgesics and perhaps a neck collar have sufficed?"

"Not in my judgment."

"Did you call any consultants in to substantiate your judgment?"

"Dr. Paris from orthopedics."

"What do you have to add to this, Dr. Paris?"

Paris was short, with a bossy forehead, wire-rim glasses and a snappish, crisp presentation. "What is there to say? Peck called us to see Conroy. He had a whiplash, and we advised traction." The editorial "we" gave Paris a numerical advantage, even though it was common knowledge that he was in solo practice.

"Did you also advise him to use the Krutchfield tongs?"

"No."

"You're a goddamn liar." It was Peck, standing, shouting and pointing at Paris. "You told me to go to Krutchfield."

"The hell I did, Burton. You asked me what other form of traction could be used, but I never told you to use it on Conroy."

"You said we'd never get a decent settlement from a neck collar, that we'd have to go to traction."

"One moment, gentlemen." It was Caspar, quietly. Peck and Paris, both on their feet, sat down. "Are we to understand that there were indications other than medical for the course of treatment?"

"I had no part in the treatment. I advised only by consultation. And you'll find no note from me recommending the Krutchfield."

"Dr. Peck, do you have a comment?"

"No comment."

Shaver signaled for the floor. "Dr. Peck, and Paris too, I guess, what were your fees for this case?"

"None of your business," shouted Peck.

Paris said, "The question is impertinent, and has no place at this meeting."

"It doesn't matter," growled Shaver. "We'll ferret that out at the credentials committee."

Caspar resumed. "Dr. Peck. Did you have a discussion with Dr. Weaver about the possibility of the right prong penetrating the skull?"

"Yes. In his office. But the plane was off center and that accounted for the appearance of the penetration. There was no penetration on X-ray."

"But apparently there was in real life," Pier intoned smoothly.

"I didn't know that until the wound became purulent."

Pier pursued him. "Then why did you start tetracycline?"

"Because just in case Weaver was right I figured I should protect the patient."

"But to protect against a possible meningeal infection tetracycline is precisely the wrong drug. It is dangerous because it masks the meningitis and abscess, prevents systemic spread and delays the development of fever. Which is precisely what happened."

Caspar again: "Dr. Weaver, there is no mention of possible penetration in your X-ray report."

"I explained that to Dr. Lapius. My secretary misheard the tape."

"But don't you check the reports before you sign them? Surely you would have noticed the error and been able to correct it."

"I usually do, but I must have missed this one. We have so many . . ." His voice trailed.

"Or perhaps," Shaver said, "you were afraid that you would provide evidence for a malpractice suit against Peck."

"Ridiculous. Why should I protect Peck?"

"I'm sure I don't know," said Shaver.

Caspar quickly summarized the inane medical reasoning that prompted Quackenbush to advise against surgery. Peck had simply followed the recommendations, feeling safe in the protection imposed by higher authority. Shaver whispered caustically to Pier and then made some notes on a scratch pad removed from his breast pocket.

"Gentlemen," Caspar asked, "is there any discussion?"

"I don't think we need belabor the case," Shaver barked. "It's clearly a case of malpractice. There is a strong suspicion from what I've heard that much of the treatment was motivated by other than medical indications. But that is of no concern to this meeting. On the bald facts of the case it was mishandled, mismanaged. A patient is dead."

Pier took the floor. "I suggest that the tissue committee include Dr. Shaver's remarks in its report. I second his interpretation."

Weaver squirmed. "Don't you think that the word 'malpractice' is a little strong? Everyone makes mistakes in medicine. I have a closet full of them in my office, X-ray films over the years—"

Shaver literally spat the words: "Don't you know the difference between mistakes in diagnosis, errors in judgment and malpractice?"

Weaver retreated. Caspar stood up and called for order. "Gentlemen, there is no other business for tonight. The meeting is closed."

Peck was first to the top-row exits of the amphitheater. He held his briefcase aloft. "You see what I have here," he shrieked. "It's a tape recorder. I taped this meeting. I taped those scurrilous accusations of malpractice. I'm going to sue the whole bunch of you for libel. You won't dare put the word 'malpractice' in the report." Then he barged out.

Afterward Lapius said, "Harry, you're quite right. Peck is crazy."

Letters were sent, meetings were held. Peck refused to resign, so he was kicked out. Quackenbush would not be recommended for reappointment by the credentials committee. Weaver suffered the embarrassment of exposure, and Paris was instructed to show all bills for compensation and insurance cases for a period of five years to assure that there was no contingency fee involved to motivate his practice in injury cases. Quite a month.

Lapius and I ate at Spinelli's. Five steps down from the street level. Spinelli himself ushered us in. "Ah, the great Dr. Simon Quentin Lapius. To what do we owe this honor? You finally accede to the supremacy of the Italian cuisine over the Chinese?"

"Please, Spinelli, don't badger me tonight. Just simmer some manicotti on your alcohol burner. If you'd buy a decent stove, you wouldn't have to add condiments to make your food hot."

"That wasn't nice, Lapius. You have to buy your wine tonight. No gifts."

"I'll buy if you promise not to water it."

Spinelli dove into the wine cellar.

Lapius was in no mood for banter. He brooded. "The meeting you just witnessed, Harry, is an interesting example of medicine policing itself. It doesn't always happen. Less blatant cases of medical malfeasance often go unpunished. There's a bond of professionalism spelled out in medical ethics that prohibits doctors from criticizing each other. They figure, there but for the grace of God, etc. I think one of the problems is that hospital privileges are tenuous and dismissal can be quite arbitrary. Of course Pier and Shaver are safe, too big to be molested. They can afford to be fearless. Particularly when a bad apple like Peck shows up. He's so unimportant. But let us suppose that Pier or Shaver fell into a malpractice situation. Who at the hospital would be big enough to bell the cat? No one, Harry. Because their judges would be their underlings, clearly an impossible situation. With more and more doctors on a full-time basis as salaried employees, their voices become muted. They become beholden and subordinate to the institutes they serve instead of to their patients.

"More wine, Harry," Lapius urged. "Spinelli dredged a dry vintage wine from his catacombs tonight. But don't tell him I said so. We must be careful not to finish the bottle entirely. I don't want to give him that satisfaction."

Suddenly the year was over. Rush was gone. Dr. Lapius, having reached the mandatory retirement age, resigned as Medical Director and went into semiretirement. He called me into his office just before he left. He was in his shirtsleeves, bustling about, stuffing papers and journals into packing cases. His beige vest with the gold buttons was draped over the back of his chair. He waved me in. "Harry, it's quite a wrench to leave this place. I've had a hand in its development for almost fifteen years. But I didn't call you in to listen to my mournful reminiscences. Actually, I wanted to tell you that your friend Rush has located in California, at University Hospital. They wrote to me for a recommendation.

"Rush's new job will offer him career opportunities that he couldn't have obtained at The County."

"And Foreman?"

"A war hero. We have to give him time to recover his sensibilities. But I feel that everything will work out." He took my hand. "I've enjoyed watching you grow in medicine, and become a doctor. Keep in touch, Harry."

The year had been enervating, so I decided to concentrate on Elspeth for a while. Love with Elspeth was a continuous interaction of demand, challenge, acceptance on her terms and, hopefully, fulfillment. To Elspeth life was passion, which led her to moonscape moods of loneliness and fear during which she became a stranger to herself. She loved to hear me talk about medicine. She listened to all of this attentively until a highlight danced beckoningly in dilated green eyes. A signal that I was about to enter the passionate world of Elspeth.

She had a lithe, fluid body that drifted into space. Wraithlike, soft, compliant, resilient, her love embrace was a wrap-around

141

coil of soft-skinned beauty. But afterward it was the scaly coil of a cobra, so quickly did she convert from rapture to indifference.

"Talk to me, Harry."

I talked. I talked to her about the heady sense of high adventure in medicine. I described the tiff between Rush and Foreman. She interrupted me.

"Men! You live in a world populated only by men."

"Frankly, Elspeth, I almost swore off women."

"What changed your mind?"

"You."

"That's a great compliment, Harry. I'll try to make you remember that." Her green eyes became bright disks. She pulled me to the floor.

Afterward, sitting apart, I watched twin columns of smoke stream from her nostrils.

She extended her hand and stroked me generously. "Come with me again," she pleaded.

When she woke me, I still had my arms around her. She disentangled herself. "It's getting late," she said.

"Elspeth, when will I see—?"

"Jesus, do you have to badger me with questions at this hour?"

She disappeared into the bedroom, slamming the door. She reappeared fully clothed. "I'm going for a walk," she said diffidently, and left the apartment. When I wakened in the morning, she still hadn't returned. I washed, toileted, made some coffee. The phone rang.

"I'm mad for you," a distant voice said. Then she hung up. It was Elspeth, rearranging my memories.

Lapius continued to edit his journal and pressed me into service as an assistant, ex officio. He taught me the precision of language. Evening hours shortened as we scanned articles submitted for publication. "In science, Harry, you have to say exactly what you mean in brief descriptive sentences. Each word carries part of the message of a sentence, and none can be wasted or superfluous. The author must think out in advance what it is he wants to say, marshal his thoughts in orderly sequence, and then find the spare words to express them."

Lapius would have me write editorial material, then go over my drafts with a heavy pencil, crossing out, rewriting, rephrasing obscure thoughts inexactly expressed. "What is it you are trying to say?" he would ask. I would tell him in lumbering phrases. "Good. I understand. Now write it so I understand."

I would write and rewrite the same paragraph ten or more times till it precisely expressed the thoughts. "We are not writing a novel, Harry. We are not reflecting on things past nor wondering about the future. We are trying to make a definitive statement. Don't shy from repetition or from cliché. After the thought has been precisely stated you can brighten the syntax and search for appropriate synonyms, but at no point must you sacrifice meaning. In scientific writing style is secondary to content."

It was tiring. It was instructive. It gave me a place to sleep.

Then Charley Crow offered me a fellowship in cancer research.

7

POSTERS ADVERTISING that the United States Government would subsidize research started appearing on the bulletin boards. At first we all thought it was a gag. Research was the potter's field of medicine. Everyone knew research workers were paupers who forsook the golden calf to pursue impossible dreams for no palpable reward other than the satisfaction of solving unstated problems. Graffiti appeared on some posters, and some were torn down. But more appeared.

Until then medical research was performed mainly on monies embezzled from department budgets, during moments stolen from busy clinical schedules. Of course every professor in a medical school was expected to be performing some research or other, but only the wealthiest institutions had endowment to support coordinated projects.

Then suddenly, in a brief quarter of a century, billions of government dollars propelled science from a cottage industry to a slick industrial enterprise. Laborious techniques that heretofore had demanded hours of tedious precision became automated and could be performed by clever high school graduates at the push of a button. A growing army of scientists, biochemists, biophysicists, physiologists, physical chemists, physicians, engineers multiplied like rabbits to populate a complex skein of research laboratories that crisscrossed the country, and often made big names of little towns. Complex chemicals which only a few sophisticated chemists in large universities could synthesize over a period of months and years were suddenly produced by the vat. Radioactive isotopes were attached to the organic radicals so that infinite numbers of biochemical substances could be traced when introduced into the body, and thus the function of all the body organs became almost "visible." Their complex machinery lighted like neon as the labeled stuff was fed through scintillation counters which measured radioactive bombardment by electronic impulses that could be counted to reveal quantity and concentration.

I visited several department heads in their creaky wooden offices and asked whether they were interested in a young doctor who would like to do research. They looked at me blankly, except Charley Crow. He had read the posters.

Charley Crow was professor of gastroenterology at Church Medical School. Church was affiliated with The County, using its clinical facilities for teaching. The staffs were interlocked.

I took a three-room flat in one of the row houses a block from Church Medical School. It was squalid, but I could always stay with Lapius in an emergency. Then, one brisk November morning when the air was nippy, and the trees struggled to retain the last of their browned leaves, I showered, shaved nervously, dressed and walked into the cool blue of autumn to meet Charley Crow.

Charley Crow had gracefully suffered the loss that attends upward mobility, namely old associates who felt that Charley had used and abused them, purloined their energies and cheated their intellects to vault into his present position of prominence. He climbed to the higher social echelon of the medical fraternity, with neither remorse nor regret. He had never made a pair of boots, but had learned early in life to polish them to a bright shine if they were worn by someone he needed. He was expert at splashing mud into the faces of those no longer useful and of attacking *sotto voce* and from behind, with indirect slurs, the intellectual probity of associates who became too competitive.

Those who accused Charley of stealing their work and ideas consisted of a watery slurry of past associates from which Charley Crow rose like cream to the top.

Why, knowing this, would I work for Charley Crow? Quite simple. He directed a huge, well-subsidized research laboratory with ongoing original projects. I wanted to dwell in the laboratories, mire myself in the animal stench and chemical fumes, plan experiments, dissect, study, examine, collate, write—in short, I wanted to be a research man. Charley Crow was willing to let me try. I would have worked for Dracula were he to let me experiment on the blood he drew.

Charley Crow had charm. He enjoyed people, and they responded, even his enemies, to his broad-grinned, sincere delight at the encounter, and then to the allure and mystique of the private person.

He challenged the curious to investigate.

He was seemingly propelled through life by a primal energizing burst, his progress simply a function of the inertia of this initial thrust. He moved forward like an iceberg, and when the waters around you started to get chilly, you had best move out of the way. Of course, he would encounter other icebergs. He liked people, but was numb to the pain he caused them.

I tried to sound out Elspeth, who was always interested in being sounded. Afterward, entwined in each other like vines, I told her about Crow.

"So use him. You'll use each other. You don't know anything about gastroenterology, he doesn't know anything about pathology, and neither of you knows anything about cancer. You'll be all right until you develop a community of knowledge. Then watch out."

I told Lapius what Elspeth had said about Crow. "It might work out, Harry. Crow is well funded. You know the story of subsidy, of course?

"Some industrialist called Simon came to his office with probably nothing more than a stomach-ache. He made a line of toiletries, called Simon Pure Products. Was also a food faddist and had curious ideas about diet. For instance, that proteins, starches and carbohydrates were digested more efficiently if introduced into the stomach separately or that water should never be taken during a meal. Simon was an important man, and Crow treated the theory seriously. He suggested to Simon that the theories be tested. Simon gave Crow some money to run experiments. Actually they proved that digestion was more efficient when the three types of food entered the stomach together, and I don't recall the outcome of the experiments with water. But the point is that Crow had the techniques to run valid experiments. Simon was impressed that these physiological phenomena could be quantitated. They published and Simon even had his name on the paper. That's how it all came about. Despite his detractors, Crow has actually produced a hell of a lot. The two of you might hit it off. As a matter of fact, you need each other. At the moment your paths are converging. Only when they meet will you have trouble. If you're smart enough to anticipate that moment, you will be able to separate gracefully.

"Until then, Harry, you'll see what research is all about. We live in what we like to think is a rational world. Given all the facts, any good bridge player can piece together an answer. But in research you may not possess all the facts. You must seek them out. Your job is to find the apparent irrationality, the paradox, the piece of information that seems wrong because it doesn't fit the logical pattern. Then, if you aren't bound by convention, not afraid of appearing to be wrong, you may construct an information series that will disassemble and replace the old logic."

"You would dispense with logic then?"

"Not at all. It is the gear of the workaday world, tongue and groove following in symmetrical procession so that things function. But in research the ultimate aim is to discard the old gear and create a new one. You apply logic, to be sure, but to the new data. Logic based on a false premise leads you to false conclusions. You will have a wonderful opportunity, Harry, even with Crow. You can let your imagination soar, you can be brazen and discard accepted theories if they don't fit a new fact that you have observed in the laboratory. You might not believe it, Harry, but there are 'researchers' who will discard a fact that they have seen with their own eyes if it fails to support acceptable patterns, because they don't want to be criticized for being different."

"They want to belong."

"Precisely. And if you are any good in research, you never quite 'belong,' because you are dealing always with apparent unrealities. A great editor of a prestigious journal in physics said that when there was room for one more paper and two were submitted, he always chose the one he didn't understand completely. He figured that if he understood a new paper completely it wasn't really new and didn't offer anything original."

"What do you figure makes a research man?"

"Oh, who knows, Harry? Ambition, iconoclasm, a desire to create order from disorder . . ."

I tried this out on Elspeth. She closed her green eyes and thought for a while. Then she said, ". . . and spite."

Mumford described the motivating forces of research beautifully:

> . . . the sheer delight of using the mind to discover ordered relationships and to create intelligible symbolic structures that reveal the underlying causal sequences or the emergent patterns of seemingly haphazard events.

I'd have to find out whether Crow would agree with that.

With that type of encouragement I trotted off to Crow's laboratory. The Crow's Nest, as it was called, occupied a perch atop the medical school building, a penthouse constructed as an afterthought.

Crow was an internist who had become involved, inadvertently, with cancer, and I was an embryonic pathologist.

Charley Crow was a brief man, brief in word and stature—scarcely five foot five, and even that height diminished by the absence of a single strand of hair across a bald and freckled pate. He looked positively dwarfed enfolded in a huge swivel chair behind his elaborate and neatly arranged desk. He came around to greet me, and folded my hand in both of his, with pontificate paternalism.

"I'm so glad you could join us, Harry." Why didn't anybody ever call me by my last name?

"Thank you, sir. I hope I can be of assistance."

"I'm sure you will. I'm certain of it."

Years later, after having written a number of his papers, synthesized his data, interpreted the results of our experiments, and created a separate research program, I received a letter from him saying I had been of assistance. But for now he was content to show me my working quarters.

If a hair shirt could be made of cold stone, the architect who designed Crow's research laboratories could weave it. The areas were poorly lighted by a reflecting bulb suspended from a high ceiling. The portals were barricaded by a huge metal door that scarcely yielded to a shove that would start a car rolling.

"We spent half a million dollars building these labs, Harry," Crow was intoning as we strolled around puddles that hadn't found their channel to the drain. I learned later that about three-quarters of that sum had gone into reinforcing the foundations of the building so it could hold the new superstructure.

He introduced me to Lil Blazer, a redheaded fat girl with cheeks like pink pompons. "Pleased tomeetcha. I do the blood counts." To Bianca Fiore, short and fat, with a center of gravity hovering somewhere around her knees. "How do you do?" extending a plump hand that gripped firmly. To Margie, Mavis, Shirley, Mabel, all scurrying in and out of the animal rooms clutching rats to their white coats, or charts beneath their arms, or hauling animal chow, or water, or the execrable paper filled with droppings from the animal cages.

"Okay, Harry. It's yours. Go to work," Crow said and disappeared into the elevator. Several hundred rats were awaiting sacrifice, and an equal number, already sacrificed, their organs stuffed in small Formalin-filled jars, waited to be sectioned, processed and studied microscopically. During the initial hours I worked amid the fumes. The formaldehyde vapors made me anosmic, unable to detect hospital odors and, worse, the smell of perfume. My hands became starched from the picrates and my fingertips insensate.

"It's like sandpaper when you caress me," said Elspeth, and restricted our relationship to the telephone until I could do something to unshrivel my skin. Since Elspeth was a palpable person entirely, the phone calls did little but serve notice that I was still alive. She took up with Joe Finley in obstetrics, and there wasn't much I could do about it, at least until my fingers softened. I tried to explain that my other probes were in fine fettle, but she suddenly failed to remember my voice, and kept asking, "Who is this on the phone?" And when I told her, she would say, "What do you want?" As if I were a salesman.

149

Down sex, up science. I entered a celibate life of discovery. The project involved feeding to rats cancer-producing agents which caused breast cancers and a few leukemias to grow. Bianca Fiore was the main line of communication between Crow and the rats, the ferret who noted every shiver and chill in the animals, grew alarmed when their noses were encrusted, excited when their blood counts jumped, and exuberant when small tumors first became palpable in the mammary glands. It was she who first found the tumors and called them to Crow's attention. He had been trying, logically, of course, to produce stomach tumors by putting cancer-inducing substances into the stomachs of rats. But nothing ever grew in the stomach. But to Crow's credit, he stopped worrying about stomach cancer and went into the breast-cancer business.

Crow told me that I was on loan to Caspar for a lecture series on inflammation.

The next day Caspar called and told me to plan a series of lectures on inflammation. I spent the night in the library. Who the hell was worried about inflammation?

It turned out that a lot of people had worried about inflammation. Aside from those who suffered from it, there was Metchnikoff, and maybe some great doctors before him. I read rapidly and made notes. At the first lecture, I dealt only with the historical introduction, buying time to study the rest of the subject. I bought one week. That was the week I met Machaon.

It seemed that almost every article in the contemporary literature on inflammation had been written by Ari Machaon. Inflammation is clinically characterized by four classical signs—tumor, calor, rubor and dolor—and anyone who has ever had a boil can translate these into swelling, heat, redness and pain. Every time an irritant enters the body, the body responds by pouring forth at the site a sticky broth of proteins, chemicals, cellular material and the cells themselves, which erect chemical and physical barricades to limit the migration of the foreign substance. Having localized the invader, cellular mechanisms attempt to isolate and destroy it. The conflict results in inflammation.

To Machaon the process wasn't just a "natural" response. You can say, "Naturally if you stick your finger, it will bleed." But the

150

reason it bleeds is because small blood-bearing channels are disrupted. Of course if you get a splinter, the site will become inflamed. Machaon wanted to define each chemical signal that called forth the inflammatory response.

To determine these factors, he injected irritating substances into laboratory animals, then collected the exudate at different stages of the development of the abscess, and submitted the material to crude chemical and physical fractionation. Body fluids of this sort can be separated into component parts by a number of methods. Through heat, the protein coagulum can be separated from the part that remains fluid. Or certain salts can be added that coagulate different fractions of the proteins. Machaon used these methods to separate a number of fractions of inflammatory fluids. He had labored for many years, using little more than kitchen salt and a centrifuge. He would reinject the separate samples into laboratory animals to determine which aspect of inflammation each would incite. Some stimulated the migration of leucocytes to the site, others caused edema, others temperature elevation. Simple. But Machaon was the guy who did it. His papers came from Harvard, Chicago, Duke, a government agency. He'd been all over the lot. It took most of the week to wade through his arguments, which were comprehensive and often repetitious. But when I reached his later papers, I was astounded to find in italics at the bottom of the title page: *"Director of the Department of Experimental Pathology, Alice Fremont Foundation for Cancer Research, and Associate Professor of Pathology, Church Medical School."*

Ridiculous. I'm giving the lectures on inflammation when Machaon, on whose work my lectures are based, is in the laboratory right over the library. I'm studying his articles to prepare lectures he should be giving. It was as though the janitor at the Vatican came out on the balcony to give the Christmas blessing, while the Pope remained upstairs studying.

Machaon's laboratory was guarded by empty animal cages in transit to the cage washer. Encrusted with foul excreta, they stank.

A door half ajar failed to yield when I pressed against it. I wormed through the tight opening, ducked under a shelf of books that bridged the entry, trod carefully around some crocks filled

151

with formaldehyde on the floor, straightened up, and found myself two steps from the bent back of a man intent on some papers spread untidily on his desk.

"Dr. Machaon?"

He turned slowly, and his gaze rose gradually from my midriff to my face. He pushed his glasses up to the bridge of his nose and held out his hand. "Hello, Harry. Dr. Lapius told me to expect you. Welcome to the kingdom of Rhadamanthys, the land of honor and integrity. Sit down."

"Where?"

Machaon looked about dubiously. "On that pile of books over there," he pointed. "I don't have too many visitors," he apologized. I balanced myself gingerly on the book stool. Machaon probed the pocket of a vest that he wore beneath a long, smudged white coat, and withdrew a wrinkled cigarette. He poured two cups of coffee and added some milk.

"What can I do for you?"

"Nothing really. To tell you the truth, I didn't even know you were here until this week. But Crow told me that I have to give a few lectures on inflammation to the students in pathology."

"Oh, you picked me up from the references."

"Yes. As a matter of fact, I feel foolish about the whole thing. Why don't you give the lectures? It's your subject."

"No one asked me."

Was it possible that Caspar didn't know Machaon was available? Ridiculous. Machaon was an associate professor of experimental pathology.

"What brought you to the stone-cold hallowed chambers of the Crow's Nest?" Machaon asked.

As I talked, Machaon sipped his coffee reflectively. Then he said, "Keep in touch with clinical medicine, Harry. Don't leave yourself out on the research limb. When they cut your budget, you'll fall to the ground, and won't have any roots in medicine."

After leaving Machaon I went to see Caspar. He was in the morgue, autopsying an eight-year-old girl. She was very pretty, allowing for the smudges of blood on her still and tranquil face. Caspar was bent over her body snipping sections from the psoas muscle.

"Those idiots will never learn," he said without looking up.

"She came in to have a hammertoe revised. After surgery they wrapped her foot in an airtight cast, and everything went swimmingly, except no one thought about the excavation. She developed tetanus and died. Can you imagine? No one thought to give her a tetanus booster, with all that dust circulating from the excavation, for the extension to the hospital, distributing tetanus spores everywhere. I'll roast their fat orthopedic asses at the next conference."

He did no such thing. A note went out from the pathology department suggesting that tetanus boosters be given prior to operative procedures, particularly if the postoperative dressing is airtight and conducive to growth of anaerobic bacteria such as tetanus. That way they could all stay friends. The family of the dead girl was told that it was just one of those things, the risk inherent in any operation.

Caspar looked up at me. "Look!" I said. "Shouldn't Machaon give the lectures on inflammation? All I know is what I read in the books. And they were all written by him."

"Good training for you, Harry. By the time you're finished with the term you'll know inflammation inside out."

"Machaon already knows it inside out. It's in his bones. Frankly, I'd like to sit in on his lectures. Why doesn't he give the lectures? The students would have a chance to come in contact with a medical great."

"He mumbles." Caspar was clearly annoyed.

I walked slowly back to the Crow's Nest. The ginkgo trees lining the boulevard were putting forth their pussy odors. It was a balmy day, and I was angry as a thundercloud. Caspar was a milksop. I remembered the stupid slide conferences we used to have in pathology. Every day the histologic tissues from surgery were laid out on trays for diagnosis. We would sit around the table and look at the slides and write our impressions on a pad. So far so good, great teaching exercise. Interns, residents, the professors and, at the head of the table, Caspar. Then after each slide he would tote up the ballots and the vote would be the basis for the final diagnosis. Benign, five to four; or cancer, by majority decision. It took Caspar off the hook each time, but it didn't always do the patient any good, particularly since, regardless of rank, specialty or experience, each of our diagnoses was given equal weight.

One great advantage of research is that the weekends are free. This weekend I had promised to teach Lapius how to ride a bicycle. Shod in sneakers, Lapius wore a crocheted salt-and-pepper tam and a light raincoat over a sweat suit of purple. At the park, we rented bikes. I suggested that he get the feel of the thing by mounting it while it was still safely rooted in the rack. The seat disappeared entirely beneath a cushion of purple-swathed thigh and nates.

"It seems quite simple," Lapius announced, gripping the handlebars till his knuckles turned white. I agreed and by way of illustration pointed to children scooting around on smaller bikes. I instructed him carefully. "If you feel unsure, or that the bike is falling," I said, "simply take your feet from the pedals, and spread your legs. Then if the bike falls to one side or another, your foot will break the fall."

With him on the bike I rolled it back from the stand. "We're going backward, Harry," he exclaimed.

"Yes," I reassured him, "but from now on you'll go forward." I held the bike firmly while he wiggled his ass from side to side trying to establish secure purchase on the small saddle. "Now then," I said, "the main thing is to keep your balance."

"I think I've got it, give me a shove."

"But—"

"No buts, Harry. Shove me off, let's see how I do."

I gave the bike a shove and off he went. Lapius maneuvered in a straight line for about twenty feet, then tried to turn the bike gently. This brought him to a slope and the vehicle started to pick up speed. He swerved the wheel frantically from right to left. The bike went faster. Suddenly he started pedaling backward to reverse direction, veered off the path, let out a mighty bellow—"Watch out!"—crashed into the brambles and lay still. To extricate him I got two men from the bicycle shop. We took long boards and levered the prickly branches off his body, and when they seemed safely out of the way, I started slowly to extricate him from the tangle of bars and spokes which held him firmly. Finally he was free enough to point his purple beachball rump to the sky and crawl backward on hands and knees. He stood up, brushed some clinging debris from the cotton togs, assembled his dignity and turned away forever from the stricken tangle of bush and machine.

"Fetch my coat, Harry." I draped it over his shoulders and bundled him into a taxi. He was mute until we got home. I prepared tea for him while he sulked in his overstuffed armchair. His brows were knit in studious thought. He sipped slowly at his tea, no sugar, no lemon. It warmed him. I told him about meeting Machaon, and what Caspar had said.

"I don't like it," he murmured. "They are starting to isolate Machaon. There's going to be trouble." Then suddenly he said, "Harry! Where do they hide the fucking brakes on that infernal contraption?"

"On the handlebars. You squeeze them with your hands."

"How was I to know that?"

"I was about to tell you when you demanded that I shove you off," I said sweetly.

The next time I saw Lapius he was mellow. "How goes it at the Crow's Nest?"

"Pretty good."

"Do you like Crow?"

"Sure I like Crow." He was precise, energetic, worked as hard as any of us. He had a slow, tentative way of expressing himself, as if expecting to be interrupted or corrected. He didn't come to any conclusions, but kept throwing out provocative questions. "He always encourages me, makes me feel clever and useful—"

"And lets you do his work," Lapius said.

"Not exactly," I told him. "After all, he originated the problem and initiated the experiments."

"There will come a time, Harry, when you will have progressed on your own to a certain point. Then you will have a proprietary interest. You will want to strike off in new directions. There will be friction. You will be in danger then. He's your Rhadamanthys."

"Machaon mentioned that."

"Yes, the judge of the dead. The man with the power to consign you to heaven or hell. Just remember, Harry, lurking beneath the idealism and nobility of the research dream there's a competition as vicious as is found in the world of business. The incentives are the same, greed and fear."

And spite, I thought to myself, remembering what Elspeth had said.

"Incidentally, do you know why they didn't ask Machaon to lecture on inflammation?"

I shook my head. But Lapius didn't know either. "Let me know if you hear anything," he said.

Later, I asked Elspeth what she thought. "Because he mumbles, Harry. Isn't that what Dr. Caspar said?"

"Do you believe that, Elspeth?"

"That's what you told me. Talk to me, Harry."

I did. I told her about Machaon, his isolation, the hermit's nook surrounded by musty books; about the man walking entirely in a world of tubes and rabbits and exudates, and chemical fractionation. About a man sacrificing all worldly contacts to pursue his compelling obsession to discover secrets the gods have taken pains to confuse and disguise. Suddenly, Elspeth beamed the light of her widened green eyes into mine and sparks shot off all over the limbic area of my brain. Afterward, Elspeth, enunciating each word slowly, said, "Harry, people are afraid of hermits."

Machaon spun on a different axis. If you could enter his frame of reference and develop a community of interests, he was great. But his scope was limited to particular objectives in experimental pathology. He ate to obtain the fuel to work. He bedded with his wife because it relieved him of tensions that fogged his concentration. He flew planes to get to places where inflammation was being discussed; it never entered his mind that the plane might not get there. On arrival, he was all set to probe the infinitudes of inflammation. Since most of us haven't the capability to live in exclusive worlds, Ari Machaon was estranged.

At the Crow's Nest there was much work, and Lil Blazer kept the assignments coming. She was like a tight end continually taking plays from the coach into the huddle. And what was worse, she reported to the coach little tidbits of information she managed to overhear in the huddle. It wasn't unusual to get a call from Charley Crow and have him question me about some finding or other which I had mentioned during the coffee break, or muttered to my technician. I would reassure Crow that I wasn't keeping secrets, but that there was no point in reporting something before I had checked it out.

The next day Crow would call again. "Harry, I'm not trying to breathe down your back, but—" When my voice grew edgy, he became disarming. "Look, kid. You're here because I have confi-

156

dence in you and appreciate your integrity. It's just that I'm under pressure. I have to report our progress to the board. As a matter of fact, I urge you to be precise and careful. If I push too hard, well, give me a nudge, eh?"

Crow took me to lunch almost daily and listened attentively as I rambled about statistical methods, or conceptualized the interplay between carcinogenesis and the endocrine system. He would nod appreciatively. I soon realized he was learning, not confirming. "I like the way you think," he told me. "Oh, incidentally, John Griffiths is coming in from Denver. It would be embarrassing if I could not make a complete presentation of our work to date. You could check out some of the discrepancies more rapidly, eh?"

"Of course." Sure, if I gave up dinner, Elspeth and sleep. But somehow Crow got under my skin, and after a while I became motivated mainly by a desire to please him.

Victor Krouse, chemist, felt differently. "Fuck him," he said. He minced tumors and analyzed their intricate chemistry, but minced no words. "That sonofabitch doesn't understand a damned thing I'm doing, yet he'll take the data and report it at a meeting, or after I write it up he'll put his name on it."

"But he originated the project."

"He found a way to make tumors. Hooray. But I'm the one who is tracing the oxidative pathways. He don't know a farvel about chemistry. What the hell am I supposed to do, carry him on my back for the rest of my life?" Krouse never smiled. At first I thought it was his lip, scarred in the brutality of the concentration camps of Europe, from which he had graduated, somehow, otherwise unmarked. Bianca confided in me that it was because of his unhappy home life. I was prepared to believe her until I learned that she ascribed this root cause to all the real or imagined disaffection that she detected in the private lives of the laboratory people. The only two whose home lives were ideal were hers and "The Chief's." She dwelt in a gilded cage of exalted dreams, she the fat, dumpy charmaid who would be turned into a lithe, beautiful princess every time Charley Crow thanked her for finding a pea-sized tumor under the mattress of hair on one of her animals. Frankly the whole damn place was sticky with some cloying idolatry that began and stopped with Charley Crow. Except for Victor Krouse, of course, so I turned to him for refreshment.

We held a staff meeting the day before Griffiths was to arrive. Immaculate white linen coats were draped across the backs of our seats. "The visiting coats," Bianca whispered in answer to my inquiring glance. "We return them after Dr. Griffiths leaves."

Crow went over the details of the visit briefly. "I expect that you'll be able to answer any questions that Dr. Griffiths asks. If it borders on the unpublished work, be informative but vague." He turned to Krouse. "Dr. Krouse, I've arranged an appointment between you and Starrett in the Cancer Biochemistry Division at the National Institutes of Health in Washington. Unfortunately, it's set for tomorrow, so you won't be here. Would you leave a summary of your work for me?"

"I'll give you the data books. I won't have time to write a summary. I've got to prepare for the meeting in Washington."

"You've had two weeks to prepare for that."

"I have some loose ends," Krouse said, looking into the distance. Crow said nothing, but his lips were drawn.

Afterward, Krouse was gloating. "Let these wise-ass doctors make sense out of the data books. They don't know the difference between a high-energy phosphate bond and a government bond. You M.D.'s with power and money push us Ph.D.'s around all the time. Things will change, because we're probing molecular biology and they don't teach you guys anything about that in medical school."

The morning of the visit Crow bustled around the animal room, and ordered the trays beneath the cages to be changed at noon, an hour before Griffiths would arrive, even though the liners had been fresh that morning. He carried a little atomizer which he sprayed intermittently to eliminate unseemly odors. He had Bianca ferret out Krouse's data books and cart them down to his office.

"That shouldn't be a problem," I offered consolingly. "Griffiths will have enough to see and we can sort of sketch in the work that Krouse has been doing."

"Sketch in?" Crow barked shrilly. "You can't just sketch in for Griffiths."

"Will he understand all that detail? Has he the background?"

"He doesn't need the background. Griffiths doesn't come alone, Harry. He brings his entourage—his biologists, his chemists, his endocrinologists. They sketch in for him."

158

"So why all the agitation?"

"Because Griffiths is connected with every study section in Washington. If he doesn't come away impressed, not only with our data, but also with the entire operation, we'll never get any grant money."

At one o'clock sharp Crow escorted Griffiths and his pride of young lions through the halls and made the necessary introductions. Griffiths was medium height, and his hair flowed in a long, well-combed white mane. There was liquor on his breath. His handshake was firm. As soon as he and Crow had gone, the Griffiths boys swept down on our data like Internal Revenue agents. They watched carefully while Bianca displayed the animal room and demonstrated how the little rubber catheters were passed into the stomachs of rats through the gullet. One of them asked if he could try. He was clumsy at first; the tongue and nose of the rat turned blue, while its eyes popped.

"You squeezed its neck too hard," Bianca admonished.

On second try he succeeded and the group moved on. I spent half the afternoon going over data, demonstrating the consecutive histological changes as tumors developed, and explaining what I felt to be the important interplay between stroma and parenchyma.

Griffiths' pathologist listened politely, but was unenthusiastic. There were strange things about the tumors that our rats were growing on their breasts. When tumor growth was induced in female rats by powerful chemicals, they grew as glandular and malignant tumors. But in males, fewer developed, and they grew as fibrous and benign tumors. As far as I was concerned, the male hormone caused the cells to grow in a benign form and the female hormone caused the same cells to develop a different appearance and a malignant potential. For Griffiths' man, and almost everybody else, the male hormone stimulated the fibrous cells to dominate the gland cells, and the female hormone did the opposite. I believed that the fibrous and glandular cells were two different forms of a single cell type, and had pictures to demonstrate it.

The argument had important implications, because if the dualists were correct, there was no sense bothering with the male rats because their tumors weren't malignant. But if I was correct, then we had the right to ask what change the male hormone

159

created in the potentially malignant cell that altered its pattern of growth so that it became indolent, benign and lost all resemblance to functioning glandular tissue.

Late in the afternoon we all gathered in Crow's spacious office—Griffiths and his group, Crow's friend, Vincent Heller, and the rest of us.

I'd met Vincent Heller several times—a soft-spoken, business-like chemist with the aplomb of an important physician. In those days the chemists, despite their obvious importance, were underpaid, wore scrounge clothes and always were obsequious in the presence of physicians, because it was the doctors who more often than not paid their salaries. The advent of government grants would eventually liberate them from this serfdom.

So it was no mean accomplishment for Heller to be invited to sit between Crow and Griffiths, power brokers in science who knew less than he about the chemical intricacy of cancer. He was impeccable in dress and bearing. He was a member of cancer councils in Washington. At least once he kiboshed grant requests by the "opposition" at Crow's request. He would, one day, have Crow's job.

Crow called for questions, and Griffiths nodded to one of his men in a gray suit, who said, "We were hoping to meet Dr. Krouse today."

Crow was expansive. "Dr. Krouse was called to Washington to consult with the biochemistry sections. However, Dr. Heller was good enough to review his data, and will answer any questions."

The questions were polite and searching. Heller answered them indirectly. He drew diagrams on a blackboard. He sketched chemical cycles, drew arrows and wrote formulas. "These are the areas in which Dr. Krouse is working."

"Has he explored the high-energy phosphate components?"

"He told me he intends to complete that."

"What about energy-transfer mechanisms before and after carcinogen administration?"

"He has just set up his controls."

"Is the carcinogen recoverable in any recognizable form from the induced tumor?"

"You'll have to wait for Dr. Krouse to return to get an answer to that, but I believe he's working on it."

My pathologic counterpart leaned over and whispered to me, "Heller is very informative, isn't he?"

"Yes, he is," I whispered back.

"Why the hell is Krouse in Washington?"

"Krouse was shipped to Washington. Crow didn't want him here."

Crow ended the meeting.

Krouse returned from Washington. He shrugged when I told him that Heller had been through his data books.

"Crow uses Heller to check up on me," Krouse said. "He's just a flunky. Crow thinks Heller can referee this stuff. No one can. All Heller can do is assure Crow that the data are correct. If the data don't point to Crow's preconceived notions, it's just too bad. Anyway, the trip to Washington wasn't a total loss by a long shot."

"What happened?"

Krouse looked blank and moved away.

Bianca told me confidentially not to consort too much with Krouse. "The Chief doesn't like him."

"Why not?"

"He's too independent."

"Isn't that the way it's supposed to be?"

"Perhaps. But within limits. He shouldn't run off with the Chief's work."

"Has he done that?"

"He resents that the Chief's name is on his papers."

"Did the Chief do the work?"

"Well, he started the whole thing."

"Sure, but at some point it's no longer his. After all, Crow isn't a chemist. He's a practicing physician, he teaches at the medical school, he has people gathering his data for him and writing first drafts of the papers. As a matter of fact, what the hell does Crow do around here?"

"You shouldn't talk like that."

"It was just a question." Crow had a patron, so he had the power. But now the government was becoming a patron of research. Money was available to thousands of young scientists all over the country, who were thus liberated from the shackles of institutional authority by a granting program that would endow

161

them with sufficient funds to follow lines of research distinct from those pursued by their department heads. Crow wanted some of that money. That was what the Griffiths visit had been all about.

Crow approached the grant problem with precision. He collected our data sheets and made us write interpretative accounts. He pored over the data, phoning all hours of the night for explanations of puzzling points. He sent us streams of references he wanted checked. I virtually lived at the library. He worried Washington daily about the meaning of various questions on the grant application. Bianca kept the animal rooms going, but all other aspects of experimentation, except for the sacrifices of scheduled groups, came to a standstill. It took a month. The grant asked for a lousy fifty grand plus 10 percent for overhead to the medical school. We were exhausted. Crow flew to Sarasota for a rest.

He called every day. He changed orders, started new animal groups and in general was as active as if he had been downstairs in his office. He returned with a nice tan. "I had a sunlamp in my room," he explained.

The grant game proved to be lots of fun. The work started to produce interesting offshoots, one of which was the leukemias. Bianca discovered the first ones and learned to transfer them from animal to animal. At first she injected the blood of the leukemic rats into the other rats, and nothing happened. Then she found out that if you injected the stuff before the recipient rats were ten days old the transplanted leukemic cells grew in the new host. Crow put me to work on the pathology of the transplantation process. I made some interesting observations quite apart from the mainstream of the work and quietly wrote up my own grant application. I brought it down for him to sign.

He read it over briefly. "Don't you think you're gilding the lily, Harry?"

"What the hell," I told him. "It's just an interesting sideline."

He signed it. Then Krouse brought one in on the chemistry of the leukemic cells and Crow signed it also. Within a year we each had our own projects alongside of the main Crow experiments. Krouse and I became independent researchers. That was the beginning of the end.

We put in a full day for Crow, but the nights were our own. We decided that as long as we provided Crow the raw data we had fulfilled our obligations. If he wanted the material written up, he'd have to do it himself. After all, his name went on the paper. But Crow wasn't good at synthesizing the data and at first had a lot of trouble with the editors of medical journals. So Krouse and I had to go over it after all. But at least Crow gave us the skeleton of what he wanted. Between us, Krouse and I could bat the thing out in a couple of nights, and hand it back to Crow for polishing and the measured syntax that was his imprimatur.

Successful research is often initiated by an accidental finding or perhaps a unique collision of events. As Lapius put it, "There must be a point of departure from the predictable. Once embarked on the new direction, the research is pursued by logic. Finding the point of departure is a matter of luck, intuition, unforeseen accident. Crow inducing breast cancers when he was looking for stomach cancer is a case in point."

When Bianca started transferring leukemic cells to infant rats, Crow asked me to look into it. "You know, check it out."

I couldn't get specifics from him, so I decided to study the pathogenesis of the transfer—that is, the route by which the transplanted leukemic cells became seeded in the tissues of the suckling host.

The two classic leukemic types were transferable: myelocytic leukemia, which originates in the bone marrow, and lymphocytic leukemia, which originates in tissues outside the bone marrow, probably in lymph nodes or thymus or spleen. The myelocytic cells formed green masses and fluoresced red under ultraviolet radiation, but both forms of leukemia could be traced microscopically because their cell colonies were distinctive when found in tissues in which they didn't belong.

Experimental groups of newly transferred rats were set up and I did serial day-by-day studies of the bone marrows. It turned out that between the ages of seven and twenty-one days the character of the rat marrow underwent sudden and startling changes independent of which type of leukemia had been transferred. Normally the marrow has a few lymphocytes, a plain cell of undistinguished characteristics; large numbers of erythrocytes, dark cells which give rise to the red cells of the blood; and granulocytes which spawn the so-called "polys," which are the first line of defense against invading foreign bodies, including microbes, the cells that form the essential substance of pus in

163

infections. I was intrigued, therefore, to find that in rats one to three weeks of age a sudden transformation had occurred in the marrow. The indolent, mysterious lymphocytes suddenly crowded in and comprised more than 50 percent of the cell population; then suddenly within seven days, like a receding tide, their numbers dropped back to the more usual 5 to 10 percent.

I recounted these findings to Bianca at lunch one day.

"What do you make of it?" she asked.

"I'm not sure. I'll have to study it."

An hour later Crow called me. "Harry," he said, "I understand there's something very exciting going on upstairs."

"I don't know if it's exciting or not."

"I'll be right up."

He peered intently through the microscope at the slides I had prepared. I pointed out to him the various cell forms, and the unusual distribution of the small round exceedingly plain lymphocyte-like cells.

"They shouldn't be there, Harry. We've found something, my boy, we've found something. If this proves out, Harry, it means that the injected cells release something that prompts the marrow to fill with undifferentiated cells, which then give birth to the particular leukemia that was injected. Maybe they release a viral particle?"

He leaned back in the springback swivel chair and polished his glasses before mounting them on the bridge of his nose. "Hurry with this, Harry; we've got to publish it."

He called me daily for weeks, prodding, pushing. I fended him off for a while. Suddenly, there were no more calls. He had flown to Argentina. While he was away I had Bianca set up groups of normal suckling rats, sacrificing batches of ten for each day from birth to three weeks. Then I set about the laborious task of counting thousands of marrow cells for each age group under the microscope. The daily counting was onerous, a task I learned to dread; to sit hour after hour hunched over the enemy microscope, moving the slide in measured paces and orderly fashion, counting, turning gnurled-head controls that activated a mechanical stage. Since the classic grouping of cells was no longer applicable, I designed new categories to account for the in-between forms.

Clusters of numbers gradually began to fill the spaces of columnated data sheets. The end of the day brought little joy, because it meant only that I had to repeat the chore on the following day. My nightly vision swam with orange-colored spheres, blue bodies and pinpoint granular images, the afterimages of a universe of microscopic things. My vision became restricted to the tubular world of the microscope focusing incessantly on a galaxy of matter as far removed from a world of smaller things as the giant starlit cosmos from the earth. The lights and shadows of each of the cells revealed only the coarse outlines of the minuscule engine that drove the cell to its predestined and particular cycle of life; the engine itself composed of cojoined organic elements of universal parts that carried the message of energy values, growth patterns, function and longevity.

By the time Crow returned from Argentina I had proved that the flood of small round lymphocyte-like cells to the marrows of rats between one and three weeks of age had nothing to do with the leukemia transplants; it occurred normally in unimpaired animals. It was part of the natural pattern of marrow development.

"Are you sure, Harry?"

"See for yourself." I unfurled pages of tabulated data, went over the slides of the normal baby-rat marrows. He immediately lost interest in the project. Thereafter he left me alone to my "hobby," as he called it.

Within a few months I had compressed the raw data into a meaningful format and was invited to present it at one of the monthly research seminars. Machaon sat in the first row, and became increasingly intent as I talked and demonstrated pictures of the cells. He cornered me afterward. "Come, Harry, you must be dry, after talking so long. We'll go to my office and I'll make you some good Russian tea." He filled an Erlenmeyer flask with water and set it over a Bunsen burner. The water should come to a boil about dusk, I thought.

"You know what you have done this afternoon, Harry? You have explained to me a mystery in my work. Here, I'll show you." He rummaged through his slide files, plucked out a few of the one-by-three-inch glass rectangles and placed one under the microscope. "Look, Harry. Does it look familiar?"

I found myself peering at a field that replicated my material, a marrow composed almost entirely of lymphocyte-like cells. I was momentarily crestfallen. Machaon had beaten me to it. He read

165

my thoughts. "No, Harry. This is not marrow from a baby. This is from one of my mature animals that I injected with a substance that produces granulated leucocytes. As you said this afternoon, you believe your little round cells eventually differentiate into all the other marrow forms. You showed pictures of the gradual transformation. Your numbers are convincing. This can't be seen in adult marrow because it doesn't happen fast enough or frequently enough, but in your baby animal it's clearly visible. Your little cell is the progenitor of the erythrocyte, the granulocyte. You've got a classic finding, my boy. But few people will be interested in it because it contradicts current concepts."

"But you have the same phenomenon in your slides."

"Yes, Harry, I do. But I misinterpreted it, or rather I didn't interpret it at all. Now, however, I know that in order to produce leucocytes, or probably any other cell form, these small, round undifferentiated cells are necessary. And when I provide a powerful stimulus for leucocyte production, the marrow first gets flooded with these small cells. You have shown me something today that explains my own work. I want you to present this talk again for some of my colleagues, and then, Harry, you must publish." I thought I was going to kiss him. *"You* must publish," he had said. When Crow said it, it came out *"We* must publish."

Lapius was not sanguine. "It will be difficult to publish, Harry. It is controversial."

"Machaon said something like that. He said it contradicted the German school."

"Actually, Harry, your finding isn't entirely new. The early histologists interpreted their findings in much the same way you do, that is that all hematologic cell types derive from a single source. But their techniques lacked the precise detail of the dry smears. With the dry smear, nuclear detail and cytoplasmic granules became visible. Some of the Germans, using this technique, believed that they could distinguish definitive cell lines, each deriving from a specialized blast cell. You are not the first to assume that a single small undifferentiated round cell can give rise to all the blood cell types. But you are the first to demonstrate these changes clearly within the context of normal mammalian growth.

"Despite the lip service paid to Darwin and the descent of man from other life forms, many biologists continue to treat mammals

166

as a biologically separate species, and won't accept the fact that the cellular phenomena of lower life forms are predictive of events in the mammalian species. This may derive from some religiosity that claims man to be an independent creation of God. And of course there are political considerations that enter subtly into European research."

Lapius was rambling about things I didn't feel like trying to understand. I excused myself politely.

I called Elspeth from a phone booth. She wouldn't see me. "You're too wrapped up in blood cells, Harry."

I prepared an abstract for the spring meetings and it was accepted promptly. Then I composed a long article replete with photographs, drawings, charts and tables. I submitted it to *Hematologica*. Ludwig, the editor, sent me a letter of acceptance. What the hell is so hard about publishing?

A week before the spring meetings in Boston, Ludwig called me. "There are a few minor changes I would like to suggest. I see you are giving a paper in Boston. I'll be there. Can we get together on the paper?"

"Sure." I liked Boston.

Victor Krouse heard I was going to Boston.

"Can you get the travel money from your grant, Harry?"

"No, I bought some equipment with it."

"Who is going to pay for your trip to Boston?"

"The Institute."

"You better get the money in advance then."

"How so?"

"Is Crow's name on your abstract?"

"No."

"Well, last year when I gave a paper in Chicago the Institute failed to reimburse me."

"How come? The paper came out of the Institute."

"But Crow said it wasn't an important piece of work and that I hadn't asked for permission to give it in advance."

"Had you asked permission?"

"As a matter of fact, no. I simply told him I was giving a paper in Chicago. He said, 'That's nice,' and walked away. Then, when I returned, he wouldn't give me the expenses. 'You knew I was going,' I told him. 'Sure I knew,' he said. 'You can give a paper any place you want to. But that doesn't mean the Institute has to pay for it. I have a responsibility to my board of directors.' "

"That's very interesting," I said and started to leave.

"Where are you going?"

"To see Crow about something."

"Aren't you going to thank me?" he whined.

"Thanks."

Crow was going over papers on his desk. He was dwarfed in the high-backed green leather chair, which for the moment was the most imposing object in the office. He glanced up as I entered.

"Yes, Harry."

"I've had a paper accepted at the Boston meeting."

"Yes, you've told me that."

"I was wondering whether I could have my expenses in advance?"

The phone rang and Crow discussed a clinical case for five minutes. While he talked into the phone, chuckling graciously at appropriate moments, he stared stonily at me. I fidgeted.

When he hung up, he folded his hands across his plump belly, leaned back and glanced up at the ceiling with the bemused look that Newton might have worn waiting for the apple to drop. "That's a highly irregular request, Harry."

"It's just that I don't have the money to lay out." They weren't paying me a hell of a lot, and I figured that I had brought in about five thousand dollars' worth of instruments and a few thousand in cash overhead with my grant. What the hell was he so tight about?

"Then you won't be able to go to Boston. They'll read the paper by title and publish the abstract. After all, Harry, I can't sanction irregularities. I have a responsibility to my board of directors."

The phone rang and soon Crow was chuckling again. It was the dean. They were talking about additional space for the Institute. I used the time to think, trying to slip my eyes from the noose of Crow's cold stare.

When he hung up, I said, "Okay. I'm sorry that I can't go. I'll have to withdraw the paper."

"You can't do that."

"Why not?"

"It will look bad for the Institute."

168

"Well, I sure as hell can't give the paper in Boston if I'm three hundred miles away."

Crow turned white and compressed his lips, a mannerism I learned to associate with his attacks of chest pain, while he silently calculated. Then a blush appeared on his cheeks and he smiled. "Well, if you're that hard up, I guess we can advance you the expenses this time. But in the future, Harry, you'll have to lay out your expenses and we'll reimburse you on your return. It's a matter of policy, you realize."

I drove to Boston, nursing my jalopy along the slow lanes of the turnpikes. If the transmission went again, the ten cents a mile Crow was paying for the trip would barely cover the towing charges. For most of the way, I practiced my brief ten-minute talk, trying to time it out exactly and anticipate questions. I was pretty skittish about my first lecture to a group of professional researchers. Lapius had given me some useful hints.

At the hotel there was a message from Ludwig. Could we meet in the morning to finish the paper? I called his room and made a ten-o'clock date. I spent the night reading the program for the meeting and noting the talks that I wanted to hear during the next few days.

Ludwig was a rosy-cheeked expansive fat man, his pink, balding pate partially obscured by a horizontal panel of bright gray hairs. He smiled broadly and pumped my hand. "So nice to meet you, so good of you to come. I know that you'll excuse this informality, but it will save us both time, and enable me to meet an earlier deadline with your paper. Come, let us sit in that quiet corner and talk, shall we?" We sat in the quiet corner and he started to talk.

"I like your paper very much, but one or two points require clarification." He unzipped a brown vinyl briefcase, souvenir of a previous conference, and removed the copy of the paper I had submitted. He riffled the pages and stopped at a large red X. "Ah, here it is. You state here:

> The question of the myeloblast must diminish in significance because, far from being the only pathway of granulocytopoiesis, it is only a link in an occasional pathway of hematopoiesis, and can be bypassed in many instances by more direct transformations.

You recall that?" I nodded. "Well, I would suggest that you delete it."

If my face didn't betray astonishment, my voice delivered the message. "*What?*" I said loudly enough to attract curious glances from transients in the lobby.

Ludwig smiled incongruously. "I'm afraid I don't understand," I said in more modulated tones.

"I would like you to delete that."

"But if I delete that, I have to delete everything that leads up to it. What's left?"

"I thought your comments on the myeloid metaplasia of the spleen were germane, original and important. As a matter of fact that observation led me to accept the paper."

"But that's only minor. It has no great implication. The other material, about the lymphocyte-like cell being a stem cell from which all marrow elements can arise, is a substantive observation."

"Of course you are entitled to believe that, Doctor, but it's simply not true."

I quietly tried to assemble badly jumbled thoughts. Suppose an editor had asked Mary Shelley to leave the monster out of her book *Frankenstein,* or an editor had said to Proust, "I would like *Remembrance of Things Past* better if you wouldn't write about yourself so much."

Finally I said, "But I thought you had accepted the paper."

"So I did, my boy, so I did. But it requires some editing."

"I should imagine that editing refers to phraseology, or to definitions, or to the order of things, not to dismembering the paper."

"Editing is more than that. I can't publish foolish things. I can't compound scientific error. In your paper I am simply trying to separate the original contribution from the repetitive controversial argument."

"It's all original."

"It is not all original. The material on the spleen is new and the observations have not before been published. The material on the lymphocyte-like cell or whatever you call it has been discussed for the last forty years, and I don't want to get into it again." He was becoming acerbic.

170

"But my data and observations are valid. The animal and the particular age limits for the changes have not been described before. It offers another model in which the argument can be examined."

"It contradicts Naegeli. His is the final word. He has been accepted by leading scientists for thirty years."

"You didn't even read the paper." I grabbed it from his hands. "Here," I said. "I quote Naegeli's original observations in 1909. They support what I have described in the rat."

"But he eventually came to different conclusions."

"He was right the first time," I said.

"That is just a matter of opinion, Doctor." I was getting nowhere. Ludwig compressed his lips. His blue eyes were cold and angry.

"Suppose I can't agree to these changes?"

"Then I am sorry, but we can't publish the paper."

"I don't see how I can cut the heart of—"

"Please don't be hasty, Doctor. I want very much to publish your data. Think it over. Please excuse me, I have another appointment. Give me your answer by Wednesday." He popped the manuscript back into the vinyl case, zipped it shut with finality and bowed slightly as he left. My hands started to shake and soon my whole body was trembling.

Later, after the shakes had subsided, I called Lapius. He was unsympathetic.

"What did you expect from him, Harry, fanfares and flourishes? He publishes a journal that thrives on confirmations of well-accepted theories. You're a threat to him because you've come up with something a little different, although I must admit it's not going to revolutionize hematology." He chuckled. "Ludwig probably didn't read it carefully first time around. But he shows signs of progress, Harry. He's never before come this close to publishing something that's original. Are you going to meet his terms?"

The hotel dining room was filled with clusters of men whose baritones were embellished by the fluty voices of the few women present. Conversations at most of the tables were intense and orchestrated with scientific jargon. Ari Machaon was seated in the corner, eating alone. I joined him and poured out my story.

171

"I'm truly sorry to hear that, Harry. But there are other journals."

"It's just that I find it hard to believe."

Ari smiled. "When I was younger, I submitted a brief clinical note to a prestigious journal. I had noted that in about 2 percent of cases in which the appendix was removed incidental to other surgery, a mild appendicitis was present. I had been puzzled by this. After all, I doubted that 2 percent of the general population had appendicitis at any given moment. I had to ask myself: Does a patient about to be operated on differ from the general population? I concluded that appendiceal irritation was probably produced by the enema given prior to surgery. I dutifully wrote my findings and conclusions and had it promptly rejected."

"On what grounds?"

"The referee, a pathologist, flatly stated that what I had seen couldn't have been pus. I was most impressed by that man. A genius. He could tell from seventeen hundred miles away that what I was looking at wasn't pus. What eyes he had."

I sipped my wine. Tension evaporated. The whole business was ludicrous. Everybody played it safe.

"Let me have a copy of the paper, Harry. There's someone here I would like to show it to."

I steered clear of Ludwig for the next few days. The Boston hematology group hospitably had arranged a picnic clambake at a shore estate. We bussed out there through the traffic matrices of the staid, begrimed center city, over skyways and through tunnels, finally to the shore points where cold winds had delayed the arrival of spring. A stately mansion defied the fresh breeze that tore open the surfaces of the water to expose the bubbling froth. Needle sprays drilled against its cold stones.

Scientists took cover behind the massive colonnades of the veranda, or huddled beneath the balustrade pillars which lined the stone patio. A series of banked charcoal braziers found haven in alcoves on the leeward side of the mansion. The doors and windows were locked. We couldn't get into the building, but the grounds were ours. The buses were scheduled to return at 4 P.M. We were stranded. We strode forlornly, hands in our pockets, the collars of our inadequate jackets unfurled to protect our necks, our shoulders hunched to exclude the probing windspray. Picnic tables were dispensed with. They would have blown away. We queued for food and cold beer. A small gazebo offered moderate shelter. Clutching a paper plate of slithering lobster claws, jamming an unopened bottle of beer in my coat pocket, I leaned against the wind and forged slowly to the crowded sanctuary. I found space on a peripheral bench and spread my picnic things. The crowd in the center of the gazebo was stamping on lobster parts to crack the shells. I retreated to the bench, wondering how the hell I would get the beer bottle open when a large, balding man approached. His beefy red face radiated good cheer and smiles, like the sun coming from behind a cloud. "I'm Artemus Strong," he said, extending his hand. I clutched at it since mine had been frozen to a lobster-claw posture. I knew the name Strong. A venerable, great anatomist, probably in his late sixties. He was unruffled. His hand was warm.

"Dr. Machaon showed me your paper last night. I will come right to the point. I believe it is a classic of sorts. I would like to publish it."

"That's very kind of you," I stuttered and shivered. "In what journal?"

"In the *Anatomy Journal*."

"Everybody who reads the *Anatomy Journal* is a believer in the monophyletic theory. I want to reach the disbelievers."

"What difference? Get it in print and you can refer to it in your next article. Eventually you'll reach those who need it."

"Why do you want to publish it? It isn't exactly in your line."

"Quite the contrary. It is pure evolving anatomy. Furthermore it confirms developmental facts that we observe in other species and in man during embryological development."

"Aren't you cold?"

"No." He smiled and radiated the only heat within forty miles of the place. "Are you?"

"I'm too cold to think now. Maybe back at the hotel we can talk about it."

"Please do call me when you get back." He vanished like an apparition into the crowd of lobster-stomping scientists. The gazebo trembled threateningly from time to time, as the stompers generated rhythmic harmonics. Soon the entire structure started

173

to shake and the great multitude plunged through the weakened floor with a crash. The last voice I heard as I scrambled over the side to escape the collapsing roof was "At least it's warmer down here."

The chill was wreaking its physiological wonders, and despite the fact that I had had neither food nor drink for six hours I had to take a leak. Two gaunt New Englanders, jut-jawed, blue-eyed, furry-browed, were still busy, to say nothing of warm, nursing the charcoal fires of the lobster roast. I ambled over. They were discussing the weather, in dry citric inflections.

"Treminds me of thyh stoahm in '48."

"Hwhat does?"

"Thuh stoahm does."

A minute went by, then two. Finally, one of them peered into the mist, examined the haze, stuck a finger into the wind and sniffed diagnostically at the damp air.

"I'll contradict chya," he said, and the conversation was finished.

"Where can I take a leak?" I asked.

"Down thatahways, 'bout a quahtah-mile, if you walk fast."

"Thanks," I said, departing. Perhaps if I ran, it would be only an eighth of a mile.

The small stone building hidden from the mansion by a copse of trees was easy to find, surrounded as it was by the stale odor of urea. I dipped behind the wooden partition that screened the doorway. A trough on one wall was the urinal. Ludwig stood there pissing. I joined him. He glanced over his shoulder at me.

"Hello—I've been expecting to hear from you."

"I've been meaning to call, but I've been busy."

"Well then," he said, "I guess this is as good a place as any. Are you going to delete that paper according to my suggestions?"

"No."

"Then I can't publish it," he said impatiently. He dug into his breast pocket with a hand suddenly freed from its appointed task, and handed me the bulky folded document that represented one year of monkish effort, concentration and emotional investment. "Here, take it." This gesture in the pissoir had an air of finality. I was so surprised that I forgot what I was doing, and when I turned to accept the rejected manuscript, I pissed all over his leg.

He stamped his foot angrily. "What the hell are you doing?" he yelped.

I tried to apologize but couldn't get the words out. He wriggled uncomfortably as the liquid seeped down his leg. Zipping his pants, he turned away. His foot made squishing sounds in the drenched shoe. He straightened his tie, ran a comb once quickly through his hair, looked despairingly at his soggy cuff and limped out. "You insufferable squirt," he gasped.

"This was just a sample, Ludwig," I shouted into the dusk. "Next time you try to crap on me I'll drown you."

The buses arrived on schedule to transport a shuddering, bedraggled mass of medical scientists back to their hotels.

The meeting ended. At the final banquet, we toasted the hospitality of the host, the Hematological Society of Boston, and voted a resolution of sympathy for seven members hospitalized with pneumonia.

Machaon stared blankly for a long time when I told him about the encounter with Ludwig. Finally he chuckled and uttered a Latin couplet to himself:

> Inter pedes est figura
> Ex quae fluvit aqua pura.

Charley Crow smirked when I told him about Ludwig. It confirmed his opinion that no work from the Institute other than his own had worth. In my absence he had rearranged the animal schedules to concentrate on the rat breast cancer problem. Inquiries flooded from all over the world after his first publication on the induction of breast tumor in rats, and his technique was copied and applied in numerous laboratories. It was a good technique. For the first time, researchers had a consistent rat model in which developing breast tumors could be studied.

Krouse and I partitioned the experimental data into several small abstracts that Crow could present at various meetings, then put the whole thing together for the big annual cancer meeting. Principe, the large pharmaceutical house, established a strain of our leukemia in their research laboratories. Krouse continued to examine the chemistry of the peroxidases and protoporphyrins that the leukemic cells produced so abundantly. I supervised a pathological production line, sacrificing, dissecting, processing

175

the tissues, examining them under the microscope, categorizing them and building an invaluable complex of data. Periodically, I would tabulate the material. Tumor characteristics were scored numerically, then treated statistically, and demonstrated on revealing graphs. The data were arranged so that comparisons between different treatment groups could be examined. Then Crow, myself, Bianca and Krouse would digest the information, and the next day Crow would outline other experimental animal groups that could be established. He was in constant touch with friends in the pharmaceutical industry, and they sent him hormone analogues to test against the tumor. Some would inhibit tumor growth, some would exacerbate it. Crow pursued the possible dream, the dream of a cure for cancer. Prodded by Crow, our work was developing an irresistible momentum. My work on the bone marrow was shunted aside. Krouse was skeptical. But, daily, I could see some tumors shrinking. Control of cancer, at least in experimental animals, seemed attainable.

Then, suddenly, unexpectedly, Crow was given the means to hurdle the rats and demonstrate the inhibition of tumor by the application of chemical treatment in man. Principe Pharmaceuticals used the transplanted rat leukemias procured from Crow to test the anticancer effect of a new series of chemicals they had synthesized. The leukemias were a natural, since leukemic cells in the blood, sometimes numbering one hundred thousand per cubic milliliter, appeared within weeks of inoculation. Chemicals that inhibited or destroyed the leukemic cells could be screened within a matter of days. Structural analogues of the most successful chemicals were synthesized and the tests repeated.

Finally Principe forwarded to Crow a melamine derivative, neatly packaged in multiple-dose vials to be used for clinical trials on cancer patients. Crow arranged with the departments of hematology and surgery at the hospital to have patients with terminal leukemia and breast cancer referred to his service. He started administering the new drug to them.

It worked at first. As tumors grew smaller, and blood counts improved, Crow marched to the beat of distant applause beneath the cyclic chemical halo of melamines. Principe Pharmaceuticals was long forgotten as the source of the material. Crow was the doctor who was saving lives, actually the first to demonstrate direct chemical inhibition of tumor in man. Despite his incorrigible preening cockiness, the disappearance of cancer was awesome and inspiring.

However, the results, miraculous to observe, were short-lived. The tumors recurred. The revived hopes of the patients were dashed.

Probably the hardest task a physician faces is to deal with the emotions of the patient stricken with cancer. For one thing, the name itself inflicts terror. Cancer, the crab that claws its way through a living body leaving in its tracks unwanted, useless, pain-producing, cellular matrices. Initially, the cancer patient has no sense of illness. Cancer is established insidiously, and the patient's first knowledge starts with the discovery of a mass, bleeding, or abnormal blood count. Gradually, as the doctors become more intent and industrious, ordering X-rays, analyzing body fluids, performing explorative surgery, the curtain of immortality parts, revealing to the patient the backdrop of his own death.

To survive the reality of daily trips for radiation therapy, visible signs of malignant encroachment, ugly scars of extirpative surgery, or pain, patients eventually must make an accommodation with death. The adjustment is enervating and soul-searing. A new frame of references must be created. New values must be sought. The patient must face the darkness while there is still plenty of light. The terms of this disparate struggle are continually altered by the medical attack on cancer, and its fraudulent prolongation of life.

The advent of chemotherapy aggravated the terms of the conflict. Initially, as tumors melted away, leukemic cells disappeared, belly-filling spleens receded to normal contour, even the doctors were misled. Months passed before we realized that we were dealing only with a delusion of cure, a temporary remission, before the final recurrent onslaught of the disease.

Because the doctors were honestly optimistic, the confidence of life returned to the patient. His defenses against ensuing death dissolved. He regained his normal dreams and visions. But the recurrent onslaught of the disease forced him once again to establish a psychic barrier against the terrible truth, and once again to come to terms with death.

We learned this agonizing lesson from Harold Sklar. For, after a brief month of giddy expectation, his belly again filled with tumescent spleen. His breathing quickened due to loss of oxygen-carrying red blood cells as inevitably his marrow again, but this time irreversibly, became destroyed.

When the truth of our failure dawned on Sklar, he hurled himself at Crow, screaming hysterically. We tried to restrain him, but he broke free and ran crazily through the halls, opening the doors to all the examining rooms, as if seeking the one door through which he could escape this terrible nightmare place of torturing needles that had treacherously offered him the false hope of life. But he found no door and was dead within a week.

Of course, the cruel joke of life is that fundamentally we are all in the same predicament.

Crow presented the preliminary results at the monthly research conference to his colleagues at Church, who sat silently throughout the demonstration. Patient after patient was presented, as before-and-after Kodacolor slides were flashed on the screen. There was neither awe nor wonder in the audience of doctors who were privileged to view for the first time a phenomenon they had never expected to live to see. They accepted with a restraint amounting to indifference the first unfolding of the chemical secrets that would certainly lead to the control, if not the cure, of cancer. During the question period they displayed the irritable perturbation of people whose complacent way of life had been suddenly dislocated by progress.

Someone asked the inevitable idiot question "Did you keep controls?" They quibbled about the term "remission." They would settle for nothing less than permanent cure. Departing the amphitheater, muttering dubious judgments, they marched complacently back to the nineteenth century.

Crow received a better reception among strangers in New York. The *Times* wrote appreciatively of the well-organized, unpretentious material, which heralded a new stride in the search for a cancer cure.

Griffiths called Crow to congratulate him and invited him to Denver. Crow flew out there, and Krouse took the opportunity to run off to Washington.

Crow was ebullient on his return. "Griffiths is in advance of his time. He appreciated our work, Harry. He questioned me minutely on all the details. He will do as much as he can to help us. He is influential in Washington, you know."

Suddenly Dean William Chamberlain fired Ari Machaon. Machaon was in England when he received the letter. Ari supposed it was some supplementary data his technician was sending to update the material for his talk the following day. He stuffed it into his pocket and went off to the meetings. Johnny Harper, who was in London coincidentally to present a paper on work that Machaon had helped him with, ran into him at the Chester Beatty. They were close friends. Johnny was an assistant professor in the anatomy department. Later Harper told me that he was chatting with Machaon in the great rotunda of the Beatty when suddenly a cluster of scientists entered and, spotting Machaon, shouted, almost in unison, "Ari!" They greeted him effusively, shunting Harper aside.

"I always felt that Ari was a great scientist," Harper told me later. "I knew his quality from the help he gave me on my project. But I never realized how highly the Europeans regarded him. My God, there was Harrington, Voisin from Paris, Karnofsky from Leningrad, even Thannhauser—you know, the guy who wrote the nasty review of Ari's book. All of these great scientists crowding around Ari as if he was their leader.

"Finally they drifted off to the various meeting rooms, and Ari absent-mindedly dug into his pocket and came out with this crumpled envelope. He opened it and started to read. Suddenly he turned gray and handed me the letter." Harper showed me a copy.

DEAR DR. MACHAON:

The research committee of Church Medical School at its summer meeting has reviewed your work. It decided that you have made no progress in the last two years, and questions the validity of some of your recent findings. It is my responsibility to administer the funds of the Alice Fremont Research Foundation. Guided by the findings of the research committee, I will have to terminate your stipend as well as funds granted for equipment and assistants. You will please vacate the research premises by the end of the month.

Of course, your tenure with the university will continue but unfortunately at the moment we do not have funds for your salary.

Sincerely,
WILLIAM CHAMBERLAIN, Dean

179

The singular relationship that exists between a scientist and his institution is altered by such a letter. It is a plague that poisons the institute, taints his colleagues and divides his family.

Meg, Machaon's wife, had learned over the years the lonely esteem of scientific wifehood. When she had worked for Ari, before they married, she admired him as one might admire some organic masterpiece; not all at once or continually, but in brief appreciative moments: his ambling walk, his imperturbability, his continued reassurance about her work, his kindness. Then, suddenly, she needed him.

The mechanics of marrying him were simple. All she had to do was to replace his first wife, Dorothy. A year of faithful service in the laboratory, a weekend in bed during a convention were sufficient.

Meg and Ari had been married eight years when the letter arrived. Till then his paltry salary had been further diminished by support payments to Dorothy. Ari traveled alone now. And with the letter, even this poverty was threatened.

Before they were married, Meg had Ari. There were no gray dawns. Each morning glowed expectant pink. Their laboratory hours were filled with tender currents. Her nighttime loneliness was luminescent.

With the vacuous vanity that masks judgment, Meg believed that once she moved into his home she would possess Ari. But she possessed the home instead. He bequeathed it to her. She could decorate, redo the bathroom, change appliances, bear his children, cradle the young. But at eight each morning he left her for his other home, his house of worship, his goddamned science. The goddamned labs and tubes, rats and rabbits. Rats and rabbits housed in family clusters, nibbling fitfully on compressed cubes of scientifically formulated food, sucking water from glass nipples. Rats and rabbits felled by the poisons Ari fed them, crawling fearfully, too weak to stand. Sickened with raging fevers, their nostrils crusted by bloody secretions. Morning brought the sulfide stench from animals that had died the night before, some rotted, some cannibalized by their brethren. She used to love it. Now it nauseated her. When she had worked for Ari, love transformed every stink into special perfume. She left to marry and lose him.

180

When Ari returned from England, he walked hunched over, a broken man trying to make himself invisible. He was overwhelmed by the possibility that on a certain morning he would no longer be welcome in his laboratory, that his precious notebooks would be removed from the shelves and jammed into packing cases.

There was a message in his box. The dean wanted to see him.

Machaon was seated in the anteroom when Assistant Dean Bookman came out of Dean Chamberlain's office. Bookman did not bother to say hello. Ari wondered how he could have remained so long at Church and still been a stranger.

"Dr. Chamberlain will see you now, Dr. Machaon." Ari aborted his ruminations and entered the arched portico.

Chamberlain turned from the bay window, strode over to meet Ari halfway across the room, gripped his hand and placed his left hand paternally over the back of Ari's. "Did you have a successful trip, Dr. Machaon?"

Ari nodded.

"Well, do sit down." Ari occupied a red leather armchair facing Chamberlain's desk. Chamberlain returned to the helm.

"Well, Dr. Machaon, what can I do for you?"

Ari looked at him blankly. "You asked me to come to your office, Dr. Chamberlain. I had assumed you wanted to talk with me about something."

"No, not really. You received my letter, no doubt? I just wanted to tell you how sorry I am that that conclusion has been reached. You realize, Dr. Machaon, that not being a research man myself I have to rely on the opinion of others."

"What others?"

"Your peers on the faculty."

"I have no peers on the faculty."

"Of course that is a matter of opinion, Dr. Machaon. Well, sir, in either case, you don't have to rush. You can have at least a month to clear—to clean up your affairs and conclude whatever you are engrossed with at present. But I wouldn't embark on any new experiments." Yellow light pierced the gray window to blind Ari. He stood, but turned before he had reached the door.

"Oh, Dr. Chamberlain, could you remind me who comprise the research committee at this institution?"

"They don't come immediately to mind, Dr. Machaon, but you can pick up the list from my secretary in the morning."

Bianca Fiore knew of the deed before Machaon got the letter. She pressed her mouth into a thin grimace when I asked her about it and stared at the floor. We were in her office.

"It's terrible," she said.

"What do you think is behind it?"

She waddled to the large door, kicked away the wedge and allowed it to swing slowly shut. Only then did she look me in the eye and say, "I wouldn't go around making waves if I were you. If the dean felt you were unfriendly to him in any way, one word to Crow and you would be out."

"What the hell threat do I pose to the dean?"

"What threat does Machaon pose to the dean?" She opened the door again, and wedged it with the small triangle of wood, signaling the end of the conversation. As I left she called after me. "We'll talk about the hormone groups tomorrow after the sacrifice." Bianca rarely voiced an opinion in front of witnesses. Those who adhere to the conspiratorial theory of life live in a world populated by conspirators.

Victor Krouse sat lackadaisically at his desk, hands folded behind his head, leaning back in his swivel and contemplating the smoke figures from his pipe that diluted the chemical fumes of his laboratory. Two technicians performed secret chores silently at the lab bench.

He scarcely glanced at me when I entered. "I got the grant, Harry." He paused, waiting for me to react. I did a handspring, and kicked over an Erlenmeyer on the way down.

"That's great, Vic," I said. "Say, did you hear about Machaon?"

"Yup. You know, Harry, when that grant comes, I'm going to be a big man around this place."

"Gee, that's great, Vic. I always felt you were cut out to be a big man"—appraising his five-foot-five total length. "Why the hell did the dean fire Machaon?"

"Because he moves in mysterious ways, his wonders to perform. You know, I'm going to get three thousand square feet of space."

"What?"

Krouse looked at me through lids that were squeezed half shut, like someone with blepharospasm. His forehead was wrinkled. He repeated every word with measured pace to be sure I heard each carefully enunciated syllable. I forgot Machaon for a moment. Victor pursed his lips around the stem of his fetid pipe and sucked a little smoke, while some brown juice drained from the corner of his mouth. "Crow is in for a big surprise. He'll never be able to screw me again. I'll have my own place, and when I write a goddamn paper, it will have my name, and the names of people who helped me, not some jockey riding my coattails."

"Vic, that's great news, and I'm glad for you. Congratulations. But I'm a little upset now, so pardon me if I'm not as effusive about your good luck as I ought to be."

"Luck," he interrupted, "who said anything about luck?"

"I didn't mean it that way, Vic—"

"I hope not—there's plenty of experimental pathologists around, you know." And he took the pipe from his mouth and tapped its inverted bowl against the ashtray.

The place was a looney bin. Threatening people was getting to be an indoor sport. I tried once more. "Vic, why did the research committee send Chamberlain that report about Machaon?"

"Schmuck," Krouse said, "when will you grow up? There ain't no research committee here. Chamberlain made it up for his letter."

Lapius was subdued. "Like the syndicate, you say. My boy, the syndicate of the overworld is known as the establishment. The syndicate and the establishment both have their code of ethics, their laws and their penalty system. In the overworld there is more latitude, so there is more dishonesty. To compensate for that, a system of contracts has been established that can be tested in a court of law. In the underworld there are no written contracts. Everything is by word of mouth. A handshake is an inviolate promise. A man is as good as his word or else he is removed."

"Why do you think this happened?"

"It's simple, Harry. Did you ever hear of the Chamberlain Pavilion?"

"No, should I have?"

"As a matter of fact, you shouldn't have. It doesn't exist. The Chamberlain Pavilion is the name of the new building that the dean is going to erect. It is his monument, the new building that

183

will replace the crumbling catacombs, built in 1873, that we call the hospital. It will be the capstone of Chamberlain's career."

"What's that to do with Machaon?"

"Chamberlain needs money, Harry. He's scraping the barrel."

"But Machaon is a great scientist—"

"Rubbish, Harry. Machaon never will be missed. By the time he vacates the place he will be like a foreign body. No one will talk to him. He will be hermetically sealed off by the frosted glass of indifference, even despised. People don't like martyrs, Harry."

"He's no martyr. He's a scapegoat."

"There's little difference. A martyr is a scapegoat that fights."

"Will Machaon fight?"

"Abortively, after he gets over his bewilderment. So this is what it was," he mused.

"What what was?"

"I knew something was in the wind when you told me you were teaching his course. They don't shove a guy out of a course, deprive him of contact with students, unless something is up."

"How come?"

"Oh, you know students, Harry. If they got to know Machaon as a teacher and this happened, they'd be the first to smell a rat, and raise a rumpus. The dean wouldn't want to take a chance. One of them might be the son of a wealthy influential alumnus, and all hell could break loose."

I had become a little heady on the rich port that Lapius served up. "You should sip it, Harry, not bolt it," he said.

"I guess you're right," I said and excused myself. I wobbled over to Elspeth's. She had warned me never to come unannounced, but tonight she seemed glad to see me.

She opened a muscatel that went down like a rasp file compared to the port Lapius offered. I told her about Machaon.

She listened politely, stroking the back of my neck. "Why does that upset you?" she asked.

"Doesn't it upset you that a man who has given his life to research suddenly gets chucked out of a job, and has to fish around? Maybe he needs the money. Isn't that a little disturbing?"

"A little."

"That's all you have to say about it? Wouldn't you be upset if I got chucked out of my job?"

"I don't know."

"It seems to me that you'd be a little concerned over a guy you've been so hospitable to, whom you've been so intimate with."

"Let's go to bed, Harry."

"Wait a minute. I asked you an important question."

"I'll answer it later."

"I want you to answer it now."

"Later, Harry. Right now I want you—" She started to undo my shirt. I helped her. Elspeth. Know Elspeth and you know the world.

"I love you," she whispered, "I'm mad for you."

"And in the morning?"

"I won't need you in the morning, darling."

The next morning Crow needed me. He invited me to his office. Machaon came out as I entered and barely looked up at me. He was an old man. His hands dug into the pockets of his wrinkled coat as he shuffled slowly away.

Crow was beaming. He removed his glasses and polished them to a high reflective brilliance. "Harry, I'm setting deadlines. We must be ready for the meetings in England in the fall."

"We're going to England?" He looked up sharply, but let it pass. "What's the occasion?"

"The International Conference on Cancer. Griffiths says that our work is the first new information to come along in a decade. That we have an important technological advance. He's taken a real interest, Harry. He's a remarkable man. He was so kind and hospitable to me in Denver. He opened his laboratories to me. I was a weekend guest at his home. He is so warm. He's a very sincere man, Harry, and a great scientist," Crow said with satisfaction.

"What's his laboratory like?"

"Oh, like any other lab. Busy people doing little things with their hands and machines cranking out data. The man has remarkable judgment. You'd like him, Harry."

"I'm sure I would. What's he working on now?"

"Oh, the same stuff he's been doing for years, the effect of adrenal hormones on cancer. But he's taken with our work, and

185

exceedingly generous. He offered to set some groups up for us if we ran out of space."

"What did Machaon want?"

"Oh, a personal problem he wanted to talk over."

"Can you give him a job here?"

"He didn't ask me for one."

"He could use one."

"You know I couldn't do that; it would embarrass the dean."

"Are you going to go to bat for him?"

"Of course, I will." Crow refused to elaborate. "These delicate matters, Harry, must be settled privately."

Bianca Fiore waddled in and plumped herself into the armchair. The vinyl cushion whooshed under her weight, emitting a soft, sibilant sound. Bianca looked about her apprehensively to be certain that no one misunderstood. Krouse trooped in with a sheaf of papers under his arm.

Crow smiled benignly, then leaned forward, businesslike, and said, "I was explaining to Harry, Griffiths has encouraged us to give a series of talks at the International Cancer Congress in London. For the next several months the first order of business will be the preparation of the data, the slides, the photographs, the papers. If we do a good job, the Institute will be made. The board of directors insist on it. They are excited about the prospect."

"You mean the board authorizes a subsidization for us to go to England?" Krouse asked, incredulous.

"The Institute will pay for your food and lodging in London."

"How do we get there?"

"Don't submit individual papers unless you can get travel fare from your grant or from another source. The board will send only Heller and myself."

"Heller," said Krouse, "is not even a member of the Institute."

"He's an eminent man and a consultant to the Institute."

"Shit," murmured Krouse under his breath.

"Incidentally, Victor, congratulations on your grant. We'll have to start looking for space. As a matter of fact, I've already spoken to the dean about it.

"Victor," Crow continued, "I want to see your data on the chemistry, perhaps this afternoon if you have time."

"You're not going to present my data there, are you?"

186

"We'll decide that together. Some of it may be pertinent. Also, we'll go over your new grant." Mollified, Krouse shut up.

The meeting ended. On the way upstairs Krouse said, "I'll give him the goddamn data. After I get my institute, I'll set up my own experiments and he can go screw."

"What do you mean, your institute?"

"Three thousand square feet of space, equipped, is an institute."

I hadn't thought of it that way. Until then, I hadn't related the numbers to the actual space, but if it materialized, he would have more space than we were working in now.

When we reached the labs, Bianca jerked her head and I followed her into her office. She kicked the wedge, the door swung shut, and she said, "The Chief will never go for it."

"For what?"

"For an independent institute within the Institute."

"Why not? It can't do anything but enhance the place. Krouse is a damn good chemist."

"You'll see." She opened the door and let me out.

The weeks passed quickly, as they always did when we were compiling and interpreting data. There wasn't a buzz about Machaon. I visited his laboratory. He was bewildered and unsure of himself. Johnny Harper burst in.

"Ari, old friend, I'm terribly sorry." He leaned over slightly and placed his hands on Ari's shoulders, squeezing them, as if to infuse strength into the shrunken figure. "Anything I can do to help, Ari, anything at all—I mean it." Harper was about the only one besides Machaon and Crow's group who was doing any research at the school. Machaon looked up at the hulking figure, reached one hand across his chest and patted the hand gripping his shoulder. His eyes were moist and uncomprehending. "Thank you, Johnny. I appreciate it."

"What are your plans?"

Machaon appeared defeated, so it was surprising to hear him say, "Well, the first thing I'm going to do is get a lawyer."

I called Johnny later and we went for a beer.

"You knew about the Machaon affair before he got the letter, didn't you, Johnny?"

"I was at the faculty meeting where the thing was decided, but I didn't know about the letter."

"A faculty meeting? You told me that Machaon got a letter saying that the research committee—"

"There is no research committee."

"That's what Krouse said."

"He was right." Harper sipped his cold beer. "My chief was away and asked me to cover the department for him. The first order of business was the faculty meeting. They were droning on as usual when, suddenly, the dean says that he wants to clear up the Machaon business. Apparently he had sounded out the key figures beforehand, and the matter had been decided, but he had to bring it before the faculty. Also, he was looking for an instrument."

"Apparently he found one."

"The fascinating thing was the number of crazy ideas that came to the floor. Durwin, that whore who runs the medical department, had a great idea. Why not say that Machaon was insane? He suggested that we call him paranoid. They batted the idea around as if it weren't venal and absurd, as if it had merit. After a while it became a question of problem-solving: Machaon was to be kicked out—how best to do it. I even found myself getting intrigued by the problem, particularly since no one questioned the premise."

"The dean wants him out, so out he goes. Now all we have to worry about is the technique."

"Exactly."

"Nice guys."

"They are our leaders. The teachers of our children. Finally Bookman came up with the idea of the research committee. Durwin questioned that. After all, Machaon is internationally known. But Bookman trumped him. He pulled out a document and read it to the group. A review of Machaon's latest book by Thannhauser. Here, I have a copy of it."

I read it slowly:

Machaon's book is a prolonged diatribe against those who disagree with him. He attacks them for misinterpreting his data, for failing to duplicate his results, for using alternate terminology. He flails at his critics and defends his own thesis at length, and often in poor taste. For those who want an objective review of work on inflammation, the book will be a disappointment.

Machaon excludes many references that disagree with his own conclusions, while including several hundred of his own references. The book certainly isn't worth the price of purchase or study.

"Wow."

"Precisely," said Harper. "When they heard that, they had the basis on which to discharge him. Then Chamberlain said somberly that Machaon might actually be a threat to the reputation of Church. Professors nodded sadly at this sober judgment. They had been vindicated, and what started out as a fantasy witchhunt suddenly became legitimate."

"Thannhauser is a big man too. Maybe there's something to it."

"Perhaps," said Harper. "But I know Machaon well. He has helped me immeasurably with my research. He has been sort of an unofficial adviser to me. He's brilliant."

"Then why should Thannhauser write that?"

"Machaon embarrassed him at a meeting. He never forgave Ari and has been taking off on him ever since."

The following day there was war at the Institute.

Crow had postponed some of Krouse's experiments by fiat. Bianca had been told to clear out his cages. She didn't want to do that without telling Krouse. "I have to tell Krouse. Otherwise he might think I did it on my own."

"That's silly. Tell him you were ordered to do it."

"The Chief won't back me up. He'll let me take the blame. I'm not in the mood for that now."

She informed Krouse, and he went on a rampage. Crow handled him cleverly. "Victor, I was just going over your work with Dr. Heller. We think it has promise. Only I have to get the groups out for the England meeting. I have an appointment with the dean today. We are considering buying some space to house your new grant. You'll have a separate building with your own cages and animals. I'll never have to embarrass you like this again, and you will be free to pursue your own lines of investigation."

"Someday I'm going to get that bastard," Krouse told me later. "These goddamn entrepreneurs running around the world, parading as research men, and that pimp Heller. He wants to succeed Crow, so he sucks his ass all the time."

"Well, if it weren't for entrepreneurs building institutes like this you wouldn't have any place to work. You'd never pull three hundred grand out of the government if you were doing the very same work at some unknown hospital. Crow has to be political. The board comes marching in here once a month looking for a cancer cure. Anything less doesn't satisfy them—unless it gets into the newspapers."

"You're always in the middle, aren't you, Harry?" Krouse sneered. "You manage to understand both sides, don't you?"

The cages were cleared, and Krouse spent his free time drawing plans for his new laboratory.

Ari secured the services of a lawyer, Le Brum, who quickly assured him that he didn't have a leg to stand on.

He told him that the most the courts would assure was that Ari received due process, that the institution goes through a proper hearing according to its own by-laws. Once this procedure is followed, the courts do not get involved in whether or not the verdict of the hearing is in accord with the evidence.

Crow was on the phone with Griffiths several times a week. It was John and Charley now, and each conversation was prefaced by polite inquiries about their families. Crow confided the results of our experiments, and Griffiths was continually encouraging. "After all, Harry," Crow told me, "Griffiths isn't a novice in this field. Wasn't he the one to show that prostatic tumors were sensitive to estrogens?" Strange, I thought. The principle of hormone-dependent tumors in man had already been established by Griffiths, and now we were proving that the same principle held in rats. What was going on? "But we have an experimental animal, Harry, and it's breast, not prostate."

Chamberlain didn't like the idea of Machaon going to a lawyer. I met the assistant dean, Bookman, in the cafeteria one day. "What the hell is the matter with you guys?" I said with a smile. "Why destroy Machaon? He's produced more research out of the pinkie of his left hand than the entire faculty of the medical school has produced in the last ten years."

190

"The faculty, Harry, would disagree with that statement."

"Of course they would. Who disagrees? Keim, who lectures with his eyes fastened on the ceiling trying to remember the texts he has had to memorize for the day's lesson? He never did an original piece of work in his life. Broadbent in physiology said, 'Don't talk to me about this, it's a dangerous subject.' Or your famous medical chief, high in pedagogy and low in the decency of common ethics, who wants to accuse Machaon, a man he scarcely knows and of whose work he is entirely ignorant, as is most of the faculty, of paranoia. Goddamn it, Ari Machaon isn't paranoid now, but he will be when you guys get done with him."

"Where did you get that? Who tattled?"

"Oh, there are rumors."

Bookman was simmering. The flush drained like an ebbing tide from his whitening cheeks. "Come to my office." He strode in angrily, fetched a heavy book from his shelf and handed it to me. "Here," he challenged. "Find me one reference in the index to the work of Machaon."

I riffed the index to the *M*'s. There was no mention of Machaon. Then I closed the book and inspected its title, *Textbook of Surgery*. "Why the hell should there be a reference to Machaon in a textbook of surgery?" I asked.

"Surgery has to do with inflammation, doesn't it?" he stated triumphantly. I stared at him.

An administrator is an administrator is an administrator. That night I went to a bookstore and mailed a copy of *Love, a Bible of Sexual Technique* to Bookman with a note: "Please check the contents and find me a reference to God in this bible." I'll bet that bible became his hymenal.

After Le Brum got done with him, Ari was quite pessimistic. He still wanted to fight, but was hedging his bets, clearing some of his personal effects from the laboratory, and placing discreet phone calls.

I loaded a pile of his stuff into my car and took it to his home. Meg looked mousy in a plain gray dress that would soon do service as a dustcloth. Her light hair fell on either side of her face. She was distraught, but managed a smile.

Ari gripped my hand. "Harry, you will never know how much

your friendship means to me at this time. I was just telling Meg that I better get a new lawyer. This one isn't even neutral." He turned away. "Did you hear what I said, Meg?"

She had heard, all right.

"Your lawyer is right. You should resign," she said.

Ari stared at her. "And let them trample my reputation?"

"Oh, wake up, Ari—what reputation? You've been piddling around that damned laboratory for years. What have you gotten for your pains? You've become a hero to a few dozen scientists throughout the world. Can you convert fame into dollars? You can't even afford to take me on your trips, and if you didn't have some grant or other, you couldn't afford to go yourself. You call yourself a doctor. Can you earn a living as a doctor? You've been sponging other people's money for years, steeped in the illusion that you were sacrificing yourself to give something to the world. Well, you've sacrificed all right, but not yourself. You have sacrificed me and the children in the name of this magnificent hobby of yours, this damned obsession that occupies you day and night so that half the time you call me Dorothy. Do you remember Dorothy, Ari? She was your first wife. I'm Meg, your second wife.

"I've gotten wise to the whole research game, Ari. You are all about nine years old. Spoiled, arrogant in your talents, protective of your unearned prerogatives, fantastically selfish, mean and spiteful to each other, fighting for priorities, cutting each other up like jealous schoolgirls. Academe, my ass."

I unloaded the cartons and cleared out.

At the Crow's Nest the pace quickened. The camera of time was suddenly racing at one hundred and twenty frames a minute, as if the place had suddenly become hyperthyroid. All except Krouse, that is. He dawdled over his drawings and prodded Crow daily about his space.

"He thinks that that is all I have on my mind. How selfish, how self-centered can a man be, Harry?" Crow complained.

"That's a hard question to answer," I said, playing it straight.

"It seems strange, though, Harry. Suddenly everyone wants a place in the sun."

"Don't you?"

He stared at me as if I had uttered a *non sequitur*.

Harper was becoming conspicuous, mainly because now he was

192

the only one who ever lunched with Machaon, or accompanied him through the halls. I joined them in the cafeteria one day.

Machaon was drawn, his face was the color of heavy cream. His hair seemed suddenly thinner, his forehead higher and more waxen than before. "I've contacted the American Association of University Professors and they'll help, they say, as long as I have tenure. But what in reality can they do, except make noise? They can't pay my salary, they can't call a strike. Perhaps they present a muted threat. I've retained a lawyer—" He cast his eyes at the table and appeared forlorn.

"Actually, Ari," said Harper, "you need inside help."

"Well, I have talked to Crow. He is sympathetic."

"Will he help?"

"He said he would."

"What can he do?"

"He's close to Rudolf Rand. Judge Rand is president of the board of trustees. But I don't understand why this is happening, yet the dean has the active or passive support of most of the faculty. A conspiracy of indifference is a lethal hangman."

Crow and Chamberlain had their heads together in the corner. They munched and chatted busily, in exclusive community. Ari was hoping that Crow was going to bat for him. Machaon glanced hopefully at them.

That afternoon Crow called Krouse to his office and greeted him warmly with a wide smile. "I've sold the dean. You'll get your space."

Krouse beamed and murmured, "Thank you."

"The old man came through after all," Krouse said later. "He knows good work when he sees it."

"You've always claimed he would steal your work in preference to that of anyone else in the Institute. That's high praise indeed."

"I never said he'd steal it. You know, Harry, you shouldn't misinterpret what I say. I'll have to be careful around you. Sure, Crow and I have had some differences about credits, but we've settled them. He's been a gentleman. Considering his background he knows quite a bit about chemistry."

We were to inspect the new space. Crow was ebullient, and Chamberlain gracious, as he pushed open the door to a long-forgotten storage room at the dead end of a corridor near the old

193

anatomy laboratory. Krouse wedged himself between the two, like a bride between the father and the groom. The door swung open. Light flickered slowly in the grayed fluorescent tubes to reveal the dusty confines.

Krouse stopped, stunned. "What is this?"

"Your new laboratory, Dr. Krouse." The dean smiled.

"This is all?" asked Krouse incredulously.

"At least eight hundred square feet. You should be able to establish a beautiful laboratory here."

"But the grant calls for three thousand square feet."

"I'm sorry, Dr. Krouse, this is all we have available."

"I think the dean is being generous, Victor," Crow murmured.

The dean spoke sharply to Crow. "I thought you said that this would be satisfactory, Dr. Crow."

"Well, we're certainly appreciative, Dean."

"I'm not," Krouse said. The silence was dreadful. "I have money for three thousand square feet of space. I can't accept less than that."

"Keep your men in line, Crow. We can't have subordinates making demands," the dean said testily.

Krouse continued to sputter. Crow told him to shut up, and the dean walked away.

"I did everything I could for you, Victor. How dare you embarrass me in front of the dean?"

Krouse's scarred lip twisted into a snarl. "Where the hell do you get off accepting a deal like that, Crow?"

That broke it. The hierarchy was torn asunder. It became a gutter fight.

"Who do you think you're shouting orders at? I picked you up out of a second-rate job. Take it or leave it."

"I'll leave it. I am going to turn the money back."

"You can't do that." Crow blanched.

Krouse remembered how upset Crow had been when I threatened to withdraw my paper from the Boston meeting. "Oh, yes, I can, and I will."

"If you do, you're finished around here."

"Not with three hundred thousand dollars, I'm not."

"What do you mean by that?"

"I'll buy that building next door and renovate it."

"You'll do what I tell you to do." It was Crow's turn to leave. Krouse was sweating and trembling. He turned to me.

"That sonofabitch. Cutting down my space is tantamount to misappropriating funds. I won't let him get away with that. I'm going to talk to the dean."

He did. The dean was courteous. He explained that he simply didn't have three thousand feet available. "As a matter of fact," he told Krouse, "the medical school agreed to pay half for the purchase of an adjacent building providing you could renovate it out of your grant, but Crow said he didn't want any part of his Institute to be physically separate from the medical school."

So it was Crow who killed the deal. The dean, upset at the prospect of losing the overhead on all that loot, was sure that minor adjustments could be made that would be agreeable to all. He had underestimated Krouse. Chamberlain tried to impress upon him that no one at the National Institutes would be concerned with the details, as long as some space was allotted and an honest, creative piece of work came out of the laboratory. But Krouse insisted that he couldn't be party to a misrepresentation. He appreciated the magnanimity of the government in sponsoring research, and of providing people like himself with an opportunity to work independently and with dignity. "When I accept the grant, I'm promising to carry out the agreement to the best of my ability. Eight hundred feet of space is an evasion of the contract, and I won't accept it."

Chamberlain called Crow and Krouse to his office, and failed to budge either. They stared at each other in silence and addressed themselves only to the dean. "I don't understand either of you," he told them. "Here the school has an opportunity of adding to its physical plant, of getting thirty thousand or so in overhead cash which we sorely need, and neither of you will yield an inch to gain something that on almost any basis would benefit all of us." He turned to some papers on his desk. "You will have to thrash this out yourselves."

Crow went to his office and put in calls to the board members. He garnered enough support to quiet his nerves and assuage his anginal pains.

Lapius followed the ins and outs of the matter with great interest. "Harry," he said, "Crow has to lose. He will lose Krouse and a large government funding. Even with a separate institute, Krouse could never be a threat to Crow. Actually he would embellish the Crow's Nest. Charley is making a mistake."

Krouse sensed this too. He had already concluded that he could

195

no longer function at the Crow's Nest even if the problem were resolved. He started peddling his grant to some of the other professors. It was nice bait. Professors who had ignored him for years suddenly put out the welcome mat. The dean, who was kept informed, did nothing to discourage the effort.

Crow had several conferences with Rudolf Rand. The judge told Chamberlain that Crow would consider it a personal insult if Krouse received another position at the university. Chamberlain shrugged. "I have no authority over Crow. He's funded by the Institute and its endowment. If he feels insulted, he'll simply have to get used to that feeling."

Krouse got a nibble from physiology. The dean said that it was okay with him provided the faculty agreed. Invoking the faculty was clever. It would blunt criticism by the trustees no matter how the affair ended. The faculty agreed to hear the proposition at the monthly meeting, and decide, on merit, whether Krouse would be allowed to swing his grant to physiology.

Crow had never expected the matter to get out of hand. He was trying to piece his data together for England. The faculty meeting was coming at a most inauspicious time. He had no friends on the faculty, which as a body begrudged his independence. Now he had to go before the same faculty and state that any connection Krouse maintained with Church would be a personal affront. He was going to demand that the faculty voluntarily divest Church of a three-hundred-thousand-dollar grant. Crow would pursue this destructive course because Krouse was threatening to take away his Teddy bear.

Machaon visited Lapius frequently, renewing, almost of necessity, an old friendship and professional relationship. Lapius was powerless to affect the outcome of Machaon's problem. "The only way I can help you is by pointing out the realities," he told Machaon. "You can fight, but you are going to have to leave Church. So you had better concentrate on locating somewhere else."

"I have nowhere to go. At my age I haven't the energy to create another laboratory and research team. I've decided to fight. I have a lawyer; I have the Association of University Professors to back me."

"That's ludicrous, Ari. What the deuce will they do for you?"

"Crow spoke to Rudolf Rand."

"That's a possibility. Rand is chairman of the trustees. If they back you, then Chamberlain may have to retreat. But eventually you would have to leave. Chamberlain would submit you to unbearable pressures. There would be delays on your funding. Equipment orders would be lost. You would have to dot all the *i*'s of the by-laws, and Chamberlain would compile a damning list of technicalities you had neglected. Chamberlain can harass you a thousand ways, and he will. What does your lawyer say?"

"Much the same. He wants to know how much money I've donated to the school. He wants to talk to Rand and be able to tell him how invaluable I am. But he measures value only in terms of money. I can't get through to him about the intrinsic value of research."

"But the research committee has voted you out."

"We know that's a fraud."

"But no one else does. It stands on the official record, on the dean's stationery."

"I want a hearing. I want the dean to have to admit in public that no research committee existed. I'll call every faculty member one by one as a witness. They wouldn't lie."

"Five of them will lie and say that they were on a long-forgotten research committee. There will be minutes of old meetings available. Ari, you talk like a child."

It was true. He fumbled to collect his thoughts and to express them coherently. He said, "I've done a lot for the school. I can't allow Chamberlain to attack me arbitrarily, destroy my work, impair my reputation and get away without a fight. He's going to have to show a bill of particulars."

"He will, Ari, he will," Lapius said sadly. "How's Meg?"

"She's upset, of course. What little money we have will be used up with lawyers. If we move, the kids will be uprooted. Ah, maybe you're right, Simon. What's the use? However, if Rand gets involved . . . Thanks. You've been kind as always. I must go home. Meg will be worried. Good night, Harry."

"Ari," Lapius said, "I will speak for you."

"I know you will, Simon. Will it do any good?"

"No."

"Thanks anyway, Simon," Machaon said over his shoulder as he walked to the door.

After he left Lapius stared upward. "How selfish, how narcissistic we are, even in the name of good works, Harry. Machaon

197

never made enough to make ends meet. He always rationalized the poverty into which he thrust his family on the basis that his work served the needs of mankind. But he was serving himself, of course. His first wife griped about this ad nauseam.

"She used to complain to me that Ari had sacrificed her and her children to his work. She had little use for the research establishment. Yes, Dorothy was perceptive about some things. Not all, however. She failed to perceive that Ari was having an affair with Meg. There was a muted scandal at the time of the divorce, but it really made no difference to anybody."

Ari had been away from the laboratory for a few days and called to ask me to bring some of his notebooks to his house. I stayed for supper. During the meal, Ari had his head down, peering soberly at the tablecloth as if he were saying grace. Meg had gotten the kids off earlier. She sat opposite Ari, the corners of her mouth twitching involuntarily, her long thin fingers drumming nervously on the table. Ari kept muttering a single theme with numerous variations. "Why are they doing this to me?"

Finally, Meg uncorked a bottle of carbonated frustrations that for years must have been bubbling to get out. "They're not doing anything to you. That's really the trouble. It's not even a personal matter. You are simply the victim, anonymous, incognito, of some inner political scheme. You're a nothing, which makes it worse than if you were the object of a vendetta. Because you think research is noble," she shrilled, "you think everyone connected with it is noble. When are you going to come to your senses? Chamberlain thinks it is noble only when it brings in money. When is the last time you brought them any money?"

Ari looked up in surprise. "You sound like my lawyer."

"Your lawyer has sense. The fact is, Chamberlain wouldn't care if you discovered the cure for cancer unless he could spend it. The fact is, you have nothing to sell. You may be the most brilliant researcher in the world, but it adds up to a big zero." She flung her napkin angrily on the table, whirled from her seat sobbing and rushed from the room.

Machaon was so spiritually destitute that he was beyond embarrassment. "She's right, Harry. Research, what is it? An act of faith. I have to have faith in my work, and my patrons have to have faith in my work. And they don't. Until now, Harry, no other world existed for me outside of medicine and research." He didn't mean to say it that way, but, obviously, that nonexistent world included his wives and families.

"You know, Harry, I've had plenty of time to think lately. I've tried to approach the problem deductively, defining each of its components. I've tried to organize them into modules, hoping to find a capstone of logic, but nothing interlocks. The sequences are unreasonable, therefore meaningless. Meg is right. I am victimized by a bizarre convergence of random acts by an assortment of individuals who, although physicians and purportedly scientists, deal from a frame of reference that is foreign to me. Until now I had assumed research was sacrosanct, that research men, as disciples of science, would automatically be revered. An inner logic is becoming clear to me. In the course of my career I have systematically poisoned and destroyed thousands of rabbits, rats, dogs, cats. I watched their suffering dispassionately, my mind fixed only on the experimental results. I killed these animals to pursue *my* goals. Now Chamberlain is sacrificing *me* to pursue *his*."

Ari shuddered. He rose and withdrew a half-filled bottle of cheap Chianti from an otherwise empty rack, got two water glasses and divided the harsh wine between us.

"I have been forced to conclude at this late stage in my life that I am merely human. And the human species, whatever the rationalizations, is characterized by its inhumanity." He gulped the wine. "Here, let me show you a letter," Ari said.

There was a letter from Europe, from Italy, from the Institute at Perugia. I read it slowly.

DEAR ARI:

I am in the process of submitting your name in nomination for the Nobel Prize in medicine. Would you be kind enough to send me your bibliography?

It was good to see you in London.

Regards,
FRANCESCO PILOSI

Chamberlain's office submitted to Le Brum the document of charges against Machaon.

Written on the dean's stationery, the papers looked imposing:

1. The research committee has lost confidence in Dr. Machaon's work.
2. The school has been embarrassed by a severely critical review

199

of Dr. Machaon's latest book written by the eminent professor, Thannhauser, who himself is probably the world's foremost student of inflammatory processes.

3. Dr. Machaon is rarely in the laboratory. His trips to meetings of late have occupied an increasing amount of his time, which could better be devoted to his research, to teaching, and to the betterment of the school.

4. Dr. Machaon is personally untidy. His offices and laboratory appear unkempt. He sets a poor example for the students.

Ari was aghast. "Garbage. You don't take this seriously, do you?"

"Of course I do."

"But you'll defend me?"

"Of course. I said I would. Is there anything else they can bring against you?"

"No."

"Are you sure? Think hard."

"But these are the charges. That closes the book, doesn't it?"

"Don't be silly. That's only openers. They can throw up anything else they find out between now and the hearing."

Victor Krouse was euphoric. He scurried between departments politicking with professors, hand-writing reams of material which he condensed into about ten pages of single-spaced type which he guarded furtively. He was preparing for the faculty meeting, where he would seek approval to switch his grant to the physiology department. "I think I'm gonna make it, Harry," he said, twisting his lip into a parody of a grin. "The dean is all for it, and couldn't care less if Crow balks. He'd shove that three hundred grand right up Crow's ass if that was the only way he could keep the money at the school."

Those were the last words Krouse spoke to me. One day he was there, and the next he had vanished, like the fumes from one of his chemical reactions. After this Crow, who had aged perceptibly, bent by the struggle like a branch laden with snow, straightened a bit and developed some spring in his step, his complexion no longer the leaden gray of a stormcloud.

Harper filled me in on the details. The faculty, with the dean's backing, was willing to allow Krouse to switch to physiology. Since the Institute was semiautonomous, independently funded, bringing Krouse into physiology would be like a transfer from another institution. They felt that it would be appropriate to honor the request of the head of the department of physiology. They would be polite to Crow. If his feelings were ruffled, they were sorry, no slight was intended. Also, if Crow decided to keep Krouse on his staff, they had no objection to that. They would be impartial, like the net in a tennis game. Low balls would be stopped.

Crow showed up grim, urbane, dapper. He wore a salt-and-pepper tweed, resplendent with vest, crossed in front by a gold chain from which the golden keys of honor societies were suspended. Krouse had never been to a faculty meeting before. He wore his white lab coat.

Crow, when given the floor, was restrained. He briefly summarized the basis of the conflict, detailed the terms of the grant, and even apologized to the faculty because adequate space wasn't available. "Thus," he said, quietly and effectively, "when Dr. Krouse refused to accept the maximum space we were able to allot, and this in conference with Dean Chamberlain, and when he threatened to embarrass the faculty and the school by returning the grant to the National Institutes of Health, he left me no recourse. We had to terminate his employment." Crow went on disarmingly. "Gentlemen, I have high regard for Dr. Krouse as a chemist. He is a careful worker, fastidious with data, scrupulous with detail. But research is a team effort. It requires the subordination of one's self to the project, to the team. I cannot give Dr. Krouse high marks on that score. He is divisive. He is angry with me and has said unkind things. I understand the basis of his disappointment, but he is young and talented, and better advised to work his way up slowly and cooperatively than to follow the course he has, which places him and his own work above the established goals of the Institute. He has become openly rebellious. His continued presence on the faculty will be a source of constant annoyance and irritation to me. I request that his dismissal from the Institute be construed as a dismissal from the medical school faculty, that no place be made for him in any other department. I have the unanimous support of my board of directors in this request." He nodded stiffly, smiled and returned to his seat.

Harper said that the crack about his board of directors was ominous, and Chamberlain didn't like it at all. The contract

201

between the university and the Institute was up for renewal, and if negotiations fell through, Crow would have no difficulty locating the Institute, with its fat endowment, elsewhere, but it would leave a big gap at Church.

Then Krouse rebutted. "Everyone in this room heard Dr. Crow pay tribute to the care and attention I give to my work. Yet he has fired me because I try to apply the same principles to the administration of a grant of monies by the United States Government. And I wish I could say kind words to Dr. Crow in return, about the way he runs research at the Institute." Krouse paused and peered at the professors. They were attentive.

Then Krouse proceeded to dismember Charley Crow. "He represents himself as the sole researcher surrounded by his satellite technicians. Quite the opposite. Certainly in chemistry, the work has originated with me. The argument that it belongs to Crow because he devised the way to produce the tumors and leukemias is invalid. Bianca Fiore discovered the leukemias, yet you never hear of the important role she played. He tosses her name onto some papers as a sop, papers that couldn't have been written if it hadn't been for her. And the same holds true for the rest of us."

Krouse warmed to the task, his lip tied by the scar into unpleasant grimaces. "The bald fact is that Crow has purloined our work and published our data without consulting us. By incorporating our original contributions into his own papers, he assures that no concepts other than his own can ever emerge from the Institute. That, of course, is what is behind all of this. He could have bought me the space my grant called for. He refused. Not because of the money. He's spent that much on a single trip to meetings. It was because he couldn't bear the thought of any of his employees achieving independence. As long as he remains, presiding as a dictator over the Institute, there will be no growth there. His good people will leave him one by one as they struggle for independence. And as long as he has the power to demand the job of one of his employees who refuses to misappropriate government funds, the public endowment of the Institute will shrink, not expand.

"I have no board of directors to stand behind me. But I claim that the highest human purpose of research becomes mutilated by such actions, and that the faculty should disassociate itself from that kind of business.

"By having you accede to my ouster, Crow is corrupting you. As a matter of fact, the continued presence of Crow on the faculty is a corruption. I would find it difficult to accept the position in physiology if Dr. Crow were permitted to remain."

Crow was fuming, his face taking on all the colors of a pinwheel. All eyes riveted on him. Suddenly, Crow leaped to his feet, and as he did so (Harper chuckled at the memory) he loosed a rousing, execrable fart which flattened the silence like thunder. Suddenly, there was bedlam. What an answer to Krouse's impassioned demand! Krouse, stunned, walked out. I found out later that he had mistaken the laughter for a response to his speech. Crow, blushing, returned to his seat.

In Krouse's absence the faculty, after quenching its ribaldry with the tears that laughter brings, quickly passed a resolution to bar his transfer to physiology, after which it prevailed upon Crow to allow Krouse the privilege of resigning so that his record would be clean. The dean rapped for order and turned to Crow. "Well, I guess it could have been worse, eh, Charley? On behalf of the faculty I would like to say that we are thankful for little favors."

Le Brum called Ari Machaon at his home. The dean had requested a meeting to be held before the hearing, with Machaon, Le Brum, himself and the lawyers for the school.

Ari was resolute. The meeting was brief. Before it was over he had resigned.

When Ari arrived for the meeting, Le Brum was already in Chamberlain's office, chatting amiably—too amiably, Ari thought —with Chamberlain and Morris Little, a member of the board of directors, as well as the lawyer who handled the affairs of the school. The introductions were cordial, issued by Chamberlain standing behind his desk, with an expansive sweep of his hand. Ari sat down and was treated to the remainder of a story Little was telling that obviously had been interrupted by his entrance.

Little continued his story. "I said, 'Mark, you know if they indict you we'll have to drop you from the board. Why don't you resign now?' Well, of course, he's a brash sonofabitch and refused. He said an indictment isn't a conviction."

"Of course, it isn't," remarked Le Brum. "You're in a ticklish position, Morris. You've got to measure the embarrassment of keeping him on the board against the money he contributes—and raises—each year. Frankly, I don't think you can afford to antagonize him."

"Gentlemen," interrupted Chamberlain, "Dr. Machaon is here. We can discuss this later. Let us get to the matter at hand."

Ari was amused that Chamberlain had to call attention to the fact that he was in the room. The process of depersonalization, already begun, was deepening. He was becoming invisible, erased by neglect. It won't be quite that easy, he mused. Chamberlain droned on.

"—the hearing date has been set, and if it is agreeable to you and Mr. Le Brum—

Ari hoped that Le Brum had studied the documentation he had submitted, and would be prepared to defend—

"—put it on the agenda. It will be three weeks from today in the amphi—

—the proposition that a man devoted to research was performing a public service—

"—theater of the new medical building. The purpose of this meeting is to acquaint you with the general charges that will be brought against you.

—and that no public institution had the right to merely shunt him aside to suit their own unpublicized purpose—

"—you have read a partial list that we submitted, but the main charge that we thought it advisable to issue privately at this meeting to avoid having it appear in print, or otherwise advertising it unnecessarily to your detriment—

*—because research was a
public trust. He hoped Le
Brum would open channels to
the press and demand that the
hearings be public.*

"—first and foremost is the
charge of moral turpitude—"

With difficulty Ari brought Chamberlain into focus. Le Brum
was startled. "Hold it a minute, Dean. You're not going to bring
any charges like that out at a public hearing?"

"No," said Chamberlain in measured tones. "I should expect the
hearings to be private."

"Ridiculous," Le Brum almost shouted. "No hearing in front of
a faculty committee is private. My client will sue you and the
institution for defamation of character."

"We realize that, Claude," said Little soothingly, "but that's
the risk we'll have to take. After all, we have the right to create
and try to maintain the standards for our staff. Dr. Machaon
while on our payroll indulged in scandalous activity. He committed adultery which resulted in a divorce, marriage to the
adulteress, the breakup of a family. After all, we are a Baptist
institution. We have a letter which categorizes the events, demanding his ouster."

He handed a document to Le Brum, who read it quickly.
"Why, it's anonymous. This is garbage. It wouldn't be admissible
in any court."

"Of course not, Claude. But we're not going to court. We are
going to a hearing. A hearing that you and your client demand be
public."

Ari grabbed the letter and read it. It formalized the gossip
circulating during his affair with Meg. As gossip it was inconsequential, but categorized in print it became irrefutable because it
concentrated the emotional turmoil of a two-year period into
three words: infidelity, adultery and divorce. Ari stiffened spas-
modically, and then became limp as if a bullet had shattered his
spinal cord. He spoke hoarsely.

"This is incredible and hopeless." He mustered some remnants
of reserve strength, rose from his chair and faced Chamberlain.
Then he spoke firmly as if nothing in the past existed and the

205

statement he was about to make was the purpose for which he had entered Chamberlain's office.

"I regret, Dr. Chamberlain, that I must offer my resignation as director of the Alice Fremont Research Foundation, and as associate professor of experimental pathology."

Le Brum shot up like a fighting cock. "No you don't, Ari. This is the filthiest goddamn thing I've come up against in my entire career. Don't quit now. I'll grind these bastards into the ground." He turned to Chamberlain. "I've read his papers. I've checked his credentials. You're destroying a great man who has made great contributions."

Ari turned to face the angry voice. "Sit down, Mr. Le Brum, and contain yourself. The time for righteous indignation is long past. It's all over."

"I accept your resignation with regret, Dr. Machaon," said Dean Chamberlain, imperturbably.

Even as Ari was walking out, Le Brum turned to Little. "Do you really think Mark will be indicted, Morris?"

Months later, when I was at the race track with Lapius, we encountered Judge Rand and Lapius introduced us. "He works for Charley Crow," Lapius said.

"Indeed. I've heard of Harry. Charley has spoken of you many times. Thinks you have fine talent. You must enjoy the work."

"I don't think there's much future in it," I answered.

Rand looked puzzled. "Harry is being sardonic, Judge. He is still upset over the Machaon affair."

"Oh, yes," Rand said, "the chap who resigned."

"He didn't volunteer to resign, it was forced on him," I said, trying to control the edge of anger in my voice.

"But according to Chamberlain, Machaon was not very productive," the judge remarked in an offhand way.

"Did it take Chamberlain twenty years to discover that, Rudolf? As a matter of fact, I understand that Charley asked you to intervene in behalf of Machaon."

"He did more or less, but then another matter came up which Charley felt took priority. I told him I couldn't buck the faculty on two issues. Charley said if that was the case, to forget about Machaon for the time being. Of course I owed Charley a favor or two."

206

"You mean," I asked the judge, "your decision on Machaon was based on political factors—not the merit of his case? That wasn't a good decision."

"I don't always make the 'right' decision, Harry. Which may be why I am still in a position to make decisions."

After Rand excused himself Lapius and I went to the paddock to size up the horses for the next race.

"They are all beagles," Lapius sniffed disdainfully.

"They look like horses to me," I said.

"I was referring to Rand, and Chamberlain, and Machaon's colleagues at Church. Many years ago my research called for the sacrifice of beagle dogs. We herded them into the autopsy room, where they milled about, pissing in corners and sniffing each other. One by one we put them on the table, injected poison into their veins, and when dead, we autopsied them to remove the experimental organs. While each was being sacrificed the others sniffed the entrails, unaware of what was transpiring until finally none were left alive. There are a lot of beagles in the world."

After Krouse left, Crow became buoyant. He commandeered data like a hilltop commander arranging his troops for battle. Heller was in constant consultation with us, trying to reconstruct pertinent areas in chemistry that Charley would need for his brief talk. "It's not the talk that's so important, Harry," Crow told me confidently. "But we'll have an abstract, and will have established priority in the field. Before it's over we, our Institute, will be known as the center for tumorigenesis. We will be the recognized leaders in the field."

I was still sore at him about the Krouse affair, and felt that he had let Machaon down, but his forcefulness was irresistible. He marshaled his energies, harnessed ours and drove us mercilessly to produce more data that he would need for his talk.

Crow was a great catalyst. He could implicate himself in various aspects of the assorted projects without participating, but because of his presence interaction became smoother, communication more comprehensive, and the work was accomplished at greater speed and efficiency. There's something almost orgasmic about taking a hodgepodge of data bred in the bloody entrails and organ systems of laboratory animals, and creating orderly schemata to interpret the results, synthesize meanings and re-

207

arrange preconceived concepts to fit the new information. Suddenly, you possess knowledge that is yours alone; your mind has culled it from the apparently random shapeless crop of latent information that a biological or living system actually represents. For a brief moment, you are the sole proprietor. When you publish, you can be assured that somewhere in the *cumulus index medicus* there will be a reference to that work, a record that no one else can claim. And, of course, it turns out that no one else gives a damn either. The moments of glory are brief and impalpable.

After a few months it's all over, except for the not insignificant inner knowledge that you have influenced colleagues the world over to build upon your work. It's like growing a perfect rose, for the brief exhilarating period of fragrant joy before the petals wither.

There is more to it than that. There is the transcendental quality, this rooting around at the origin of things to forge links to the future. And also something sinful, the holding hostage and destroying the creature-children of nature to force her to reveal herself. This is predicated on the concept that inhumanity is acceptable as long as it benefits humanity.

I tried this out on Crow, but he became impatient. "I'd kill any number of dogs if it would benefit one child."

"Maybe Krouse was doing work that would have saved one child."

"If so, he can do it someplace else."

"The sacrifice in research doesn't always stop with animals," I remarked sourly.

"You're not indispensable either, Harry," Crow said sharply. "Are you becoming unhappy here?"

"Frankly, I like to do research at the pace that the research demands. I don't like making a factory out of the place just for the aggrandizement of . . ." I let him complete my thought.

The auditorium of the Festival Hall in London was filled to capacity by scientists involved in the struggle against cancer, drawn from almost every country in the world. Charley Crow was expansive in his greetings, and almost as sleek as the interior decor. He sat back, content, awaiting the convocation.

Seated at a long table on the lighted stage were a representa-

208

tive of the Queen, the president of the Congress, an assortment of officers and John Griffiths. Crow poked me. "I told you he was important. Amazing how he has been able to work himself into the center of things. His work isn't that impressive."

Suddenly trumpeters bedecked in gaudy green and gold-brocaded pantaloons marched to center stage and blew flourishes and fanfares culled from a thousand years of English heraldry to convene and initiate this scientific congress.

The Queen's representative was crisp and hospitable in welcoming us to England. Then John Griffiths was introduced. He stood gravely, soberly, before the microphone, placed one hand on each side of the lectern, peered at the audience for a moment, then turned slowly and thanked the British Government for their hospitable welcome. He turned back to the audience, and slowly launched into a historical review of the induction of cancer by carcinogens. He described the observations of Sir Percivall Pott in the eighteenth century, who deduced that the scrotal cancer noted in chimney sweeps was probably caused by the encrustation of tars in the folds of the scrotal skin. He described the first artificial induction in the skin of mice by Yamagiwa and Ichikawa, told of Loeb's work with hormones and cancer, of Lacassagne's and Bittner's work with breast tumors in mice. In fact, the gist of the entire talk inevitably had to lead to Crow's latest work. Crow was beaming, his bald head shining, as he combed at it with his handkerchief in his excitement. Sure enough, Griffiths told about Crow's experiments, and that was where the talk should have ended, but he continued. He mentioned Crow only as a matter of passing historical interest, before describing the work that was now going on in Griffiths' own laboratory.

He had gotten hold of a carcinogen that worked about five times as fast as the one we were using, so in a brief period of time had been able to repeat all the work we had done and then some. His work was more comprehensive than ours. His tumors were produced so rapidly that he had moved into dose-response experiments, and, in fact, by the time he had finished, Charley Crow and his work had been relegated to the dust bin of medical history, and Griffiths had established that the crown of legitimate ascension to the throne of carcinogenesis rested solely on the head of John Griffiths.

Thus, before his eyes, the entire edifice Crow had built over the years was suddenly smashed. Had someone put a bullet through the forehead of Charley Crow at that moment, it might have been the kindest act. When it was all over, Griffiths received a resounding ovation and Charley Crow virtually staggered from the hall, his face assuming the sick slate hue of a damp pavement at dusk.

He glared at me, and that night wired to Bianca Fiore to discontinue all my experiments, and clear the cages for new work he would embark on upon his return. The king of the beagles was dead, long live the king.

Afterward, Crow could no longer disguise his angina. "I've been a fool. I didn't think Griffiths would do that. He drew information from me about our experiments, and all along he was merely measuring our rate of progress against his own."

The oppressive anger of his melancholy increased the intensity of his constricting chest pains. The spasms gradually became more intense, more frequent. Over the months, he became increasingly a prisoner of the high green swivel chair behind his desk.

Finally, as each step invited calamity, his options dwindled. All that remained was the option to die. He concluded deviously that if his gallstones were removed his angina would improve. He was warned that he couldn't survive the operation, but he insisted on it. He died on the table.

REQUIEM

Death is not an event that we fashion, shape or create. At best, it's a meager, spiteful moment that unceremoniously interrupts a stream of biological continuity. There is a commonality to death, and Machaon's was no exception. He was stricken suddenly with crushing chest pain. There was time to call an ambulance, time for him to feel the lethal grip of a profound visceral disorder that prompted him to turn to his wife and say, "This is the end." There was time for him to reflect on the vulgar disaster that terminated his career in research, and time for him to realize that, compared to the agonizing vise that slowly squeezed his breath and consciousness into pulpy death, the past was terribly unimportant. I was sorry, but felt no sense of loss. Machaon was a private person, but perfectly comprehensible, impelled as he was to rearrange the tangled threads of information into a skein of knowledge.

But, curiously, when Charley Crow died, I sensed the loss. I didn't grieve. Even after years of working together, I scarcely knew the man.

Lapius understood. He said, "Machaon was a great researcher but a remote man. Charley Crow, on the other hand, was a public man. People you hear about and read about constantly have a transcendental quality. When they die, a piece of your personal experience, a fragment of your generation, dies with them."

"It's a good thing Crow didn't live to see Griffiths win the Award."

"It probably wouldn't have mattered, Harry. Crow's dream ended at the London meetings. The irony is that Griffiths got the prize for work he had done twenty years before. But he had slipped from public view. Crow had demonstrated the same phenomena in rats, and Griffiths legitimately built on Crow's experiments to become conspicuous again, to promote his prior claim. And it worked. Griffiths deserved the prize for his early work, but I wonder if he would have made it without the involuntary assist from the work of Charley Crow.

8

I WAS BETWEEN JOBS now and not in the practice of either getting up early or rushing anywhere. When the phone rang, the clock said seven.

It was Lapius. "Harry, hurry up, will you!"

Usually I would zip into the bathroom, make the morning toilet and buzz off to whatever my destination, leaving the housekeeping chores for a more convenient time. But now I spitefully dallied. I folded my pajamas, made the bed, took some extra time to create hospital corners, dusted a bit. Showered, dressed and, since it was a lovely spring day, walked slowly to Simon's place. The phone rang again as I was leaving, but I ignored it.

Lapius was grumbling. "I don't know why you're so late."

"Housekeeping, Simon. I have chores to do now that I'm living alone and out of work. I can't afford any help."

"Well then, Harry, maybe I can help you. I have a job for you."

We moved to his drawing room–office complex. He seated himself behind the large mahogany desk.

"Harry, there's a problem. A woman called Dolly Matson claims that there is an attempt to kidnap her child. She claims she is being accused of child abuse and the youngster will be made a ward of the state."

"How do I fit into this?"

"I'm not able to get about the way I used to, you know, and there will have to be some distances to cover. I thought you might be able to help me."

"Of course I'll help you. Where do I start?"

"At the Community Health Center."

I looked up at him sharply. "That's a coincidence," I said. "I've applied for a job there."

The Community Health Center was supposed to bring Health, with a capital H, to the inner city. Blacks, lured by the hope of freedom, poured northward through migratory funnels, and became buried in the granite maze of city life. They were joined by the Puerto Ricans who swarmed by planeload to explant their Spanish patois to mainland America. Schools became daytime prisons. Night people marauded and commerce was throttled by brutality and crime.

Inner city is a place of rats, lice, drugs, a torpor bred of poor nutrition, of filth bred of ignorance. It is a place of junkies, pimps and gaping wounds. The dirty attic of America, it is hidden by the shadows of commercial skyscrapers, by concrete concourses built over and around it to speed a stream of cars between the suburbs and the center city. Occasionally the squalor becomes piercing. One such shriek must have stirred the conscience of the nation, which suddenly decided to bring Health to inner city. Money was allocated to Community Health Centers, as if a money-needle alone could drain off the pus of poverty from the ghetto abscess.

Community Medicine is a patchwork attempt to repair medically a sickness that is fundamentally economic. "It's like sending a team of economists to cure an epidemic of bubonic plague," Lapius snorted.

I accepted the position of project director of the Community

Health Center Dr. Mike Grady directed. Mike Grady, professor of something called Community Medicine, was pudgy, gray and rumpled.

Paint peeled from the cracked walls of his office at the Community Health Center. Grady's blond oaken desk was almost hidden by an array of important-looking documents. He sat in a four-legged oaken armchair, tilting it backward precariously as he spoke, hands gripping the arms for purchase. A soft brogue inflected his speech. His shoes were scuffed.

"There are few formalities here," he said. "You must meet the community board of directors who will vote on you. Then you will be interviewed by the staff. We have a lot of community participation going on. Theoretically no decisions can be made without their advice and consent, but in reality they defer to my judgment.

"Medicine is in for great changes, Harry. We no longer talk about private practice. Here in the cities we are concerned with the delivery of health care. It calls for administrative talent. It's a system that will put the physician to work. He won't be able to assume that elite role that has plagued the profession. He will not be able to order nurses and aides to do his bidding. The nursing and medical professions will cooperate with each other to the ultimate benefit of the community. I'll have my secretary give you a schedule of interviews for the coming week."

His secretary was a redhead with a wolfhound profile, Mrs. Polly Stiner. Her name was inscribed on a small sign on her desk.

The Community Health Center was a staid row house. The windows of the red-brick building were framed in white granite. The white stone steps, concave from years of use, had a marbled patina. Except for the sign over the door the building was indistinguishable from its neighbors, all of which had been upper-middle-class dwellings at the turn of the century, middle-class before World War II, and now slums. The interior was a maze of hallways and rooms with high beamed ceilings, heavy walls and sturdy oaken floors and stairs. Partitions framed small offices for the officials of the center, such as Al Roscoe.

Al Roscoe was chairman of the board of directors of the Community Health Center. His office was small. He strode toward me from behind an oaken desk. His hand, proportioned to his six-foot-five large-boned frame, covered mine like a blanket, and after shaking he twisted to grasp my thumb and made some other indecipherable movements that I later learned was the handclasp of brotherhood. He smiled. His teeth were unmarred. His hair sprang like steel wool to frame skin so dark that good lighting was needed to clearly distinguish his regular features.

"I just wanted to say hello to you, Doctor, before we meet the community board. As executive director of this community center my job is to help solve any problems you might have, and hope that you will help me solve mine. What do you think of Mike Grady?"

I looked at Roscoe and shrugged.

"Grady does a lot of shoving," Roscoe said. "C'mon. The board awaits you," he said in mock courtliness.

The social agencies responsible for the disbursement of federal funds to the Community Health Center required community participation. The idea was to give the community money with which to hire a medical team. In effect, the community, as represented by its board of directors, composed of neighborhood people, was hiring its own doctors, and could demand medical care on the same basis as private individuals. Although the board was theoretically responsible for the money, the Center was to be run by a doctor, one chosen by a responsible authority, which the government believed should be a medical school. To qualify for the directorship of Health Centers, the medical schools, enticed by the chance to apply salaries to a federal project and thus expand their facilities, created departments of Community Medicine, the exact function of which has not as yet been defined. Theoretically the community board could fire the medical director and get rid of the medical school. Although this was paper power, Grady treated Roscoe with demonstrable respect, while Roscoe issued guarded evaluations about Grady and the way he was running things, to maintain the fiction that Grady was working for him and the board.

Funds were disbursed through a subsidiary of the Department of Housing and Urban Development, HUD. Thus, in order to spend money, Grady had to get approval from the community board via Al Roscoe, then requisition it from Willie Turner, our man from HUD. The medical school really didn't care how Grady did the job as long as the government paid his salary. Thus the delivery of proper medical care depended on both the

215

goodwill of Grady and the release of funds by Willie Turner. That Willie Turner would stop the release of funds if he thought that the monies were not being properly spent was a fable, because Turner didn't know the difference between good and bad medical care.

I prepared to meet the neighborhood board of directors of the Community Health Center.

In a room not much larger than Roscoe's minuscule office, board members sat in a semicircle that faced the camp stool reserved for me.

I was introduced by Roscoe. "This here is the doctor they want to hire to help run the medical part of the center. Mrs. Ramirez, Mr. Blocker, Mrs. Pook, Mr. McGrath, Mrs. Esposito . . ." and several others. The women wore cotton dresses, the colors bleached by many launderings. The men's suits were threadbare. Their shoes were scuffed, the heels worn.

"I'll leave you to their tender mercies," said Roscoe after the introductions. "Don't be too hard on him," he said over his shoulder as he left.

Blocker spoke first. "We represent the neighborhood. Any problems or complaints the community has they bring to us and we lay it on Mr. Roscoe and Mr. Grady."

Mrs. Pook corrected him, "You mean Dr. Grady. Ain't going to do no good bringing him down from a doctor now, is it?"

"I'd like to continue with the interview, Mrs. Pook, if it's all right with you."

Mrs. Pook offered a thin smile in retreat.

Blocker continued. "What we are trying to do here is to bring a dignified type of medicine to the poor people."

"Yah, we don't want no handouts, we have the money to pay for dignified service," Mrs. Ramirez cut in. Blocker silenced her with an admonishing finger.

"You'll have to excuse some of the board members. They never served on such a body before. Sometimes they get a little rambunctious. But the real question we got to ask you is, do you think that you can bring medicine to this neighborhood like they got in the suburbs?"

I sat quietly for a while, then said, "That would depend on the patient load, the number of doctors available and the availability of hospital beds for the sick. This is only a clinic."

216

"You still ain't answered Mr. Blocker's question. Can we get as good as the sick people get in the suburbs?" Mrs. Pook interjected.

"I'm not sure that suburban medicine is what you'll settle for," I told her.

"What's good enough for them is good enough for us, Doc. Them white ladies go to any doctor they want any time they want, even for a sneeze. . . . All they gotta do is drop some money on his desk and he'll see them any time. Now the government is giving us the money to pay the salaries of doctors and nurses, and it's our job to see that the community don't get short-changed."

I answered slowly. "If you think every time you belch there's going to be a doctor available, it just won't happen. They don't have that in the suburbs either. In the suburbs there are few general practitioners and house calls are a thing of the past. Suburbanites often have to wait several hours in the office before seeing the doctor."

"You got anything better?" Mrs. Esposito asked.

"I don't know. For one thing you can't buy private medicine here. You can buy only institutional medicine. And stop kidding yourselves. You're not buying anything. The government is buying it for you. You'll have essentially a free clinic subsidized by the government, no matter how it's dressed up."

"We ain't gonna accept no motherfuckin' clinics. We been through that," said Mr. McGrath ominously.

"The old free-clinic system provided good medicine."

"What was so good about it? We'd have to sit on those benches for hours, sit there burnin' up with fever, and some mother in white pants would come out and give us some aspirin and send us home. Some of us died at home."

"That's the modern clinic. I'm not talking about that. In the old free-clinic system if you went to medical clinic, the Chief of Medicine of the hospital was directly responsible for you, and if someone pulled a stunt like that, he'd be disciplined. And if you went to surgical clinic, you were fundamentally the direct responsibility of the Chief of Surgery of that hospital."

"How come we ain't got that any more?"

"Because the whole thing is now under the department of Community Medicine of the medical school, and I'm not sure

217

what that is. One thing I am sure of, it's not surgery. It's not pediatrics, it's not obstetrics, and it's not medicine. And that's the catch. It's Dr. Grady, as far as I can tell, and he never practiced medicine."

"Man," said McGrath, "you tryin' to tell us that Doc Grady ain't no real doctor?"

"No. He's a doctor, but he doesn't practice medicine. He's trying to hire me to direct the project. And he's got to hire doctors to run the dispensary. For $25,000 bucks a year he's going to get some pretty rusty guys ready to retire, and some younger foreign doctors waiting for placement. And at five o'clock they'll go home. I don't know exactly who is going to be responsible for your welfare, but somewhere along the line someone will have to take responsibility for each patient."

"Wouldn't that be your job?"

"If I'm given the authority."

"Well, you better do it if we hire you. Otherwise we gotta hire someone else."

"On what basis are you going to judge me? How will you know if medical care is good?"

"Depends. We get bad reports from the patients."

"Patients can't always judge the quality of medical care. A setup like this needs doctors, nurses and technicians to provide good care. If the service breaks down anywhere along the line, care can deteriorate. Do you think you can make these judgments?"

"We depend on Dr. Grady for the medical judgments."

"Well," Blocker asked, turning to his right and then to the left. "You heard the man. What do you think?"

"At least he don't give us no shit," said Mrs. Pook. She seemed to express the collective judgment. Blocker smiled. "Okay, Doc, we'll let you know." Then the members of the board stood up and moved slowly to the door, shaking my hand on the way.

I followed them, right into the waiting arms of a middle-aged, gaunt, flat-chested and professional female. She said, "I'm Norah Rubin. Tomorrow, you'll be interviewed by the staff." Who the hell was Norah Rubin?

Prior to meeting the staff Grady ushered me through the complex. The clinic was in a separate building, across the street, an equally shoddy remnant, a ghettoized house, compartmentalized with plywood partitions hastily lined with cheap paneling to create the effective space for a waiting room and small examining rooms. Floor tiles were missing, and those that remained were eroded. The toilet seat in the bathroom was filthy, which didn't matter since it was unhinged and fell off entirely every time it was raised. The sink was grimy and anemic streams of cold water could be coaxed from the faucets only at certain times of the day.

I wondered out loud why some of the community people couldn't clean the place, repaint the toilet seat, scrub the floor, wash down the walls. Perhaps the board could look into this. Grady remained impassive. "There are more important things to do, Harry. You mustn't get off on the wrong foot here. We haven't the janitorial staff for that."

"But there are lots of people around, including all those teenage kids—maybe we could get some volunteers."

"And ask them to do menial chores, Harry? You'll simply be instituting the old white-master, black-slave relationship. It would destroy community relations. Come, you'll meet the staff."

The meeting was held in a square room on the second floor. There were no chairs. Staff members sat on packing cases, sprawled on the floor or propped themselves against the wall. The nurses were young, five black, three white. Norah Rubin excused herself and came back with a chair which she offered to Grady. He refused. She placed it against the wall and sat down. When I was introduced, it was as if they had gone through this procedure many times before, like a permanent cadre making temporary space for transient officers. Grady introduced me. Norah Rubin, Florence Furness, Margie Roller, Willie Turner and others. They nodded.

"Harry. The purpose of this meeting is to satisfy the staff that you understand basic principles of community relations. It's only fair for the staff who will have to work with you to evaluate your sensitivity in this regard."

Mrs. Rubin took up the thread. "You see," she said, reaching into her purse for cigarettes, "we're the first group in this city to establish a care center for the underprivileged. Except for a few people like Dr. Grady, the medical profession hasn't felt any

219

particular responsibility for the poor, and in effect has deprived them of medical coverage. We are bringing medicine to these people and hope you will be able to help us."

I was expected to say something. "I shouldn't imagine it to be a problem. The staff is here and you say the money is committed."

"We do have all these things, like you say, Doctor." It was Miss Furness, brown, businesslike.

"Miss Furness is our directress of nursing," Grady interrupted.

"But the main thing," Furness continued, "is attitude. Without the right attitude no money and no staff is worth a damn."

"The practice of medicine is built on well-known traditional principles. If people need care, we should be able to provide it," I said.

"He's missing the point," said Miss Roller, the beige, fat one. "Explain what you mean, Florence."

"It's just that you can't treat these people like you treat white patients," continued Miss Furness.

"Why not?" I asked, remembering that the board members wanted to be treated like white people.

"What the girls are trying to say, Harry," Grady explained, "is that it may be more important to protect the man's dignity than to lower his cholesterol. If you strip him of his dignity, fail to speak properly to him, you damage his pride as a human being."

"That's implicit in the doctor-patient relationship," I said. "There's no loss of dignity in being a patient."

"You're not just treating a disease, Doctor, you're treating a human being," Furness carefully explained.

"I'm treating a patient," I said.

"You'd just better be damned sure you understand that before you start here," she said cantankerously.

Al Roscoe walked in suddenly. Grady turned to him. "What did they say, Al?"

"The board likes him. They'll accept him for the time being."

"We don't need your help," said Turner. "We'll check him out ourselves." He glared at Roscoe. Grady was uncomfortable. "Are there any more questions?" he asked sweetly. "Okay, Harry, that's probably enough for the day."

As we walked out, Roscoe said to Grady, "We need someone around here to keep those hens in check."

220

Grady chuckled softly. "And to keep an eye on Turner, too, eh, Al?"

Then Roscoe turned to me to shake hands. After the first contact he twisted his hand up and around my thumb, and repeated the ritual maneuvers of manual embrace that had puzzled me before. After he left I asked Grady, "What's that all about?"

"Some black-power rigmarole," he muttered.

The medical staff at the Community Health Center consisted of, first, Joel Prentice, M.D., a licensed physician, trying to earn some money prior to entering his third year of residency in otolaryngology, which he would start in the fall. Grady told me he was already seeking a replacement. Next there was George Das, an Indian, who was waiting for his state license to practice medicine, so he was actually working illegally under the umbrella of the university. His prescriptions had to be countersigned by a licensed physician. The third member was Dr. Christina Matthews, a full-fledged gynecologist. The doctors worked from nine to five in cramped rooms, separated from each other by flimsy partitions that turned each private consultation into a public hearing once voices rose above a whisper.

On the other side of the hall an old utility room housed a wheezy refrigerator, and a movable cloth screen which guarded, but failed to assure, the privacy of an examining table used for proctologic and gynecological inspections. Accessories in the tiled room included a large sink and a partially enclosed hopper, done in early-twentieth-century chipped porcelain. Formerly a parlor, the waiting room for patients faced the street. Red-brown deck paint hid completely what must once have been high-polished oaken floors. Patients, black and Spanish, sat moodily on the stuffed musty-smelling sofas. Redolent feathers poked through lacerations in the upholstery.

My office was clean, carpeted, paneled, windowless and unfurnished. I sat on the floor next to the newly installed push-button telephone, with its blinking extension lights. This wasn't the way doctors given a million dollars a year would set up a clinic. I could see there was no laboratory. The very ill were sent to the university clinics for adequate work-ups.

Here, the finely polished, highly geared profession of medicine was being dismantled by abstraction and reassembled to fit an amorphous mold of untried theory by the uninformed, who had been granted a short cut to power by patronage. The Community Health Center was a clearinghouse, a battalion aid station for the disenfranchised. My last thoughts before I dozed off were that I needed pencil and paper.

I awakened to the eerie silence of a deserted slum house. After switching the light off in my bare office I palpated my way through a darkened corridor. I groped for the front door and blinked at the relative luminescence of the street. As I walked toward my car, Grady emerged from a building across the street. I quickened my pace to greet him. He turned away and folded himself quickly into the front seat of his car. As he pulled away from the curb, I saw the silhouette of a familiar face seated next to him. I couldn't place it. It was dusk. The day people had gone into hiding. The night people had not yet emerged. I hurried, uncomfortable in the silence, checking carefully for moving figures. My car was parked in blackness. Two hulking menacing men emerged from the shadows. I moved toward the car, turned to insert the key into the door lock. Footsteps closed in. I steeled myself; the footsteps faded. My hand was unsteady. I carefully nursed the car into the traffic lane. A stranger, in the darkness of my city, I wanted no accident, no commotion, at that lonely moment.

The morning sun ruthlessly liquidated the fearsome shadows of the night. Open screenless windows welcomed the playful breeze that wafted acrobatic scraps of papers and rustled the leaves of the lone tree that brazenly pierced the concrete. Black teenagers lounged on steps or leaned defiantly against the buildings. Pigtailed schoolgirls walked in groups, clutching their books like babes to the breast.

Within the Center a businesslike bustle trafficked the halls. Patients occupied available seats in the waiting room. Puerto Rican girls in blue smocks bustled back and forth with charts under their arms, and mothers guided frightened children to the pediatric wing. Flo Furness was seated at the desk in her office to the rear of the building.

"Good morning, Miss Furness."

"Good morning, Doctor."

"Do you have time to give me a guided tour this morning?"

"How about right now?"

"Sure. Bring a pad and pencil."

"What for?"

"To make some notes."

"I've got a good memory."

"Okay."

She followed me into the hall. "Oh, Doctor, follow me, I'd like to show you your office."

Magically it had been furnished. Modern sleek desk, lounge, swivel chair, credenza and bookshelves were neatly arranged. A brand-new Dictaphone with shiny tapes occupied one corner of the desk. I recalled the scuffed chairs and tattered upholstery in the waiting room.

Furness smiled, her teeth framed by dark-mahogany lips, awaiting my reaction. "Great, isn't it? Only the best for our doctor."

"It's very nice, Miss Furness. Thank you very much."

She seemed pleased. "Oh, Doctor, before we see the place, I've got a few problems. Could you come to my office first?"

"Sure, glad to."

She was behind her desk again. I was seated to one side on a metal stool.

"What can I help you with?"

She extracted a cluster of manila folders and opened the one on top. "This is the way we keep our charts. Each case has a number. The colored tag indicates the doctor in charge. Now since you are medical director I think you should know how some of these doctors are handling their cases."

"I'd rather determine that by observing them at work. You know, sort of get used to the procedure here."

"I am talking about our patients, Doctor, and I don't think they're getting proper care. Wouldn't you think that takes precedence?"

"Well, if you put it that way, of course."

"Now take this case. Dr. Prentice is managing it. The patient complains of headaches. There's not even a blood pressure on the chart. Don't you think he should have taken a blood pressure?"

"I'll be glad to talk to Dr. Prentice about that. Here, let me see some of those charts."

223

"Help yourself," she said.

On most of the charts there were no vital signs recorded. I mentioned this to her. "Wouldn't it be wise to have pulse and blood pressure taken on all the patients? The aides or nurses could do that before the doctor sees the patients."

"It's hardly practical. We simply don't have the time. We have to be selective."

"Well then, perhaps doctors can do it routinely, vital signs, etc."

"That's the nurse's prerogative, not the doctor's."

"You're kidding."

"No, Doctor, I'm not. Look it up in the job descriptions."

The meeting was becoming a confrontation.

"Job descriptions?"

"Yes." She handed me a notebook filled with mimeographs, introduced by a complicated table of contents that had numerous subheaded and sublettered and subnumbered indentations, and sat back.

"How about my guided tour?"

"Read the job description first."

I returned to my office. The notebook contained page after page of organizational tables and job descriptions. They represented the "regs" of the Health Center, probably drawn up by Grady and his staff in conjunction with the supervisory agency of HUD. Reading was tedious. My desk wobbled. I pressed a button and picked up the phone. Furness answered.

"My desk wobbles. Who do I see about that?"

"Mr. Turner." She hung up.

I walked into the corridor and encountered a dark-haired man in a white coat. A stethoscope hung from his neck. He wore shell-rimmed glasses, his features were regular. "Excuse me," I said, "could you point me in the direction of Mr. Turner's office?"

"You must be our new project director. I'm Joel Prentice," he said, keeping his hands at his side, giving me the option. I stuck out my hand and he gripped it firmly.

"Hello, Dr. Joel Prentice. I've seen your name on the manifest, your job description and salary, all of which tells me nothing. Exactly what do you do here?"

"Who, me?" he asked. I nodded reassurance. "I see patients from nine to five, five days a week."

"Who sees patients after five and on weekends?"

"Beats me."

"What happens to a sick patient on Friday who requires a follow-up on Saturday?"

"Couldn't tell you. Mr. Turner's office is one left, one right, another left, and keep going. It's on the other side of the entrance hall."

Turner's office was easy to find. His name was on the door. It was Turner who was hard to find. His secretary, tall, lithe, mascaraed brows offset by the blue paint on her upper lids, was dark ocher, enveloped in lilac. Even her fingernails were lilac.

"Excuse me, Where can I find Mr. Turner?"

"I'm sorry. He's in conference."

"When will he be finished?"

"I'm sure I don't know." She turned back to her typewriter to continue reading a paperback that lay open across the keys.

I returned to the clinic wing. A blue-smocked Puerto Rican girl was leading a patient out of Dr. Das' office.

I might as well meet Das. I knocked and entered. He was an Indian. His straight black hair was stiffly pomaded.

"Ah, yes, I knew you would come," he said. "I have been waiting eagerly to meet you." I stuck out my hand, and he demonstrated his eagerness by waiting about five seconds to decide whether or not to shake. He decided yes, limply.

"Won't you sit down?"

I did, but at that moment a patient was ushered in. There was only one chair aside from the one Das was using and I was on it.

"You'll excuse me, Doctor, but my patient is here. Perhaps we can talk later. I would like to know more about you."

"Do you mind if I stay here while you examine the patient so I can get an inkling of the routine?"

"Oh, of course I don't mind. But the patient might. It would probably be better if you left. You know, here we try to provide the patient with the same dignity and privacy that he would get in a private office."

"And of course the same quality of medical care," I observed wryly.

"Of course," he hissed, holding open the door for me to leave.

I headed across the hall to the old utility room. No sooner had I crossed the threshold than I was confronted by a shrill scream.

225

"What are you doing here? Get out immediately." It came from behind the screen. I walked up and peered over the screen to see what was causing the commotion. A patient was in the stirrups buried beneath paper sheets, and a doctor—Matthews, I presumed—was doing an internal examination.

"Get out, get out at once," the shrill scream repeated. It was addressed to me.

A pale, plain girl, with dark-blond braids hanging over the back of her nurse's uniform, stopped whatever it was she had been doing to assist Dr. Matthews. She pointed an imperious finger and shrieked once again, "Get out."

I realized I had no white coat, and could have been just any stranger. "I'm sorry," I said, "I'm the new project director, Dr.—"

She didn't let me finish. "I don't give a goddamn who you are," she screamed. "Get out of here immediately. Women are entitled to privacy and decency when being examined. Don't you have any feeling at all for people, Doctor? This patient may be a Puerto Rican, but she's still a human being, and she has rights." Dr. Matthews had finished the bimanual examination and had extended her hand for the speculum.

"Maybe you could protect your patient's privacy and dignity more, and also help diagnose her problem, if you would be good enough to hand a speculum to Dr. Matthews."

"I don't need you telling me what to do," she trilled, off-key like an angry canary.

"Just hand her the speculum," I commanded. She was taken aback by my anger. She grumbled something and started to give the speculum to Dr. Matthews. Then stopped. "When you leave the room, I will hand the speculum to Dr. Matthews." Until now Matthews, her back toward me, was concentrating on the task at hand. Now she turned and smiled in an embarrassed way at me. Her large black eyes indicated the door. I left, so that she could finish the procedure.

Flo Furness met me in the hall. "Commotion seems to follow you around, Doctor."

"Perhaps," I said. "We can make rounds now."

"I think I better go with you. You seem to be getting into trouble on your own." She pulled a shorthand pad from the side pocket of her white coat, extracted a pencil from the breast pocket and said sweetly, "Where would you like to start?"

When we had finished the grand tour, I asked her to have a list typed and a duplicate put on my desk as a check list. I found it there later that afternoon.

1. Scrub all tile surfaces.
2. Repair toilet in utility room.
3. Procure a microscope for urinalysis in the laboratory (including a list of other basic requirements for simple laboratory tests).
4. Waste paper baskets in all offices and examining rooms.
5. Towel dispensers and soap dispensers in each bathroom, and over the sinks in the examining rooms. Particularly in the bathrooms used by the patients.
6. Burned-out light bulbs to be replaced.

And a few other items referring mainly to supplies.

I sat in Grady's office half-listening to his litany of problems.

"—and further, Harry. You will be running the place in my absence, indeed even when I am here. One thing—I would like you to keep an eye on Turner. He has to be brought down a peg or two. Let me know whether he is functioning efficiently—"

"Wait a minute. We only met once. Isn't he the agent for HUD?"

"That's the one. Believe me, Harry, I wish these people well. I've devoted my life to Community Medicine, to the best way of delivering health care to the masses of people, but Turner is cutting the ground from under me. I can't get financing for any of the things I need without going through him. He's supposed to be under me, but in reality the way he deals, I'm working for him."

"What am I supposed to do?"

"Impose your authority, Harry. I'd do it but I'm not here enough. With you on the premises, in the same building with him, he couldn't dare buck you if he knew you had my backing."

"Can I impose your authority on the nurses too?"

"What do you mean?" he asked sharply. "There's no problem with the nurses, is there, Harry? They have a mission. They are inspired. They'll do what's right."

"Will they do what I tell them?"

"Of course they will, Harry—if what you tell them is right." There was no point in pushing that line of reasoning.

"I guess that will be all for now, Harry." I started to leave when

227

he called me back. "Harry, by the way, I have some complaints about the doctors. It seems they don't do thorough work-ups. Miss Furness documented some cases for me. Look into it, Harry. I'm depending on you to run a tight ship."

Grady, although I did not appreciate the fact at the moment, was herald to the era of the disposable doctor.

Community Medicine suddenly blossomed across the country like a late-blooming flower, the poppy most likely, to dispense its opiate brew to the community. Financed by federal grants, the medical schools created departments of Community Medicine as a specialty and staffed them with doctors like Grady and nurses like Norah Rubin, who were fundamentally social workers explanted from the profession of medicine. Medically inarticulate, they were able to leapfrog to positions of power they could never have attained either in practice or in the more traditional academic disciplines of medicine. They were the advance men of the soft sciences, empowered to create Community Health Centers to distribute health care, whatever that is, to the poor.

The morning was busy. The waiting room was filling rapidly. Petite aides in their teens and blue smocks bustled purposefully, guiding patients, carrying charts, running messages, conducting inquiries, in either broken English or fluent Spanish. In the waiting room a huge man was draped almost supine over a chair too small for his bulk. His forehead was beaded with sweat. I stopped one of the little couriers in the hall and suggested that, since he appeared to be sick, he be taken first. She nodded and hurried away. I went after her.

"Do you understand what I said?"

She said, "Sí," looked up at me defiantly and went on her way.

I went to the "laboratory," that musty room with an old wooden laboratory bench that must have been rescued from a demolished drugstore. I checked for equipment. The cupboards were bare.

Because of language difficulties between doctors and patients, because of an inability of many of the patients to verbalize, much of the medical history was a check list which had little substance and which no one took the pains to modify in instances when the case demanded a new line of questioning.

228

The nurses measured only those vital signs that satisfied their private intuitions. If a patient looked feverish, they took his temperature; if he looked flushed, they might decide that a blood pressure was in order. But there was no routine.

None of the rooms offered privacy for disrobing. In the course of an examination clothes would be scattered about the room as if a washing machine had suddenly gone berserk in the spin-dry cycle. A rude bench was provided for the palpable physical examination, which was mainly eschewed by the doctors. As Das explained, "After all, Doctor, we are, as you know, very busy here. We are conscientious, but we do not have time to perform the complete examination. And medicine isn't that complicated." He paused, waiting for me to assimilate his wisdom, then proceeded with a demonstrative lecture. "If," he said, "a patient has pain here"—he clutched his chest—"it must mean that his heart is involved. We will make an appointment for an EKG and draw blood for enzymes."

"And how long does that take, Dr. Das?"

"Oh, not long," he said. "They accommodate us at the medical center, and the results will be back in a few days, unless of course a weekend intervenes. But let me continue. If the pain is here"— and he placed his hand over the right upper quadrant—"we are probably dealing with gall bladder disease. To the left of that, an ulcer may be suspected. CVA tenderness is kidney, and so on. You must know these things, of course." He smiled generously.

"For instance, Dr. Das, suppose someone comes in with dysuria?"

"Oh, that is no problem. We take a urine specimen. If the symptoms are severe, we will initiate treatment; if not, we wait for the results."

"It can't take long to run a urine. All you have to do is to insert a chemically treated paper dip stick into the urine and see if the colors change."

"But of course. However, we don't have the facilities."

"I can go to the corner drugstore and get you a dip stick."

"Can you also get us a microscope? Of course, Doctor. You will try to improve things. We are aware of our inadequacies. That is why we depend on you." He smiled sweetly.

I returned to my office and called Al Roscoe.

"Hello, sweetheart. How's our doctor today? Everything copacetic?"

"Not bad. How's chances of my getting some equipment for the laboratory?"

"Great. Call Willie Turner. He's in charge of purchasing."

"I seem to have trouble reaching him."

"Try him, sweetheart. If you got any problems with him, let me know. I'll frost his little ass if he don't cooperate. I got the community behind me. You're not afraid of him, are you, white boy?"

"Bye-bye, blackbird," I said and hung up.

Turner's phone didn't answer. I walked to his office. His secretary was doing her nails. "Phone out of order?" I asked.

"No. It rang."

"Is Turner in?" She waved an elegantly manicured hand at his office door.

Turner, legs on the desk, was looking out the window. "Did you ever see such a crummy neighborhood?" he muttered.

"Al Roscoe said you could get me some laboratory equipment."

"When's that fucker gonna learn to keep outta my affairs?"

"He's not in your affairs. I called him, and he referred me to you."

"I'll get you anything you want, boy. Just send me a requisition."

"Do you have the requisition forms?"

"Naw, you gotta secretary. Dictate a memo and list what you need."

I returned to my office and practiced on the Dictaphone. I said "shit" three times. The fidelity was excellent. I erased and started the memo. The list was long. I left the tape on the desk for my secretary, whoever she might be.

Turner called me several days later.

"I got your memo, boy. Run over here and read it to me."

When I got to his office, he showed me the list. It was neatly typed.

> testoobs
> mikraskope
> spektrafotomita

The spelling got worse as it went along. "Doesn't she have any 'c' on the typewriter?" I asked.

"This girl doesn't know medical words, Doc. You gotta explain these things to her."

"Sure. But I expected that she would give me the rough copy, not hand it in to you. Then I could make corrections."

"Shit, Doc, we ain't got time for that poky stuff. We gotta buzz along and get things done."

"Well, if you want to buzz along, give me about twenty bucks and I can start off with some bare essentials. I'll shop for them myself this afternoon."

"Where am I going to get twenty bucks?"

"Don't you have any petty cash?"

"Who's gonna trust a po' nigra like me with twenty bucks?" He went into his drawl.

"Oh, come off it, Turner. I want to get some work done here."

"You implying that we ain't getting work done?"

"We could do better."

"Man, I'm here to oversee the funds from HUD. And they got auditors and accountants watching me. However, I think your heart is in the right place. I'll push this stuff for you."

"Actually, Turner, all I want is an old microscope for urines. We can pick one up for about two hundred bucks. Another thirty will get us some material for blood counts. That will do for starters. We can upgrade the lab afterward. But we really ought to start. The patients are getting it right up the ass here. They have to wait four to five days for results of the simplest lab tests to come back from the medical center. Treatment is delayed. They deserve better than that."

"An' you gonna change everything with a po' little ol' micro-scope?" Turner used shuffling diction.

"You're fucking well informed I'm gonna change all that with a po' little ol' microscope." I shuffled with him. " 'Cause if there's pus in the piss, I'm gonna see it, an' if there's pneumonia in the sputum, I'm gonna see it, an' if there's cancer in the lungs, I may see it, an' a lotta things like that."

Turner took his legs off the desk. "Okay," he said. "I'll see what I can do."

"I'll bet that I could scrounge up some of this stuff, discards at the medical center that have been stored away."

"We don't do that here. All our stuff is new, it goes through our purchasing agent who puts it out on bid."

231

"How long does that take?"

"Three to four months."

"It figures," I said, and walked out.

An angry voice rumbled through the hallways like a roll of a kettle drum. "What the fuck d'ya mean, I gotta wait? I been waiting, man, since this goddamn place opened." There was a moment of silence, then the deep voice, incredulously saying, "Lunch? You mean I gotta wait till you motherfuckers go eat lunch? I'm sick." His frame filled the doorway completely with angry darkness. "No, I ain't waiting. Shit, you ain't runnin' no clinic, you runnin' a tea party." He was moving through the halls now with the insistent momentum of a boat in water. No one tried to intercept him. He was the only one moving. For a moment the place resembled a crowd scene at the wax works. Flo Furness and two nurses were in the hall leading to the doctors' offices. Turner's head poked from his office. The clerks were frozen like statues. When the angry patient left the building, everyone started moving again and the sounds of clinic business took over.

I followed Furness as she returned to her office. She busied herself with papers, ignoring the fact that I was standing in the doorway.

"What was that all about?" I asked.

"You heard it."

"Well, so I did. He may have a point. What was the matter with him?"

"A sore throat."

"He looked sick. Why didn't you have him attended to?"

"He should have waited," she said brusquely.

"We should be able to prevent that. Even if you take him into the medical area solely to take his temperature and then return him to the waiting room, the patient will think that his examination has begun. If, when the girls see that there's a long wait, they will take the trouble to explain this to the patients, I'm sure there would be less discomfort. Why don't we have the girls do this?"

"What girls?"

"You know, the aides and the nurses."

"Well then, Doctor, call them nurses. They're not girls and we

232

resent this male put-down. How would you like it if we referred to the doctors as 'the boys'?"

"Dr. Matthews is a girl, or possibly a woman by now. Incidentally, we're always discussing protocol. Doesn't anyone talk about medicine around here? My job is patient care. Could we address ourselves to that for a change, Flo?"

"Sure, Harry. You don't mind if I call you Harry?"

"I don't give a damn what you call me as long as we get the job done. The table of organization you gave me says I'm the boss."

"We don't have bosses. We work together, we are equals. Dr. Grady doesn't like to have any discrimination."

"Who is Dr. Grady?"

"He's the head of this place."

"Is he the boss?"

"We don't have bosses. Ask him. He'll tell you."

"Okay, I'll ask him. Now would you be good enough to ask your nurses and aides to please do as I suggest. Start the patients through by taking temperatures, shortly after they come in. Pay attention to them. Weed out the sick, apologize to the well patients when you put someone ahead of them. In other words, Flo, just a little common sense and courtesy."

"You're breaking up our routine. We haven't time for that."

"Make time for that."

"We don't work that way here, Harry. If you insist, we will call a meeting and discuss the issue. If you can persuade the nurses that this is the best way, you'll have your way, but if not, we will vote you down."

"Will the aides and orderlies be at the meeting?"

"No."

"Don't they have a vote?"

"They work for us. We'll tell them what to do."

"Are you their boss?" She didn't answer. "Five nurses telling twenty aides what to do. Why don't the aides have the same democratic rights you reserve for the nurses?"

"They are not professionals. They are members of the nursing department."

"Will the aides obey me?"

"You have no authority over them. They don't belong to the medical department. They belong to nursing."

233

"Isn't nursing part of medicine?"

"No. Nursing is an independent profession."

"Do you treat patients?"

"No. Our job is to take care of patients."

"Do you follow doctors' orders?"

"Sure, on medical matters."

"Why don't you take the blood pressure on all the patients?"

"That's nursing. That's a procedure that we are entitled to do, and therefore we can decide when to do it, when it is necessary."

"Is the patient to be torn apart now, to be divided between nurses and doctors? Or can we keep him in one piece and each cooperate to establish his health?"

"Sure we can cooperate. The question is whether I'm supposed to cooperate with you or you're to cooperate with me. Nurses are sick and tired of being pushed around by doctors. We no longer will be the handmaidens of the doctors."

"Handmaidens of the patients, Flo, not the doctors. You're so caught up in the mishmash of women's rights, community rights, nurses' rights, that you can't even do your job right."

I spent part of the afternoon going over charts. They were not informative. Just brief notes.

Otitis media. Pain, 3 days duration. Rx. Tetracycline, ornade, span, neo syneph.

RLQ pain, 18 hours. Some guarding. Possible Ap. to hospital.

This was no clinic. It was a battalion aid station. A redeployment center.

I visited Prentice. "Joel," I said, "I see that you sent a patient home yesterday with 103-degree fever, advised her to take some aspirin and come back in a week. What happens between now and then?"

"What do you mean?"

"Well, you didn't prescribe antibiotics—"

"Of course not. There was no evidence of bacterial infection."

"Quite right. But then shouldn't she be seen tomorrow? Or can't we have someone see her, an aide for instance or a nurse, make a house call, and see how she's doing? A week is a long time."

"Well, suppose I gave her antibiotics and she reacted, or developed colitis?"

"I understand, Joel. I'm not questioning that. It's the lack of follow-up. I agree these might have occurred if you had prescribed antibiotics. But then I would have had the same question. Where the hell is the follow-up?"

"These cases are scheduled here weeks in advance. We can't squeeze in follow-ups. We haven't the staff to handle that load."

"Well, why don't you insist that in some way there is follow-up information? That the patient is contacted?"

Prentice's owl-eyes behind shell-rimmed spectacles were watery and benign. He said, "Look, Harry, before you came—"

I thought he was going to say that before I came everything was running smoothly, why do I have to stir things up, but he didn't. "Before you came here we were told that there would be patient follow-up. It's all in the prospectus we handed in to HUD. As far as they are concerned, it is being done, but actually follow-ups haven't been set up yet."

"Well, I think as a physician you should insist on it for your patients."

"Are you kidding?" he laughed. "I can't insist on anything. I'm just waiting for my residency to start, and trying to earn a few bucks in the meantime. If I insist on anything, they'll kick me out."

"Who would do that? Grady wouldn't do that. He wants the place to run. After all, it's a feather in his cap."

"I tried to talk to Furness. She wouldn't do it."

"How could she refuse?" As if I didn't know.

"She didn't. The next day I got a visit from Norah Rubin. She told me that Furness ran her own department and I wasn't to interfere."

"Grady wouldn't go along with that, would he?"

"Yes."

"For what reason?"

"Norah Rubin."

"Oh."

I was mulling that over in my office when I noticed a note on my desk. It said: "Call Mrs. Rubin in the am."

Grady called. "Harry, could you buzz over to my office?"

I enjoyed the trip. It took me outside to the city stench, a breath of fresh air after the embattled morning indoors. The kids skipped rope or played children's games with chalk. Older boys slouched in groups leaning on buildings. Heads dotting second-story windows watched the action on the street till, I guessed, the dusk occluded the view. I bounced up two flights to Grady's office. He looked like a schoolmaster in a sweater that should have been buttoned down the front.

"Well, how is it going, boy? You've got things moving, I bet. Everything under control?"

"Fine," I lied.

"Good. I understand Turner is giving you a hard time."

"Not really. He's just a slave of the system."

"Don't use words like that around here, Harry. You must develop a social conscience. You know, Harry, these people are sensitive about their past and we've got to respect their feelings."

"Look, Dr. Grady, I have some real medical problems to solve."

"The priority problem around here is public relations. If we solve that, the others will fall in line."

I got back to my office to find Norah Rubin waiting for me. She was thin, almost gaunt, titless in a blue cotton shift that followed a plumb line from her shoulders to her knees. She tried to liven her ascetic features with a pale red paint, applied carefully to her lips. Her fingernails were manicured, polished and colorless like the rest of her. Her arched eyebrows were the only curves in her entire figure. Her thin hands displayed a gold wedding band. She must have earned it through force of personality.

"I wonder if I could have a few words with you, Doctor?" she said with a forced flicker of a smile that suggested this might become an unpleasant interview.

I leaned back in my swivel and nodded.

"You are coming on a little strong, and some of the nurses have ruffled feathers. I know you want to get things done, but it takes time and tact." I was too tired to go that route again.

"You realize, Miss Rubin—"

"Please call me Norah."

"Okay, Norah."

"The fact is, you have caused a lot of tension. You should be more gentle. More politic."

"About what?"

"Well, you've ordered some changes."

236

"It doesn't matter, the girls didn't do them anyway. I felt they should pay more attention to the patients in the waiting room. Take a little time and try to schedule the patients according to degree of illness rather than in the sequence of arrival. But in either case, to inform the people who are waiting what's going on, and when they will be seen. You know, just some public relations."

"I think there was more to it than that, Harry."

"Like what?" I figured there must be a pretty serious complaint to have Rubin step in like this.

"Wasn't there something about blood pressures?"

"I asked Furness to have the girls do TPR's on all the patients."

"Do you think that's necessary?"

"Necessary? It's good practice. You can't tell whether a blood pressure or temperature is elevated until you measure it."

"They are much too busy for that, Harry. They do it when it is necessary."

I was having a *déjà vu*. "Then the doctors can do them. They have the time. The point is, they should be entered on the chart with each visit."

"That won't do, Harry. That's the job of the nurses."

"Who said that?"

"It's always been their job. In any hospital or clinic where do you see doctors taking TPR's?"

"Norah, I'm not taking the job away from the nurses. They don't do the job. Are you trying to tell me that if the nurses refuse, then it won't be done—it's not to be done?"

"We are a highly trained profession. Don't encroach on it. Nurses no longer are handmaidens to the doctors."

"Look, I'm supposed to be project director. I'm supposed to run a service for the patients."

"Are you implying that our concern isn't for the patients, Doctor?" she asked frostily.

"No—I'm not implying anything—I just can't believe that I'm involved in this crazy conversation over a simple, obvious point."

"Harry." She became soothing. "Don't you see—if we don't maintain our integrity, our professional pride, our sense of ourselves as people, then we can't perform in the best interests of the patients."

The dialogue was getting out of hand. "What is your position here, Norah? I mean, are you in charge of the nurses?"

"We won't go into that now, Harry. There's a table of organization that covers everything. Actually I work for Dr. Grady in the Department of Community Medicine. We are trying to train a cadre of nurses here, so that when other community centers develop under Dr. Grady, our nurses will be able to deploy to the other centers and train new staffs."

"And all the centers will be under Dr. Grady?"

"Exactly. And hopefully, Harry, when you learn your job, become conversant with the politics, learn how to assemble the reports and write applications for funds, you will head up new centers and break in the new medical staffs. Dr. Grady is determined to deliver health care to the underprivileged, to the poor. He wants, in his own way, to make amends for the neglect that the medical profession has shown for the deprived masses. After all, they deserve the best. They are citizens with the same rights as you or I, Harry," she said piously.

"Well, how about starting right here? Show some solicitude for these people, here and now. I mean—make this a model. Then the word will spread, and the other communities will demand Dr. Grady's brand of care."

"We can't solve all the problems at once, Harry. And in our developing phases we have to make some compromises. Right now we have to build the staff that will spread out to envelop the city. So think about what we are trying to do, Harry, and help us out. Don't antagonize the nurses. And another thing. You had a salesman come in to show you new chart forms."

"So?"

"Wouldn't it have been nice to have Miss Furness and Mr. Turner at the meeting, and perhaps myself?"

"It wasn't a meeting. I was just getting information."

"But you acted independently of the rest of us. After all, Harry, the delivery of health care is teamwork. There is no room for solo fliers. You can't introduce new record-keeping systems without getting the approval of all of us."

"Even medical records?"

"Especially medical records."

I started shuffling some papers on my desk. "If you have any problems, Mrs. Rubin, take them up with Dr. Grady. I'm busy."

She tried to mollify me. "Be patient, Harry. You'll come around to our point of view when you see what Dr. Grady has planned."

"Incidentally, Norah, I'm supposed to chair a conference—social case histories—this afternoon. Do you know where and when?"

"Across the street in the back room at four o'clock. I thought Dr. Grady was chairing it."

"Maybe he is."

I walked slowly to a small lunch counter around the corner. The street arabesque was in full swing, bright colors, fluid body movements, laughter, curses, songs from an open window, torn curtains frolicking in the warm afternoon breeze.

Polly Stiner was seated alone. "Mind if I join you?" She nodded to the empty chair.

The waitress came by, and I ordered from the black-lettered sign above the counter. I looked questioningly at Stiner. "I've ordered," she said.

Suddenly I remembered. "Didn't I see you down here the other night? You were in Grady's car?"

"No," she said quickly.

"Strange, I could have sworn it was you. You have a very distinctive profile, you know."

"Yes, like a Russian wolfhound." She stared at her coffee and folded her lower lip under the upper.

"What makes you so happy all the time?" I asked.

"Would you pass the sugar, please?"

I complied.

"I'll never go with a married man again," she said softly.

"Grady?"

She nodded.

"What happened to your marriage?"

"What marriage?"

"Well, you have kids, don't you?"

"Yes, two. But it wasn't a marriage."

"Well, you made love twice, didn't you?"

"Sure, in the dark," she said, her eyes enlarging as she looked up for the first time.

"So tell me, Polly. Why did you split? Sex problems?"

"He leaned on me all the time. Leaned, leaned, leaned. He'd go

239

out to the beach and he'd spend the whole day asking me if he was getting an even burn. But when I needed him, he was nowhere to be found. So one day I came down to breakfast and I said I wanted a divorce."

"What did he say?"

"Nothing. He moved out of the house. His things had already been packed!"

"Prepared for any eventuality!"

"Apparently."

"It's hard to believe."

"It's true."

"How many years were you married?"

"Ten."

"And that's the way it broke up? I mean, you didn't discuss it?"

"What's to discuss?"

"I mean—didn't you have an argument?"

"We never argued."

She had a strange distant softness. Her femininity was forged of a resignation that fell short of hopelessness, and a sadness that was saved by brief unanticipated thrusts. "Someday, I'm going to write a book called 'F.'" By the time she said that we had both eaten.

Grady graciously moved from the chair and offered it to me. "A signal day, Harry," he said. Then he turned to the group waiting expectantly at their seats bordering the long scuffed oaken table, and said, "This will be the first meeting chaired by our new project director."

Norah Rubin sat next to Grady, then Furness, Margie Roller, Beverly Lloyd and Ethel Warren. Broda Laine was a new name and a new face. Rubin introduced her to me. "Mrs. Laine is head of Social Service."

"Harry," Grady said, "we have old business. A case report. I had mimeographs made. There is one in front for you. If you take a minute to look it over, I'll move that we dispense with the reading of the minutes."

Rubin quickly seconded the motion, and I started to read.

Case of D.M. Purpose of conference. To discuss child abuse. D.M. is a 40 year old black female, mother of five children, each by different fathers. Whereabouts of the fathers is unknown. D.M.

works during the day and gets back home about 3:30 pm. Is reported to be out frequently at night. Two children live at home. Oldest of the two at home is a girl, age 7. Youngster, a boy, age 5. Mother brought boy to clinic at Community Health Center last week. Boy had bruises over body, contusions on forehead, ecchymoses of both eyes. Child said he fell. Mother seen late that evening, staggering in the street, obviously drunk. D.M. known to have violent temper and makes threats of bodily harm frequently. Complains about children. Has reputation as a troublemaker.

D.M. has been frequent visitor to clinic for her own medical problems. She complains of headache and abdominal pain. She fails to improve despite all therapeutic measures taken over the past six months. Each time she comes in she makes nasty remarks, and has tried to destroy our reputation amongst the neighbors. She complains that the quality of care "stinks" and that she wouldn't send her dog to the place.

During D.M.'s visits she is accompanied by her children and staff has observed her striking the children. The staff feels that her punishments are excessive, and that she has abused her child and votes unanimously to have the courts seek custody of the children.

"Since I don't know the woman and have no familiarity with the facts as presented or the role that the Center can play in these cases, perhaps Mrs. Furness would like to start the discussion," I suggested.

She nodded appreciatively. "Well, the fact is that D.M. has stepped out of bounds once too often. She is our patient, although a thankless one. But we are charged with delivering health care to the community, so that child abuse becomes our responsibility. The child is also a member of the community and we have to protect him." She stopped abruptly.

I looked around expectantly. Silence. "Any comments?" Grady motioned. "Yes, Dr. Grady?"

"To bring you up to date, Harry, we voted to bring this case to the authorities. We must show the community that they can depend on us."

"She is a troublemaker," Norah Rubin murmured.

"Yes," said Grady. "She's obviously an unfit mother. What do you think, colleagues?"

The faces of the nurses lighted up. One of them broke in. "This

241

wasn't the first time. I've seen her almost tear the kid's arm out of his socket dragging him down the hall to the pedie clinic."

"What does the community say about her, Mrs. Laine?"

"They don't like her. They think something ought to be done and they look to us for leadership," Laine said, her tight-skinned face betraying the shrinkage of tissues that often follows plastic surgery.

"Any comment, Harry?" Grady was now leading the meeting.

"What does D.M. say about this?" I asked.

"You don't expect her to admit this, do you?" asked Norah Rubin.

"It seems proper somehow that she be given a chance to answer."

"She's not a nice person, Doctor," said Broda Laine. "We must deal firmly. Otherwise our credibility with the community will melt away."

"Like snowflakes on a warm pavement," added Grady. He smiled, enjoying his lyrical platitude. "What's the follow-through, Broda?"

Broda was assertive. She spoke clearly and slowly.

"D.M. and the problem of child abuse is the subject of a petition that we had our lawyers draw up in behalf of the community at large. The petition was submitted to the Orphans' Court, and a hearing will be held in the fall term. Any other evidence in behalf of D.M.'s child will be appreciated, and will probably be useful when the petition is heard."

Broda's statement pleased everybody. Nods of assent circled the room like falling dominoes. The remainder of the meeting was trivial. Furness read into the record the monthly statistics, which would later be used in progress reports to satisfy the government that so many patients had been treated, to demonstrate how well the tax monies were being spent.

After it was over I went to see Al Roscoe. He was on the telephone. He beckoned me to enter, finished his conversation rapidly and hung up. His office, except for the telephone and decrepit furniture, was empty. There wasn't a book, a pen or pencil on his desk, nor a picture on the wall. "Well, Moses, y'all gonna deliver my people to the promised land?"

Roscoe always fell into his colloquial drawl when talking to me, and I never knew whether he did this as friend or enemy.

242

"You know D.M.?"

"No, should I?"

"Yes. A woman called Dolly Matson."

"Yeah, everybody knows Dolly. Why?"

"I want to speak to her."

"Go speak to her."

"I'd like you to come with me."

"Why? You afraid to go alone?"

"She doesn't know me. I would like you to introduce me."

"You ain't my responsibility, Harry. You scared to walk amongst us niggers?"

"Frankly, yes. Shouldn't I be? You have a high death rate and an insignificant rate of resurrection in this neighborhood. Why won't you take me? You 'fraid to walk amongst your niggers?"

"You wanna get your mouth busted, you keep talking like that."

"I just asked you to introduce me to Dolly Matson. You represent the community. She's a member of the community. Maybe I can help her."

"How could you help her?"

"They're trying to take her kid away from her."

"Yeah, I heard that. She abused that kid."

"How do you know that?"

"Man, everybody knows that."

"Did you talk to her?"

"I don't waste my time on nonsense."

"Well, I think someone ought to hear her side of the case."

He dug into his drawer and pulled out a large loose-leaf notebook and started flipping pages. Then he wrote something on a piece of paper and handed it to me. "Here's her address. Go there yourself. But not after dark."

The street was warm and the lengthening shadows loomed ominously before the setting sun, its light halo in the smog-filled sky occluded by the uneven skyline of the city. I walked past boarded storefronts. The brick and mortar of the buildings were decaying like rotted teeth. There were neither stores nor vendors, no peddlers, no pushcarts, no one with wheelbarrows probing the trash for junk. There was nothing to buy, and no place to sell anything.

Black boys swaggered in club jackets and groups clustered in alleyways displaying and comparing weapons. There were no games.

Dolly Matson lived in a people-battered building. A partly painted door showed the colors of other years and other tenants. A rusted knocker hung askew. A bell button dangled uselessly, pulled like a rotted eye from its socket. The shadow of a figure looming behind me fell across the door. I braced myself. "Can I help you?" a voice asked softly.

I turned. A huge tan man, about twenty, wearing a white shirt partly covered by a sleeveless wool pullover sweater stood behind me on the steps.

"I'm looking for Mrs. Matson."

"C'mon, I'll show you." I followed him up one flight of stairs. He pushed on the door and we entered a dingy hallway. I followed to a brightly painted deck-gray door. The knob turned easily. "Ma," he called as we entered. "A man here to see you."

The room, well lighted, was carpeted with patched remnants. The walls were freshly painted. The old furnishings were in good repair. "What's he want, Junior? I ain't gonna' buy nothing."

I explained to Junior that I had come from the Community Health Center.

"He says he's from the clinic, Ma. He wants to talk to you."

"Throw him out, Junior. He ain't no friend of ours."

Junior took hold of my arm and persuaded me through sheer strength to turn toward the door. I had remembered suddenly that she was the woman who had consulted Lapius. "Wait a minute, Junior. Tell her Dr. Lapius sent me."

Junior stopped long enough to shout that information over his shoulder. Suddenly there was a commotion in the rear of the apartment and a door slammed. "Bring him to the kitchen, Junior."

Without changing the force of his grip, Junior wheeled around and walked me to the kitchen. An old painted table, partly covered by oilcloth, was set against one wall. There was a gas stove near the window, and an old refrigerator rattled under cupboard shelving.

An obese woman with flared nostrils and full lips sat at the table. Two braids descended like ropes from her stockinged head. She wore a house coat and slippers.

"Sit down, Mister." I did. Junior leaned against the door jamb.

"I been waiting to hear from Dr. Lapius. How do you know him?"

"I do some work for him sometimes."

"I thought you said you worked for the Community Health Center."

"I do."

"Then you can't be working for Dr. Lapius."

She eyed me defiantly. Junior lounged in the doorway. I explained that Lapius had asked me to look into the matter between herself and the Health Center before I took the job, and that the fact that I now worked there was just a coincidence. "How do you know about Lapius?" I asked her.

Junior answered. "He helped me once several years ago. I figured maybe he could help Mom."

I extracted a copy of the Health Center report on Dolly Matson from my inside pocket and handed it to her. "Read this and tell me what you think of it."

"What is it?"

"It's a copy of the report by the staff of the Health Center that will be used as a basis for the court proceeding."

She picked it up, stared at it for a moment and threw it down on the table.

"Well?" I asked.

"You read it, Junior."

Junior picked it up, read it to himself and swore.

"Let me read it to you, Momma." He read it slowly, and after he had finished I asked Dolly, "Is it true, Mrs. Matson? How did the boy hurt himself?"

"He was coming up the stairs behind me with some groceries. I guess he slipped when he reached the top and tumbled down the whole flight."

"What did you do?"

"I dropped my packages and ran down. He was knocked out. I held him and after a little while he woke up. Then I brought him upstairs and he slept a while. When he woke up, I took him down to the Health Center. But they did like they always do. They give him a half-ass examination and send us home. That was the last I heard till the lawyer tol' me they was trying to take him and his sister from me."

"Where is he now?"

245

"On the street. He'll be back soon."

"Has he had any other problems?"

"Not as I know."

"Well, Momma, you tell him that baby dozes off sometime. I've seen him do that a couple of times."

"That's true. Sometimes he'll be sittin' at the table and all of a sudden his head will drop down like he's asleep, then he wakes up after a while. I think he just playin' jokes on us. He's only a baby."

"Were you drunk that night?"

"More than probably."

"What happens to your children when you go out and get drunk?"

Junior answered. "I give Momma one night a week. I live down the block and come over here and baby-sit."

"Do you know she gets drunk?"

"Hell, yes," Junior said, laughing. "When she comes home like that, I bring her to my place to sleep it off and I stay here."

"You like your liquor, Mrs. Matson?"

"I sure do. Don't you?"

"I guess I do at times."

"Is this one of those times?"

"I guess I wouldn't mind," I said. She went to the cupboard and reached in, coming up with a bottle of bourbon.

"How do you take it?"

"Water and ice."

"Junior?"

"Straight, Mom." She poured the bourbon over ice and added water and two glasses straight, handing one to Junior. "We might as well relax a little."

Junior noticed my apprehension. "Don't worry. She's not an alcoholic. The only time she ties it on is when she's off for the night."

"Does she take good care of your brother and si.ter?"

"Hell, yes. Look, Doc. They aren't going to take the kids away. She's a good mother. She's been a good mother to all of us. I got another brother and sister old enough to go to court and say that. She never abused any of us."

"Is it true that you don't know who your father is?"

246

"He died before I was old enough to know him."

"And the others?"

"I didn't know them."

"They can paint a pretty damaging picture of your mother in court."

"Maybe. But there have never been strange men in this house. Whatever happened happened somewhere else, and you can't hang me for that. I'm human. No man gonna jump fences to marry me."

"Momma didn't have too many choices. Some of those men fed us for a while, and sometimes, particularly when Momma was pregnant, there wasn't much food around the house."

"Where are your other children?"

"Two of them live with my sister. She has a husband, but they have no children. They are growing up and almost in high school."

"Do they mind the separation?"

"There is no separation, Doc. This isn't like the way you live. Momma's sister lives down the block. The kids are always together. It's just that Momma can't feed them all, and my aunt wants children."

I finished my drink quickly and thanked Mrs. Matson.

"Oh, one last thing, Mrs. Matson"—I had almost called her "Momma"—"was it true that you were loud and nasty to the people at the Community Health Center?"

"Yes."

"Are you short-tempered?"

"When people hand me a lot of crap, I gets mad. When they treat me like dirt, I gets mad. I been going to that fuckin' center for months for cramps and headaches. Week after week they give me some medicine that dry my mouth, and then when I come back the next time I ain't no better, they get nasty."

"Who gets nasty?"

"The nurses. They make wise-ass remarks. They say, 'Here come Dolly again, always askin' us to fix her hangover,' and things like that. They ain't got no right to talk to me like that. I'm going there because I gets sick—"

"What does the doctor say?"

"He says I didn't take the medicine. If I did, I'd be better. He

247

says I drink too much and that's why I got the pains. He don't ever examine me, and talks in circles so I can never get any answers."

"Look, Mrs. Matson. Give me a few days to check your records and the boy's. Then I'll call you—"

"We better call you," Junior said. "We have no phone here."

"Fine, call me. I better be going. Thanks for the drink."

Junior unfolded himself from the door jamb and stood up straight. "I better walk you home, Doc. It's dark out."

The streets were empty. Darkness had scrubbed the squalor and erased the stigmata of poverty. Lighted windows made Mondrian panels of the great walls that lined the chasms of the ghetto.

Grady's car was parked in front of the building that housed his office. Mrs. Stiner's car was parked in front of his. A lone figure sat in a car parked near the corner. "That," said Junior, "is Mrs. Rubin. She has become curious. She is waiting to see whether Mrs. Stiner and Dr. Grady travel the same route."

"How do you know that?"

"Because every move a white person makes in this neighborhood is news."

Junior called a week later. I had reviewed the medical charts of the Matson family and they corroborated what she had told me. There was no doubt that the evidence against her was insubstantial, refutable, and that she would win the case.

I made an appointment for Dolly and her boy to come to the Health Center. A complete history on the boy suggested that he was having petit mal attacks and he was scheduled for an electroencephalogram. Dolly was a different story, and after a history and physical examination I referred her to Dr. Matthews for gynecological examination, which I attended, despite the baleful stares of Ethel Warren. Positioned behind Dr. Matthews, I was able to see the thick purulent exudate that coated Dolly's cervix. Smears and cultures were done. We had no microscope at the Center, so I pirated a smear and planned to look at it at Lapius's house that night. When it was over, I took Dolly into my office.

"You haven't always been a good girl, Dolly. Not only do you have a case of clap now, but I don't think this is your first attack."

"You gonna be like the others and pass judgment on me—"

"No, Dolly. I am making a diagnosis. Your abdominal pains are from the first attack. They have been recurrent over the years. I would guess that usually you'd go to a hospital and get some treatment and they would go away. But this time, for almost eight months, you got no treatment. The vaginal discharge is from your current attack. You'll be okay."

"And my baby?"

"I think he has a mild form of epilepsy. If the tests prove it, we'll put him on some medication. He'll be okay, too. You see, Dolly, he didn't slip on the stairs. He had an attack at the top of the stairs and lost his balance. So much for child abuse."

Dolly stood up and we shook hands. "Thank you, Doctor," she said, "very much."

Billy's electroencephalogram showed evidence of a convulsive disorder, and tests proved Dolly had the clap. I made copies of the records and mailed them to her and told her to return to the Center for medication. I kept a copy, and excerpted the findings in a final report for Lapius.

I brought the chart to Grady's office. Polly Stiner was busy typing. She stopped for a moment, pressed a buzzer, picked up the phone, cradled it between her cheek and shoulder and started typing again until Grady answered. Then through the staccato of the typewriter she spoke with him, replaced the phone and motioned me in.

Grady was pacing up and down, talking into a Dictaphone. When I entered, he motioned me to a chair, and rattled off a few paragraphs before replacing the microphone in its holder. I caught phrases like "community problems," "societal ills," "behavioral reflex," "population excess," "racial prerogatives," "ecological misuses," "population" and "economic distress." Not a single medical word in the entire batch. "Well, Harry, kin I help ya with anything?" He sounded particularly Irish now, compared to the flat, dull New York tones he enunciated while dictating.

I outlined briefly my interview with Dolly Matson, and the results of the tests and examination. I opened the charts and turned to the electroencephalogram, but Grady waved impatiently. "I'll take your word for it. Why bother me with these medical problems?" He was no longer jaunty.

"Well, the point is that there was no child abuse. Billy Matson had an epileptic attack and fell down the stairs."

"But we don't need that. The girls have other evidence. Broda Laine is very careful. The nurses will testify."

"I don't think it would be a good idea—"

"You don't think it would be a good idea?" he exploded. "Who asked you to get involved with this case? It's open and shut. She's a drunken whore. The whole neighborhood knows that."

"But that doesn't mean she abuses her child. As a matter of fact, I was impressed with the way she kept her home, and the way she handled the kid when she came to the office. Junior is a married man now, and he said he would testify in her behalf. Everybody has been telling me that the main item of business here is community relations—"

"Well, Dolly has had relations with everybody in the community," he said sardonically.

"—and when I patch something up, you seem to be sore. I think you should drop the case."

"Why?"

"Because you'll lose it."

"I don't think so. I think we can show that a whore and drunk is not a fit mother for children, and the community will back me up."

There was no point arguing. He was angry and annoyed that Dolly might wiggle off the skewer.

"Okay, I just thought you ought to know. I'll send you a copy of the medical reports."

He had collected himself somewhat. "Thank you, Harry. You've done an excellent job here. Although I think it was misdirected. I am sure you will be able to apply your talents more profitably in the future."

I walked out, closing the door behind me. "Fuck you," I said to myself.

Lapius was solicitous. He handed me a drink as soon as I was seated, and insisted that I put my feet up on the hassock. "Relax, Harry. You've had a busy day. You're trembling."

"Jesus Christ. That guy is going to take Dolly to court."

"No he won't, Harry. He'll think it over and realize that if he does indeed lose, it would jeopardize his position. Grady has an acutely developed sense of self-preservation."

"What the hell is going on over there, Simon?"

"If I were to hazard a guess, the nurses were frustrated by Mrs. Matson. They had been treating her for a year and had gotten nowhere, a fact that Dolly was not loath to remind them about. Dolly lacks weapons. Belligerence serves in their stead. She was showing them up, and they decided to punish her for not getting well."

Lapius had broken open a Napoleon brandy for me. The drink was warming, and I started to relax.

"Tell me, Simon, how did you meet Junior Matson?"

He sat down, sniffing his brandy. "Oh, that was several years ago. Apparently he had been accused of molesting some girl on the subway station platform. He was working for Jack Stacey at the time as a draftsman. Junior didn't know who to call, so he called Stacey and Stacey called me. I had some contacts at the Civil Liberties Union and persuaded them to send a lawyer to the hearing. Junior was resigned to going to jail. He protested his innocence, but didn't see how a black man could beat an accusation like that from a white woman. Well, the lawyer immediately picked up a few discrepancies in the girl's testimony, and badgered her into admitting that she had owed the policeman a few favors, and that the whole thing was trumped up. The case was dismissed."

"What happened to the policeman and the girl?"

"I don't know. But Junior was freed. And when this happened, he thought of me, and wondered whether I could get him that same lawyer again. But I thought of you instead. Aren't you glad?"

Before the Dolly Matson affair, I was an outsider at the Community Health Center. Afterward, I was an enemy.

The nurses acted like pettish sophomores whose plans for a cruel sorority initiation had suddenly been discovered. A crowd deprived of the violence it has conspired to commit, be it death or some lesser form, seeks another sacrifice. I figured to be it.

I had banked on Grady's sincerely wanting to pull this act together, but he was playing games, and rigged it so that the nurses were responsible, through Rubin to him, not to me. I was window dressing.

My options were limited.

251

Furness came to my office. "You still upset because that man with pharyngitis went home?"

"Partly."

"Our job is to deal with the community as a whole. We can't do this and cater to each individual. We are here to educate the community. You think of a nurse as someone who pushes thermometers and takes pulses and cleans up the shit when the doctors leave the room.

"Well, we are women and we are nurses, and we are no longer slaves of the doctors. You don't understand anything about this job. This community is like children. We got to educate them to the facts of life and to realities. When that patient with a sore throat walked out, he got an education."

I told her that I didn't quite follow her line of thought.

"You don't think that's education?" she said sharply. "You don't think that when he wakes up at two o'clock in the morning with his throat on fire that he'll remember, and next time he won't be so quick to walk out. He'll hang around to get treated. That's what I mean by education."

"Well, perhaps you have a point, Mrs. Furness. But on the other hand perhaps by providing the very best in medical services we would also provide the community with an education of how well medicine can be performed."

"You saying that we ain't performing well?"

"How about trying it my way?"

"Well, we'll have a meeting on it and see what the nurses say. It has to be agreeable to all before we put it into action. No one person has any power here. We act as a group. So if you can make your case, Doctor, we'll do it. How's that? Fair enough?"

"Frankly, Mrs. Furness, you nurses need an education."

"You got it backward, Harry. We nurses are gonna educate you doctors and teach you what your place is. You ain't no longer an elite group lording over us. You're no better than us, and we ain't taking no chicken shit from you."

At dusk, I ambled across the street to Grady's office. There was a shadow in his car. That profile again. I got Grady just as he was closing his office and made him open it "—for a few important minutes."

"I haven't much time Harry. Be brief."

"Yeah, I saw someone waiting in your car. But she can wait a minute."

Grady paled. I recounted the conversation with Furness.

"She thinks she has your tacit support, via Mrs. Rubin. All you have to do is make it unequivocally clear that I have the authority that goes with the title."

"But you have."

"Good. Then we'll replace Mrs. Furness. That would straighten out the whole mess and we could get started whipping the place into shape."

"You can't fire Mrs. Furness."

"That's what I thought. So I don't have the authority."

"Of course you do."

"Well, how do I make decisions stick?"

"Come on, Harry. Be politic. Make them love you. You could have those girls eating out of your hand."

"I don't want them to eat out of my hand. I would just like them to do as I ask."

"But you're upsetting their routine."

"Don't be naïve, Mike." Suddenly I understood, and spoke rapidly. "As a matter of fact, you're not naïve, are you? You know exactly what you're saying, don't you? You agree with Furness that if a guy walks out of the clinic the neglect that caused him to leave will educate him to his responsibilities as a citizen of the community. Translated to double-speak, that means damn well not criticize the Center, because then they won't take care of him when he's sick."

"Well, I wouldn't put it in such uncompromising terms, Harry, but I do believe that there is an educational value in that, and I have confidence that the nurses know how to deal with their people. I have to leave."

We walked the long halls and descended the worn wooden stairs. Suddenly, a flash of lights spun shadows off the wall. It came from a room I had not noticed before, a room separated from the landing by a partly opened curtain. I peered in. Fluorescent cartoons energized by dark lanterns lined the walls. In one corner a flickering purple filament danced crazily, illuminating shadowy figures with stroboscopic consistency. Sweet incense

253

floated from glowing embers in old coffee cans, and with each flash of strobe light I perceived more dark figures lounging on chairs or on the floor.

Grady grabbed my arm. "Come along," he said, "you're not allowed in there."

"Why? What's in there?"

"That's the clubroom for the boys. We're not allowed to enter. It's their private preserve. It's important for community relations. It's something they can call their own."

"What would happen if I walked in?"

"I wouldn't want to predict. After all, this is a community center—it's theirs. We're only guests here. We can't afford to offend the community."

"What would happen if the community knew you gave their kids a private den for smoking hash?"

"What makes you think they're smoking hash?"

"I smell it. Aren't the parents of those kids part of the community?"

"We have to make peace with these boys, Harry. Otherwise, our cars would be stripped down. We might have trouble getting out at night. I don't want trouble. We have an important mission here, and community relations are the crux of our program."

"You're afraid of these kids. You buy them off with drugs and rationalize it as community relations. After they prowl at night and maybe mug a few people for dough to support their habit you provide them a nice sanctuary to return to. Certainly the community consists of more than ten or twenty punks."

"You talk like a Victorian matron, Harry. Get wise, boy. This is the twentieth century." We were at the door. A surly black kid leaned against it. He was chewing a toothpick. "Hello, Leonard, would you excuse us? We're leaving."

Leonard remained immobile. Grady and I came to a dead stop. "Anything wrong, Leonard?"

Leonard was motionless, staring at us from under half-closed lids. He brought his hand out of his pocket and a blade flashed in the dim light.

Grady yelped, "Follow me," and wheeled about. We ran to a door in the next building, from which we emerged to the street. Polly Stiner was still in his car, waiting.

"Good night, Harry," Grady said as he went to his auto. I had an idea that Polly didn't like waiting alone in the darkening street.

I asked her about this the next time I met her at the grill.

"Don't you find it spooky waiting alone like that?"

She was sipping a Coke through a straw. Her eyes were lowered. She stopped long enough to say, "Yes."

"How did you get into this anyway?"

"It—I thought it was just a dalliance. I didn't take it seriously. But then it turned out to be very good."

"Well, after all, sex is crucial to a relationship, wouldn't you think? I mean, doesn't it forge the fundamental link?"

Stiner lowered her lids. She was obviously a woman who had to wrestle her words into a suitable alignment before she uttered them. She paused, working out the script. "No, it's not crucial to a relationship. It's crucial to love."

"So, what's the problem?"

"He's married."

The community was annoyed about the way the nurses were handling things. Roscoe complained bitterly and I no longer received those encompassing handshakes he reserved for his friends. "You better shape up, Harry. Get those fucking nurses under control."

"That's difficult," I told him. "I don't exactly have a mandate, you know. Grady is running the show. I can't do anything about it unless I have the authority."

"The authority to do what? Shit, man, you are the project director. What else you want?"

I told him I needed the authority to fire the nurses before things would change, namely Furness.

"No one is gonna give you that authority."

"Well," I said, "that's the point. The place is a mess. Only Grady can change it. Don't bitch to me."

"The community wants things changed. You are the project director. If things don't change, they'll chop you."

I left and sought Turner. "I'm supposed to ride herd on you. Grady's orders."

"You just try it, white boy," Turner drawled, a big smile on his

255

face, his hand curling tightly around a letter opener, suddenly converted in his catatonic grip to a weapon.

I smiled. "Seriously, Willie. Why is Al Roscoe afraid to tackle Grady?" I quickly related our encounter.

Turner propped his feet on the window sill adjacent to his desk and stared out the window.

"It just so happens, little man, that Roscoe's salary comes out of Grady's budget. I'm paid by HUD. I'm the only guy around here whose salary Grady doesn't control. Me, I'm free. I'm the only one can frost his ass, when the time comes."

"So talk turkey to him, Willie. These are your people here."

"They ain't my people, man. I don't come from this shit hole. I'm just here doing a job."

"Why don't you talk to Grady? You could cut the funds for the whole project if you wanted to. You got a big club over his head. Why don't you use it?"

"I won't talk to Grady because I ain't got nothing to go on. Roscoe ain't talked to me. He's got to make a written complaint, and he won't put nothing in writing."

"Well, I'm talking to you."

"Maybe, but that ain't official. I gotta get it from Roscoe. And in writing. I can't go around threatening to cut funds without substantiation. And if I don't have substantiation, Grady will cut off my black balls, which is what he got you here to do. And I ain't gonna give him the chance."

"So, where does it lay?"

"Right there, man. You ain't the first project director we had and won't be the last."

"Who will be the last?"

"The last one, if he got brains, will keep his fucking eyes closed and his mouth shut."

"Well, there's a lot of people around here not getting what you're paying for, so you better do something."

"Maybe I will, but I won't speak to Grady. There is another way around this."

"What's that?"

"Rubin. She got the hots for Grady."

"He's married."

"That don't mean a shit. Where you been, man? Rubin thinks she's married to him already, only he won't make it real for her.

256

They used to go home together every night. Now he works late. And now that little redheaded girl with the big nose slips into his car and they drive home."

"Oh?" I said, as if receiving startling information.

"Yeah, I think I'll have a talk with Rubin. It'll stir things up a little. And I owe him that much for sending you to cut me down."

The next week at lunch Polly Stiner slipped into my booth. She was tense and shaken.

"I can't see him for a while," she whispered.

"Can't see whom?" I asked.

"I don't want to talk about it," she said, compressing her lips as if she had made a slip that now she wanted retracted.

"It's a nice day," I said, peering through the dirty window to justify my claim. She nodded. A tear rolled from the corner of her eye. Just one. She wiped it away. She didn't sniffle. After a while I rose, picked up her check with mine and said, "Look, if you're upset, call me later."

She nodded.

She showed up the following night. I took her coat and mixed a drink. She pulled out a cigarette and struck the match before I could unwedge a lighter from my pocket. She sat stiffly in a wing chair.

"Grady said he didn't want to get involved with another family. I spoke to my ex-husband and he agreed to take the kids."

"Perhaps it's just as well," I said.

"He said he would marry me. He would get a divorce in a few months. I'm in limbo. I'm between two shores—" Then suddenly the troubled parts of her brain became joined again. "The children moved in with their father last month. But now he says we can't see each other for a while. I feel that something dreadful is happening."

"Look, Polly," I said, trying to console her. "If Mike said he would marry you, he will. He knows you gave your children away. He doesn't want you to have to share the burden of guilt as he sheds his wife. He wants you out of the picture. You wouldn't want it otherwise. You should be flattered by his solicitude."

She rose, walked to where I was sitting, extended her hand, and said, "Thank you, Harry. Good night."

"Good night."

My office was occupied by five blacks. One sat in my chair, his filthy shoes propped on my desk. Two blocked the doorway. Two leaned against the wall. I carefully squeezed in between the two at the doorway. Touching either of them, I thought, would have incendiary consequences.

"What can I do for you fellows?" I asked. They said nothing but kept eying me. I repeated the question. No response.

I walked over to my occupied chair. "Excuse me. I've got some work to do." The black seated there rose slowly. He knocked the blotter off the desk as he lowered his feet. I bent to pick it up. A key chain swung close to my head as I leaned over. I replaced the blotter. I sat in my chair and pulled some papers from the drawer.

"Anything I can do for you?" I said, looking up. I smiled trying to hide my fear.

"Naw, Doc. We just come over to size you up to see if you're doing a good job."

"Well, if there's anything I can do for you, let me know." They stood there. Finally the one who had been in my chair said, "Where you keep the medicines in this place?"

"In the medicine cabinets."

"You want to show us where that is?"

"Not particularly."

"We would consider it a big favor if you showed us where it was."

"I couldn't do that without permission from Dr. Grady."

"But we thought you was the boss."

"That's an error. He's the boss."

"You not calling me a liar, are you, Doc?"

"No. It's just that Grady is the boss. He's my boss. Go to him." I stood up. "Look here. You have no business here. This is a medical office. I'm asking you to leave my office."

"What makes you think it's your office? It's our office. This whole place belongs to the community." The others watched sullenly.

"The whole goddamn city may be yours. But meanwhile I was hired to run the project. While I'm running it I have the use of the office. You have no business here. So clear out." I was agitated now, my hands spread on the desk.

"You gonna throw us out?"

"Obviously I can't throw you out. I'm asking you to be good neighbors and allow us to continue to work."

The ringleader turned to the others. "Should we let the man work?" They nodded, as if on signal. Then he leaned across the desk and gave me a shove that catapulted me back into the chair. My head banged against the wall.

"Okay, Doc. Go to work then. And you better do a big job, or we'll be back." My ears were ringing and I saw flashes of light. When my head cleared, the room was empty. I rubbed at my whiplashed neck. I walked from the office. The gang was making a commotion in the hall. Furness came out of her office to see what the fuss was about. I walked up to her. "Tell them to get out," I hissed. "I don't want any noise in the halls. The patients have a right to privacy, and peace and quiet."

The boys overheard me and turned sullenly. I approached the guy who had shoved me. "What are you going to do? Kill me to prove that you have the right to disrupt this place? We're trying to take care of community people here. I thought you'd like that. That was the big headline when I came here. That the community should be given good medicine and treated with dignity. Well, there's no dignity with you guys jiving in the halls."

I turned and walked back to my office. If they were going to shove again, let them shove me from behind. At least I'd see where the hell I was going. But there was no shove. The hubbub in the hall continued for a few minutes, and they filed out.

The next day I got a memo from Norah Rubin. It said that Dr. Grady was calling a staff meeting at 4 P.M. I was supposed to call staff meetings, but if Grady wanted to do it, it was okay with me.

When I entered, Grady was already seated. He motioned me to an empty chair flanked by a nurse on either side. He began as soon as I sat down.

"It is our practice when a member of our group does something that the other members feel is contrary either to policy or to the image we are trying to project, to have an encounter. Not so much a confrontation, but a sensitivity session. We take the opportunity to point out to the member his fault, and the methods he can take to remedy his errors. This is purely a staff function, and I sit merely as a witness. I do not participate in the meeting. . . ."

He droned on for a while, and I became interested in searching the faces of those assembled to see if I could find who was going to be sensitized. Norah Rubin sat with her chin thrust belligerently forward, resting on the bridge of her clasped hands. She looked straight ahead. Flo Furness sat diagonally across, doodling on some papers before her. Beverly Lloyd, Margie Roller, Ethel Warren, Willie Turner and Al Roscoe completed the circle. This ought to be interesting, I thought.

Grady continued: ". . . and so I am going to turn the meeting over to Mrs. Furness."

Furness straightened up in her seat like a spectator at a prize fight when the bell rings for the first round. "I asked Dr. Grady to call this meeting because we, the nurses, feel that the project director is behaving in such a way as to destroy what we have built up here. He is insensitive to the feelings of others. He treats the nurses as assistants, and has dealt with the community in such a way as to seriously jeopardize our rapport, and, as a result, our mission."

It took almost the duration of her speech to have it sink in that I was the star of this chamber proceeding.

"Now I want to call on Mrs. Rubin."

Norah kept her chin on the bridge of her hands, and spoke while staring straight ahead. She looked to neither right nor left, and seemed totally disinterested in what was being said. She seemed marbleized, made of pale polished stone, thrust into bas-relief by the black and brown hues of her colleagues, and the pliant mobility of their features.

"The problem came to my attention almost the first day that Harry arrived. He swung into action. He didn't wait to make acquaintances, but marched off on inspection tours, and drew up lists of improvements he wanted Mrs. Furness to carry out. Clearly, the approach was brutish, arrogant, with no thought for the feelings of the people with whom he was dealing. I think that Beverly has something to add."

Beverly was a short, belligerent, light-skinned black girl. I scarcely knew her.

"First, he called us 'girls' instead of 'Miss' this or 'Miss' that. I don't care if he's a doctor or not, unless he calls me by my last name I call him Harry. We are no longer serving the doctors blindly, saying 'Yassuh,' like slaves. I am a member of a great profession, a proud nurse. I refuse to take orders from doctors, and Harry was giving us orders. I can only work with him as an equal."

"Is that all, Beverly?" Norah asked. Beverly nodded. "All right then. Ethel?"

Ethel Warren was white, pale, her straight hair parted centrally and combed back on either side of her slim head to a short ponytail.

"Harry had no manners and no sensitivity for the feelings of others. He barged into the gynecology examining room on several occasions despite repeated warnings to knock, never to enter until the patient had been properly warned that he might enter. He had no regard for the sensitive feelings of our Puerto Rican sisters, who were being exposed." Oh, Christ, that's right. She was the one who had screamed. I had forgotten. All the nurses were starting to look alike in the eye of my memory.

"He burst in and disrupted the entire procedure. The patient was so embarrassed she begged me to cover her face. He should know that the Puerto Rican sisters are sensitive about their genitalia, particularly when they are hanging out like that—" Norah Rubin interrupted. "Thank you, Ethel."

Willie Turner leaned over to me and murmured, "That's a laugh. That spic bitch they're talking about has paraded her pussy in plain daylight in front of every man and man-child in the area. She's well known. Matthews has to check her once a month routinely for clap. Shit, man, Grady can't hang you for that."

"Great, Willie," I whispered back. "Will you address those comments or at least a reasonable paraphrase to the meeting at large?"

"Shit, no."

"You might help me."

"I don't care what happens to you, man. I might even join in, but I don't like the man Grady, so I'll stay neutral."

Grady cleared his throat. "I think Mr. Roscoe has a comment to make." That was news to Mr. Roscoe.

"Al," Grady coached, "didn't you have some feelings about what happened with the juveniles?"

Roscoe was clearly uncomfortable. "Well, there was a little problem. Harry and the kids had a sizing-us-up session, but it was nothin' serious."

Furness stood up and waved a finger at Roscoe. "What d'ya mean, it wasn't serious? Go on, why don't you tell about it?"

"Mainly because I wasn't there. All I know about it I heard from you and Mrs. Rubin." That was interesting. Mrs. Rubin hadn't been there either.

"Well," Furness said scathingly staring at Roscoe, "if some of our male community leaders are too scared to stand up and be counted, I'll tell what happened. This so-called project director insulted those young men who were in his office. He deperson-alized them. He denigrated them, he humiliated them—" Now she was getting shrill, sawing her arms up and down to create the tempo for her attack.

I had had enough of this garbage.

"Just a minute," I interrupted, but she shouted me down, her voice straining with rage. "I'm not finished. You taunted those boys. You threw them out of their own building." Suddenly it was coming from all sides. Beverly and Ethel, their voices piling up on top of Flo's, created the spine-tingling scream of bows torturing the strings of cheap fiddles.

Grady raised his right hand, like a witness taking the oath. Suddenly there was quiet, as if a sound track had been cut with scissors.

"Yes," I said quietly, "I'd like to answer some of these charges."

"Come now, Harry. We don't look at these statements as charges," Grady said. "If you start off that way, why, you will have missed the spirit of the meeting. The purpose is to accept the criticism, examine the role you have played in these incidents and, if you see fit, change your approach. Sometimes just a slight modification of behavior is required."

"Well, in that case, I would like to discuss the statements that have been made. Not necessarily to deny complicity—"

"Com—what?" shouted Furness. "It's about time you stopped speaking down to us, using those big words. Speak words that we understand. We know you've been to college."

"He means, Flo," Grady explained slowly, "that he doesn't want to deny that he took part, or was involved in these incidents."

"He was there all right," Ethel snapped.

"Yes, I was, but Ethel wasn't," I said.

I sat silently. Grady looked at me. "Do you want to proceed, Harry?"

"Proceed with what? Let the girls get it out of their systems."

Furness was on her feet again. "We're not girls, we're women. In our world there are no such things as niggers, and the way you say 'girls' is like you white men say 'boy' and we ain't gonna stand for it."

"You see, Harry," said Norah Rubin, "you have been an irritant. Abrasive. We hope that this has been called to your attention."

"Just a minute," I said. "Admittedly I might have erred walking into the gynecological examination the way I did. But the examination was taking place behind a screen. If Ethel hadn't shouted and screamed at me to get out, and spoken abusively, the patient wouldn't have known I was there. Perhaps if they had simply continued the examination and then explained the situation to me afterward—"

"That's a damn lie," Ethel screamed again. "You're lying."

"Where's Dr. Matthews?" I asked. "She could describe the incident with less bias than I perhaps." I remembered how embarrassed Matthews had been and how she apologized to me afterward.

"She's not part of this," Grady observed blandly.

"Could we ask her to present her side—"

"Harry," Grady said. "I wish you wouldn't look upon this as an attack. It is a sensitivity session, the purpose of which, at the risk of repeating myself, is to have you ask yourself why you rub everyone the wrong way."

"Look," I said, "the young fellows in my office were creating a nuisance. I simply asked Mrs. Furness to request them to leave. I didn't speak to them."

"That's precisely the point," Furness shouted. "You didn't even speak to them. You spoke to me. What's the matter? Aren't they human beings? Or are they just some niggers you speak over the heads of? You spoke around them like they were nothing. You destroyed a relationship we been building up for months, in just five minutes."

"Do you mean to tell me that the patients have no rights if it means that securing their rights will ruffle the feelings of some undisciplined kids? Why don't we ask them?"

"They won't come over to talk with you."

"Have they complained?"

"They don't have to. I'm black, Beverly is black. We know exactly how they feel. They don't have to say nothing."

"Beverly wasn't there. Ethel wasn't there. How do they get into this?"

"They have vibes," Furness continued. "When the community is insulted, it makes our job harder."

"But those kids are not the community." I turned to Roscoe. "Al, have you had any complaints?"

Roscoe said nothing.

Furness turned on him. "You know damn well they complained."

"I heard something," he said finally. "But it didn't come from them, Flo. I heard it from you."

I continued. "Who speaks for the community? I speak for the patients. They are not to be molested by some irresponsible kids marauding in the halls, who have no business there. If that ruptures community relations, then that's the price we will have to pay to establish medical care for the community. Our job is medicine. To relate to each patient who comes through those doors. If we do a good job for the sick who come to us for help, then everything else will follow. And no kids have the right to bust up that relationship between the patients and us, the professional staff. You are a bunch of pampered people with diverse motives, the least of which seems to be medical care. Meanwhile, the patient is not being served. My job is to be his spokesman, to give him care—to mend the broken toilet seats so he can have a clean place to relieve himself, to set up standards so that diagnosis will flow easily, to keep the place clean, to provide a laboratory for rapid diagnosis of simple problems. This won't be accomplished by pandering to hoods raiding the place for drugs."

Furness had the last word.

"You talk like that, mister, you won't get out of this neighborhood alive one night. We'll see to it."

I expected Grady to protest the malicious threat, but he sat, eyes averted as if nothing important had been said.

Finally he looked up. "Well, I don't believe there's anything more to be accomplished. Meeting adjourned."

All but Grady and Rubin left the room. Grady got up. Rubin remained seated.

"You know," I said to Grady, "that nothing can be accomplished here until I get some authority to tame the tigress. Otherwise she'll claw me and then you and then this project to death."

"Harry, you are too abrupt, lad," his brogue singing again. "A bit of honey and they'd be eating from your hand, like they eat from mine."

"They're not eating *out of* your hand, Dr. Grady; they've gobbled it, fingers and all. They do whatever they want and you rubber-stamp it, good practice or bad."

"How bad can it be, Harry? After all, they are nurses."

"So what? I'm a doctor."

"Harry, don't pull that doctor rank on me too. The days of the elite doctor are a thing of the past. You can't go around any longer *telling* nurses to do this or that. You will *ask* nurses to do things."

"And if they don't?"

"If they don't, we will have a conference to discuss the matter and come to an equitable solution."

"I'll tell you what. Let Furness run the project, give her the responsibility or give it to Rubin here."

"Harry, you know that's nonsense. The table of organization calls for an M.D. as project director."

There was no way to get off the merry-go-round.

I turned to Grady. "Do you know what I would do if I were you?" I asked.

"No, what would you do?"

"I would accept my resignation."

"Not right away, Harry. Please, not right away."

"Yes. Right away. I quit."

I walked to my car carefully, determined to avoid being killed in the gutter.

I got in, locked the doors, and was about to drive away from the darkness when I noticed the silhouette of Polly Stiner in Grady's car across the street. I turned off the motor, waiting quietly, invisible in the shadows. Soon Grady and Rubin, her arm through his, walked together to his car. When they reached it, Mike got in on the driver's side and Rubin went to the other side along the curb. She opened the door. There must have been a brief exchange, and Polly Stiner got out, stamped her feet and ran into the Health Center. Rubin drove away with Grady. Then I drove away, alone, for good.

My apartment was dark and lonely. I kept the lights off and stretched out on the couch.

What the hell was it with these female-dominated males that drove them into institutional work? I didn't know who Grady was married to. I didn't know his mother. But there was Grady, thinking he was using Norah Rubin, but actually dancing to her tune, as well as to the jig of the nurses. The power the dames demanded wasn't coherent, honed to converge on a single aim, but rather to feed the churlish vanity of their egos, to satisfy their envies. The mean, puny deeds Grady committed were cosmetics for the ambitions of his motherwomen. He had retreated to an amniotic past, jumping like a fetal marionette to every jerk of the umbilical cord. An umbilical jerk tied irrevocably to the institutional womb. A placental cretin, coated with the meconium of platitude. I dozed and then awakened. The bell rang. I peered at my watch. It was after eleven. I opened the door and Polly walked in. I stepped back and allowed her to pass.

"It's very warm in here, do you mind?" she said as she removed her cape. I shook my head. And then she proceeded to remove all her clothes, until she stood before me, mother-of-pearl, with cupful breasts, tipped by the roseola that guarded her secret inverted nipples. I watched numbly as the pantomime unfolded, every movement as glidingly graceful as that of a stalking cat. She walked slowly toward me. I stared. Her eyes opened widely, each pupil a deep well of space in a green luminescent iris. She reached forward and undid my belt, the button, the zipper, and slid the now useless garment down to my ankles. Then she fell to her knees and with a moan buried herself in and on me, demanding a pulsate energy I was in no mood to give, insistently drawing me into her, taking me finally beyond control, exhausting me, depleting me. There were tears in my eyes. I looked down and stroked her hair from her forehead. A dilated throbbing vein bifurcated beneath the hairline. She sat back on her haunches and looked up. Her painted lips retracted first to a harlot's grin, then to the smile of a girl demanding approval for having performed well. Saying nothing, she rose and turned toward the couch. She picked up her handbag, extracted a cigarette, sat on

266

the sofa, crossed her lovely tapered legs, exhaled and looked up at me.

"Good evening, Harry," she said, as if she had just walked in.

I finished the job of undressing and sat next to her.

"Good evening, Mrs. Stiner," I said. "So good of you to come."

"I can't stay too long," she said. "I've got to be up early in the morning. Another working day."

"I wouldn't think of keeping you," I said. "However, you must be parched. May I fix you a drink?" She nodded.

It was only the beginning. She was mistress of every maneuver in the lexicon of eroticism. Totally unabashed, she led me through what I guessed was an encyclopedic compendium of love-making. Her timing was exemplary and, sensing my every mood, responsive to every signal or call for help, she coddled my energies, laid them to rest, brought them to life, at will, like a magician waving the wand of Eros. She popped off again and again like a roman candle, and each ecstasy was accompanied by an acceleration of moans, and then a series of short tortured screams, until she lay, glowing in the sweat of our bodies, turning her head agonizingly from side to side as if something calamitous had just befallen her. And shortly was able to repeat, and, more miraculous, have me join her in repeating, the entire episode, in other manners, other modes. Afterward, I knew a peace I had never known, as if every spark of anxiety had been extinguished, every vibrant synapse in my body had been put to rest, every fear erased. All sense of struggle dissipated. I lay enfolded in her clasp, feeling totally united with this supple sample of a strange species. We parted, drank and shared the miracle of each other, then made love several times again. She magnetized every surge of neuronal energy that my body possessed into a gigantic libidinous wave of love, that entirely engulfed me. From that moment on, life owed me nothing.

We struggled, alcoholed and giggling, to bed.

She sensed the extent of her capture, and was pleased.

"Polly Stiner picks a peck of pickled peckers," she giggled.

I took the theme drunkenly into my dreams.

> Polly Stiner picks a peck of pickled peckers,
> A peck of peckered peters Polly Stiner picks,
> Polly Stiner polish please a peck of peters,
> Polly pick a peter, shine a pecker please,

Polly Stiner piece of ass and prick demolisher,
Princess Polly Stiner queen of hearts and
    pecker polisher.

The band of morning light pierced my eyes like a sliver of glass.

I arose painfully from the empty bed, groping my memory for clues to the reality of the night before. The bathroom door was closed. I turned the knob. It was locked. I struggled with the latch.

"I'm in here," her frosted voice sang out from another planet as if talking to someone in line to use the ladies' room.

"Polly, let me in. I have to pee."

"I'm in here, I told you," she said with finality.

I retreated to the bed. Finally she came out, dressed, her face composed beneath the cosmetic dust and fine painted lines that falsely arched her brows and accentuated the creases of her lids. "Good morning. Have a nice sleep?" she said, as if to no one in particular.

"Yes. You?" I rose to hold her, to kiss her. She pirouetted away, not coyly, but as from a stranger.

"Thank you for your hospitality. It was very nice. Good-bye." And she swept from the room.

I dressed, put the coffee on and raised the blinds. Sunlight poured into the room, cutting sharp silhouettes into the walls. One can't help thinking more clearly in bright light than in murky surroundings. The shower, followed by the drenching sunlight, seemed to wash away vestiges of indecision that had plagued me since the meeting at the Center. Or perhaps it was the surrealistic visitation of the night before that clarified my thoughts.

I poured the coffee and with pencil and paper painstakingly wrote a letter of resignation to Mike Grady, with copies to the director of medicine and the dean of the medical school.

DEAR DR. GRADY:

Please accept my resignation effective today. There is no point in one month's, or even one week's, notice, for indeed I shan't be missed. There is ample evidence that, between Mrs. Rubin and the nurses, things can go on as they had before I arrived, and during my tenure. I could in no way change the course of things, therefore my continued presence is noncontributive.

From the start I encountered a series of shifting boundaries designed to protect what the nurses believed to be their territorial prerogatives. I believe that you encouraged the confusion that this caused to keep the place free of any competitive medical presence, so that you could use the Center, and the services of the nurses, for purposes that extended beyond the immediate mandate of your office.

The primary mission of the Center is comprehensive health care, but this obvious fact became blurred by a babel of individual priorities imposed by each nurse in her own way. The traditional discipline and sacrifice of the profession of medicine should not summarily be displaced or insidiously eroded by the imposition of untested ideas, altered priorities or contemporary emotionalisms.

Community health starts with the care and comfort of the individual patient. If the care of the individual is sloppy, community health will be sloppy. The function of the project director is to assure the optimum in individual care. If this be done, the delivery of health care to the community will be optimum.

The job descriptions in which so much store is placed are an unfortunate device, for it would seem apparent to any nurse or doctor that his or her job description had been prescribed by their respective professional training. But at the Center you painstakingly established job descriptions to create ambiguity. The job description of the project director places the entire medical responsibility of patient care in his hands. That is proper. But the job description of the directress of nurses shows that she is under the "general supervision" (whatever that means) of the director of nurses of the Department of Community Medicine. This has been used to effectively deprive the medical project director of the authority to direct the nurses in their complementary role.

The Health Center was established as a medical, not a nursing, project. Each patient who comes to the Center, comes with full confidence that his care will be supervised by a physician, not a nurse.

The nurses' insolent requirement that the attitudes and philosophy of the project director must conform to theirs obviously reflects your attitude. It is a device which will force any project director to walk a narrow path, the limits of which will be defined by Mrs. Rubin. Under these conditions no physician can serve you as project director without compromising his professional standards.

Sincerely yours,

9

INITIALLY THE TREMOR was barely noticeable, because it disappeared entirely when the left arm was doing something purposeful. But as soon as the arm relaxed a fine to-and-fro turning of the wrist developed which slowly gathered momentum and pace, to involve the forearm. It was disconcerting, as is any involuntary movement, yet forceful enough to prevent Lapius from damping the palsy with his good right hand.

Parkinson's disease enters the body stealthily. For an innocent the initial stages of the disease might represent only a slight inconvenience, but for Lapius it was the augury of a predictable nightmare, as is any malign disease to a physician.

Alcohol seemed to soothe him, so he drank more than heretofore. He used his left hand to lift or fondle the snifter, enough activity to stifle the tremor.

"Harry, I've made a decision. I've decided to go for cryosurgery. Knowland will do it."

"Why not Cooper? He invented the procedure."

"Cooper won't take me. Says it's too early. But Knowland feels that it is the appropriate thing to do at this stage."

"What's the rush?"

"The rush is that the disease predicts my future, and I reject it out of hand. Within a year I will have a broad shaking palsy of both arms. I will develop a propulsive gait, my body bent forward in advance of my legs, as if anticipating their forward movement. The inertia of my rigid body will propel me at a faster pace than my legs will be able to control. I will salivate excessively. My tremulous mouth will fill with great volumes of fluid, much beyond its capacity to contain, and the excess will drool from the corners, chafing the skin of my jaw. Need I go on, Harry? After all, for a physician, the onset of a disease is a self-fulfilling prophecy."

During the succeeding days I helped Lapius with his files.

"Someday, Harry, perhaps when you have time, you might put these records in order and have them published."

"You'll have time," I said impatiently.

"Possibly. Knowland has scheduled me to go into the hospital next month."

The news jarred me. I wasn't comfortable with the thought of Lapius undergoing surgery. The operation was too new. The results had been equivocal.

"Simon, for God's sake, this whole scene is funereal. First, you're not dying. Second, if you were, or if you think you are, why not just leave this junk? After you're gone I'll send your lawyer, accountant and publisher here and we'll get your stuff in order.

"I promise you a posthumous volume. Maybe I can even arrange a *Festschrift* or something called 'The Immortal Works of S. Q. Lapius.' But in the meantime, I'm going sailing. Get some warm things together, I'll pick you up first thing in the morning."

At 6 A.M. the yellow morning was partitioned by the long shadows of the rising sun. One of those shadows, half as long and twice as wide as in real life, was that of Simon Quentin Lapius. Dressed in his red-flannel gym suit, he held under one arm a red sleeping bag that looked like his twin. His hair danced a gray gigue in the morning breeze as he waited for me in front of his house. I pulled to the curb.

271

"Iscariot in his chariot, I presume."

I threw open the door. "Enter O great God Aesculapius."

"Oh," he said, puffing slightly, "you recognize me, do you?"

He threw his gear into the rear of the car and settled in.

The marina was ashimmer in the morning light. The boat bobbed gently at the docking lines. I boarded first, leaned over to grip Lapius's extended hand and maneuvered him aboard. The decks and cockpit were slippery with dew. The air was crisp, the sky blue and the sun erased the night from white clapboard homes that dotted the distant shore. Their images were duplicated in the still mirror of the water's edge. Nothing moved until the crystal of dawn was shattered by the low rumble of the engine. I cast the lines and we glided into the bay. Silence was broken only by the plaintive squeaks of a lost duckling answering the throaty commands of its mother. Too early to fish, the gulls perched passively on poles and pilings.

Lapius, shivering, leaned back against the cabin wall and breathed deeply the chill air. We motored toward the wide point, watching the shoreline drop away on either side until we were a white speck in shimmering seas. I cut the engine, dropped anchor, went below and made coffee.

"Here, Simon, this will warm you." I handed him a steaming cup. He wrapped his hands around it gratefully. I stayed below awhile stowing things. Then I brought up a nylon slipover for Lapius, who was starting, despite the warm coffee in his hands, to gel, stiffen and turn slightly blue. "You'll be warm soon, Simon," I said, watching the sun move higher on its axial worm gears.

"My blood is becoming turgid, Harry. I'm sure whatever befalls me from these cruel conditions won't trouble your conscience any."

"Not a bit, Simon. This is the best thing that ever happened to you. Take a deep breath. Come on now, in with the good air, out with the bad."

"Bah. How long do I have to wait to sip the coffee without risking third-degree burns?"

"Wait till you thaw out, Simon." At the moment his body movements were as sluggish as those of a cold snake. The coal stove by now had warmed the cabin. I helped Lapius below. "Now sit here until you defrost. Then if you're feeling better you can come out and make a mutiny."

The sapphire morning, warmed by the sun, had yellowed. Sea breezes rippled the water. I raised the mizzen, weighed anchor, hoisted the main and the jib. The ketch leaned from the wind, making headway to the southeast. Lapius thrust his head from the cabin, holding tight. "My God, Harry, we are lopsided."

But as soon as he gained confidence in the vectors that govern the art of sailing, he thoroughly enjoyed the silence.

"There's a remarkable freedom and detachment about the whole thing, Harry. Does it occur to you that we are on the road to India if we choose?"

"Often, Simon, often." I set the sails to keep her on course, and moved next to Simon on the windward side. She would maintain that course as long as the wind was steady. The bay was empty. We fell to the rhythm of the boat as it hobbyhorsed into the slight chop and were lulled by the waters parted by the prancing bow.

Lapius seemed smaller in the narrow confines of the crowded cockpit than he did in his own spacious quarters at home.

The wind danced in the eastern quarter and held moderately steady, then died at noon. We ghosted quietly in light airs. I handed Lapius the tiller and went below to forage for sandwiches and again steamed some coffee. At sea under sail, the measures of time expand infinitely. Progress is incalculable, position is gauged by the unraveling shoreline. The sun, no longer a clock, is a friendly distant yellow furnace that turns to a red ember before eclipsing at the dark rim of earth.

Sunset applied impasto texture to the prismatic sky. We watched in awe as the eastern clouds were wafted like graying flocks into the funnel of night. On shore the bullrushes poked skyward like lances on parade. The gulls, their hunting done, were perched again on familiar roosts.

In the west there was light enough to read by, then suddenly we were isolated in blackness that framed a lonely silver crescent.

We sailed blindly toward the deceptive shadows of the shore-line and dropped anchor when the sound of humming crickets bade us do so.

Later, snugged uncomfortably into berths too short and narrow for grown men, Lapius suddenly called out, "This won't do, Harry."

"What's the trouble?"

"I have nocturia."

273

"Here," I said, rolling from my berth. "Use this bucket. We'll empty it in the morning."

The exhaustion of doing nothing at sea and the somnolent roll of the boat at anchor lulled us to deep slumber, and in the morning I was pleased to note that Simon's bucket was empty.

We awakened to the darts of light that sprayed off the glistening water as the sun poked over the horizon. The position of a boat at anchor varies with the currents. The color and contour of the land mass is as changeable as the shape of clouds. The bay was a torrent of wind-driven froth. As I lifted the mizzen, it luffed and snapped until, halyard cleated and sheet made fast, we fell directly into the wind. With the anchor weighed, I instructed Lapius to keep the bow into the wind, as I freed the remaining sheets and raised the main and jib. Canvas whipped furiously as the wind coaxed a wild song from the rigging. Then I loosed the mizzen, pulled in the main sheet, then the jib. Off on a port tack, our beautiful sails bent to their task. They harnessed the wind, and suddenly the violence was over. In the clutch of a friendly giant, the boat heeled to starboard, and then surged forward. The wind was an ally. On land the reeds bent double, boughs broke and shutters banged on shingled walls in the same fresh breeze that nestled tamely in the belly of our sails.

We sailed a week or so. One night we pulled into a marina to renew the larder and get some ice. It must have been during the weekend. I remember discussing my uncertainty with Lapius after. "It is the isolation, Harry. Here we are separated from familiar landmarks for only a few days and we lose all track of time. Doesn't it remind you of the elderly person whom we glibly ask to name the president, or name the date, when he's been separated and indifferent to the calendar of events for months or years? Perhaps senility is nothing more than intellectual isolation. He has no appointment to keep."

I let the matter drop. It was just after he had saved the baby, and I was still ruminating about that.

It started with a piercing shriek. A few slips away a man ran along the dock screaming, "Help, get an ambulance!" I jumped from the boat and flagged him down. "What's wrong?" I asked.

"My baby is dying."

"Where?" I followed him. The mother was cradling the infant, who by this time was blue.

"We have to make an airway," I shouted at the mother above the din of the crowd that was gathering.

"What are you going to do?" the mother cried in terror.

"Try breathing in the baby's mouth," I told her.

Suddenly Lapius appeared. He shouted, "Immobilize the infant, Harry." I grabbed the baby from his mother and pressed him to the deck, wondering what would happen next. Lapius knelt over the head of the infant and drove an implement into his neck. Suddenly the crisis was over. The asphyxial blackness receded and, although still on the blue side, the baby sucked some wind, and the horrible retraction of his belly and ribs was released.

Lapius looked up and said, "Now, quickly, call the rescue squad." Then he faced the distraught mother.

"Madam, the child must go to a hospital. There is no immediate danger. Harry, stay here and guarantee his airway." And that's how it happened.

After it was over I said, "Where did you get that needle, Simon?"

"Oh, I always carry one, just in case."

A small craft is close quarters. Intimacy is foisted upon its crew. The barriers of rank, class, accomplishment, age, wealth, position, are set awash or blown away by water or wind. At night the eternal time-flow is traced by the tracks of stars and galaxies, and slowly we become part of its tantalizing distances and infinite space.

On cold and blustery days we would anchor in cove, and stay below, listening to the rigging sing.

The cabin was crowded and headroom restricted. Lapius's indisposition was obvious. "I seem to have been looking at my stomach all day," he complained morosely. "At least on deck I can stretch and get it out of the line of vision, but here my head seems rooted to my belly button."

"Stop complaining, Simon. Next time book passage on the *Queen Elizabeth*."

Suddenly he straightened and headed to the cabin door. "Where are you off to, Simon?"

"I've got to take a leak."

"Use the bucket."

"No. The fresh air will do me good." He waved me back.

"Piss to the leeward, Simon," I shouted at his disappearing hulk.

After a brief moment there was an earthy bellow. I leaped the hatch to be met by a fine spray of urine. "Goddamn it, I'm pissing in my own face," shouted Lapius, struggling to avert his face.

"Turn off the stream," I yelled, hoping my words would pierce the wall of wind.

"I tried to hold it, but it blew right out of my hand," Simon shouted back.

"Well, stop pissing, for goodness' sake. Turn around."

"I can't stop. It takes me too long to get started. I'll just have to sponge off." When he had finished, I filled a bucket and mopped his hands and face, then my own. "Well," Lapius said, smacking his lips, "at least I don't have diabetes."

"I thought I told you to piss to leeward," I scolded.

"I did precisely that, but the wind shifted suddenly."

I warmed him with hot and buttered rum. Wind and sea and the shrill noises of nature precluded time, but the biologic clock was still running, and I could see that even during these few days Lapius had to contend with an increased tremor in his left arm, and now his right arm shook too.

Clouds, banked like ranks of silver feathers, slid across the azure sky. Black night was coming. On the morrow I would have to turn back, go home, transport Lapius to his fateful appointment.

The sailing trip failed to alter Lapius's resolve. He would have surgery. His body was becoming more rigid daily as the resilient protoplasm of his musculature seemed to gel. Only with conscious effort could he force vitality to liven his features. Even to smile was fatiguing.

I sympathized with his wish to be rid of the torment, but thought he should wait. Cryosurgery embodied risks. Its accidental discovery by Cooper opened new frontiers to the control of the disease. Almost to the day, Hornykiewytsch, in Vienna, was proving biochemically that the basal ganglia of the brains of patients with Parkinson's disease were bereft of the chemical desoxyphenylalanine amine, paving the way, too late to serve Lapius, for the medical treatment of the disease with L-dopa.

276

"Rubbish," Lapius countered my entreaties. "I haven't the time to await the results of laboratory experiments still in the test-tube stage. I'll be stiff as a board and flat on my back by the time they reach clinical trial."

"You are liable to be flat on your back and irretrievably wounded if you enter surgery prematurely," I said, smarting from his impetuous foolishness. I regretted immediately having said that, and agreed to drive Lapius to Knowland, feeling all the while like a drayman driving French aristocracy to the guillotine.

Lapius suffered only a small hemorrhage during surgery, which in any other part of his body would have been meaningless. But in the region of the thalamus it caused enough pressure, and efforts to stanch it caused enough damage, to permanently stem the neurological impulses coursing in the internal capsule, to paralyze that part of Lapius's body that Knowland was trying to retrieve. "He won't shake any more, anyway," Knowland was heard to remark morosely to one of his assistants.

The damage proved irreversible. My anger was futile, my futility frustrating.

Seymour Lapius, Simon's distant brother, decided that S. Q. Lapius should be admitted permanently to the Fifth Commandment Nursing Home and Hospital for Chronic Diseases, and asked me to supervise his care there. I agreed, then dried my tears.

I went to the Fifth Commandment to make arrangements for Lapius's admission. It had an excellent reputation. It was a non-profit private institution for the care of the chronically ill and aged, one of a kind that had sprung up in response to the commitment the nation was making to its elderly and otherwise damaged citizens who could no longer function "on the outside."

The institution was a labyrinth of cold orange brick that desecrated the grounds of what had once been a beautiful estate. Its only architectural cohesiveness resided in the necessary fact that each brick was cemented firmly to its cohorts. On either side of dismal halls heavy doors led to rooms large enough for two or sometimes four beds. Small closets lined one wall. Some of the rooms had bathrooms. The floors were tile. The halls were trafficked with wheelchairs. Suspended from the walls were handrails, that old bent figures used gingerly, as they walked precariously like steelworkers treading beams forty stories off the ground. Although the corridors and rooms were adequately lighted, the monotony of bent and twisted bony, worn bodies was like the repetitive darkness of a coal mine where life is begrimed by the dust of time.

Arthur Pegler, the administrator, was a pimple of a man with a furuncular nose that looked like a boil coming to a head. He had a boyish smile, and kept saying "Okay" in a slightly raspy voice.

"Dr. Lapius will be here Friday, okay. We haven't any private rooms at present. He will have to share a room. Okay? He will be in the infirmary. Okay? We'll do everything in our power to make him comfortable, okay?"

"He's not very old, just very sick."

"Same thing, isn't it? He's helpless, okay. Come on, I'll introduce you to the medical director, okay?"

Nothing had prepared me for the shock of meeting the medical director. The last time I had seen him truly, he was kneeling under a lamppost vomiting. Monty Foreman greeted me with the same curiously smug and crooked smile that time hadn't managed to straighten out.

"Hello, Harry."

"Hello, Monty."

Pegler took advantage of the awkward pause that followed to note the obvious. "You guys know each other."

"Take him downstairs, Peggy. There's another surprise for him," Monty said.

Indeed there was. I followed Pegler down a short flight of stairs that led to a series of interconnecting laboratories. At a distant laboratory bench, standing like the hooked figure of a question mark, leaned a tall, slim familiar figure. As it straightened I recognized Wilkie Rush.

I rushed forward and we almost embraced. "For Christ's sake, Wilkie, I didn't know you were back east."

"I guess I should have looked you up, Harry."

I turned to Pegler. "I think I'll stay awhile and catch up on things with Dr. Rush. You'll excuse us, won't you?"

Pegler nodded curtly and left.

"What the hell are you doing here? And with Foreman one flight up."

"I had been in geriatric research on the coast, and was invited to start a project here. I have enough federal support for a few

278

years, and until that runs out I won't have trouble with Foreman. We keep out of each other's hair." He took me into his office. I told him about Lapius. "Goddamn shame," he murmured.

"You look happy, Wilkie."

"I'm fine. I love the work. Getting some good projects started. Have an interesting population to work with."

"What will you do if and when the money runs out?"

"I'll run too. You know us research guys, Harry. We have short roots. If worse comes to worst, I can go into practice somewhere."

Rush, although still painfully thin, was pink-cheeked and appeared robust. "Where's your milk?" I asked him.

Rush threw back his head and laughed. "Everybody who knew me at The County asks me that. The damnedest thing happened. The army sent me to Korea. I was scared to death. I figured my ulcer would bust. But they X-rayed me up and down and couldn't find one.

"I had pains on the boat over, pains when I got to Seoul, and even had my canteen filled with milk. Then I got sent up to a battalion aid station on the thirty-eighth parallel. There was a lot of excitement, and I was petrified. Not because of the occasional shooting, but all they had was powdered milk, and I couldn't stomach it. I sent frantic requests back for fresh milk, but by the time any was smuggled up to me it was warm or sour. When they found me foraging for cows, they sent me to a psychiatrist. He told me my pains were psychosomatic, to forget them. Believe it or not, within a week or so my pains left me. I figured the shrink was right. The air was fresh, the guys were great. An occasional nurse wandered up there. Actually I had a hell of a good year. I came back just before the war started. By God, that fresh milk tasted good. As soon as I got to San Francisco my pains returned. I couldn't figure it out. I started seeing a shrink again, who took a point-by-point history, and after he had pieced the whole thing together he made a pronouncement. 'Rush,' he said, 'I've gone over your medical history carefully, and although you may have plenty of psychological problems, none of them are the cause of your stomach pains. Your problem, obviously, is that you are allergic to milk.'"

The Fifth Commandment was short-handed. I was emotionally destitute. Foreman offered me a job. They were, he explained, trying to create an accredited chronic-disease hospital to supplement the nursing home, and needed to build a medical staff. Pegler and Foreman had convinced the board of trustees that the imminent passage of the Medicare law would make the Fifth Commandment self-sufficient, and able to reimburse handsomely a staff of full-time physicians. Administration could expand, and the salary base could rise.

Committed to keep an eye on S. Q. Lapius, I decided to give it a try. Maybe I could work into some research project with Rush. The place had a rudimentary morgue, and they would hire me to do the infrequent autopsies, and supervise a small clinical laboratory managed by a fat technician who kept the place like a dirty kitchen, food stuffed into cabinets and iceboxes and crumbs on the lab benches.

"We'll be the foremost geriatric institution in the country," Foreman insisted. "I'll see to it," he added ominously.

Rita Marcus, his chief nurse, was damn near a geriatric case herself. She had been induced to return to nursing after a score of years devoted to motherhood. She sought confirmation of her gender and the fleeting dreams of girlhood by repeatedly reaffirming the details of her bridal night in a loud and phlegmy voice that knew no audible boundaries. She called Pegler and Foreman by their first names, and confided that this meant that they were her friends. She interrupted serious conversations repeatedly with pointed *non sequiturs* about her courtship, and usually ended her fables with an insistent laugh in a voice brought to raspy fullness by a nodular laryngitis caused by smoking.

Her intellectual vapidity was confirmed by her faulty judgment about hospital matters. The odds were fifty-fifty in any given circumstances that she would come to the wrong decision.

Pegler and Foreman deferred to her like men who had never properly laid a good woman. It soon became apparent, despite outward appearances and its excellent reputation, despite the figureheads Pegler and Foreman, that the Fifth Commandment, under the flabby genital dominance of Rita Marcus, was second-rate.

At first Lapius tolerated the Fifth Commandment, and displayed an affable grace. The nurses and orderlies took good care of him. His creature comforts were provided to the extent that

280

responsibility even for self-care was taken over by others. He seemed troubled by the sight of contemporaries lamed by age or illness, with whom he was destined to travel the converging paths of life's final journey. But, inexorably, as he became encumbered by disease, his isolation increased in proportion.

A violent conspiracy exists between medical progress, the institutes and illness itself, that finally robs the victim of the last vestiges of human dignity. The dehumanization is so complete that family, friends and ultimately the patient must conclude that death is the better alternative. They might remember that prior to antibiotics, pneumonia afflicting the frail was invariably lethal, and that its attack was so rapid and mercifully decisive that it became known as the "old man's friend."

But neither Lapius nor his colleagues in these throes were to be relieved of their suffering so readily. Between them and death ranged a phalanx of alert nurses and physicians whose mission it was to ward off disease at all costs, even when the ultimate salvage was a crippled carcass that could never reclaim its human content in recognizable form.

An epidemic of diarrhea struck. The patients fell ill simultaneously, and puddles of shit started appearing on the waxed tiled floor. The aides spent most of their time cleaning patients and changing beds. The laundry ran out of linens, and the absorbent paper chocks reserved for incontinent patients were distributed throughout the house.

Lapius was aggrieved because the diarrhea was a public display of his incapacity.

"It makes me smell, Harry. This is intolerable," he said beseechingly.

Rush was sore as hell. "They have these epidemics every several months, Harry. The fucking kitchen is run by some slob whose only interest in the place is how much kickback he can get on the tuna fish and chicken wings he orders. Take a look someday. Watch it when the girls mix the tuna salad. They use bare hands, they run their fingers through their hair, then back into the tuna. I even saw one of them pick her nose a little and mix the snot into the salad. The mayonnaise is at room temperature for about six hours. Bacteria, doubling their numbers every twenty minutes: the megabug, calculated at 2 to the 18th power.

That's what you can see during a casual walk through the kitchen. Imagine if you inspected it."

I took a casual walk through the kitchen. Rush was right. The food-handling was careless. I got boxes of plastic gloves, and told the girls to use them when mixing the salads and touching food, and that if they had to scratch themselves somewhere to take the gloves off to do it. If they dropped something and had to pick it up, change the gloves. If they went to the bathroom, change the gloves. Ben Nelson, who was supposed to be running the kitchen, came out of his chicken-coop office to see what was happening. "Why not keep the salads and mayonnaise iced, Ben?" I asked him.

"Good idea," he said noncommittally.

Later Pegler called me into his office. "Harry, I know you are new here, but if you have a problem, bring it to me. We'll straighten it out."

"What happened?"

"You got Ben Nelson all upset."

"Why? Because I told him to ice the tuna?"

"If you have any problems, Harry, tell me, not Ben."

"Okay, I have a problem. I wasn't going to bother you about it because it seemed simple. But the fact is that the kitchen is unsanitary. Now you know. I've reported it to you."

"Great, Harry. That's the way to do things. We'll take care of it."

Two weeks later a casual inspection of the kitchen failed to reveal any improvement. I met Pegler in the hall in front of his office. "What about the kitchen?"

"I sent a memo to Dr. Foreman. He's medical director."

After two days the shits would run their course and things would quiet down. The girls in the kitchen started wearing gloves and the tuna was iced. The cordon sanitaire lasted a week. A month later we had another epidemic.

I sought out Pegler. He sat hidden behind stacks of periodicals piled high on his desk that he kept promising to read. "We have the recurrent enteritis again," I told him.

"Harry, why do you make this your problem? Why don't you just take care of your patients?"

"That's what I'm trying to do."

282

"So be a good fellow and do it. Write nice notes on the charts and keep out of the kitchen. You get Ben Nelson all upset."

"I do keep nice notes. And what I say in those notes is that the patient has diarrhea because the kitchen is run like a—"

Pegler's voice suddenly developed a sinister edge. "Don't you dare do that. That constitutes chart warfare."

Suddenly Pegler twisted his hypermetabolic facies into something resembling a mollifying smile. "Harry, notes like that will hurt the institution. Why do you want to hurt the institution?"

"I don't want to hurt the institution. I want to help the patient."

"But if you hurt the institution, that hurts the patient, don't you think?"

"Not if the institution gives the patient the shits. What may be inconsequential diarrhea to you or me, and I know damn well you get it, because I get it too, is lethal to some of these older people. They dehydrate, and a lot of other things happen quickly and they die. After all, if my patients die, I at least would like to share the blame. As a matter of fact, that filthy kitchen interferes with my ability to care for my patients. Don't you think that as a physician I am obligated to list the probable cause of my patients' disease?"

Pegler became grim and menacing. His eyes popped. "Your obligation is to do what you were hired to do: take care of the goddamn patients when they are sick. My job is to run the goddamn institution. I don't do your job; don't try to do mine."

"Okay, Peggy. But when a patient dies, the family comes after me, not you, to find out about the sudden turn of events."

"And what do you tell them?"

"The truth."

"You are a goddamn menace, okay?" he said ominously.

Simon was developing contractures. His left arm and leg were bending at elbow and knee inexorably. Every time I passed his room I would go in and extend and flex the hapless limbs, pushing against the fixed tendons to straighten the joints out to their full 180-degree extension. It hurt him, but he understood why I was doing it. I taught his orderly, Bobby, how to do this without breaking any bones.

"Every time you come within ten feet of Lapius, go over and flex his limbs a few times," I told him. I instructed aides and practical nurses, and soon they were stealing a few moments from their appointed chores to exercise the passive range of motion of the limbs of the patients.

Suddenly it wasn't being done. "What happened, Bobby? Lapius is getting stiffer."

"They ordered me not to do it any more."

"Who ordered you not to do it?"

"That fat nurse."

I visited Marcus in her office. Her moist eyes were defensively spiteful. She attacked. "If you have any nursing chores you want done, write the orders on the chart. You have no right to go around telling my people what to do. They work for the nursing department."

Foreman knew the story. "Rita is right, Harry. She's head of nursing."

"For Christ's sake, Monty, what the hell is going on here?"

"In the army, Harry, a nurse captain outranks a lieutenant physician. Rita is head of nursing."

"Someone has to do passive range of motion on these bed-ridden patients, Monty. They'll double up otherwise."

"They are going to double up anyway. Besides, it is the job of the physiotherapy department."

"But you haven't got a physiotherapy department. You have one therapist for the entire hospital, and he's so wheezy he needs therapy himself."

I got Lapius a private nurse to be with him.

Because Rita refused to permit her nurses to do passive-range-of-motion exercises on the patients, they remained in the strait jackets of their own contractures.

Rooms in the sick wing of the Fifth Commandment were stifling during the summer months. The air conditioner in the window, when turned on, bucked and belched hot and dusty air. I wrote a memo to Pegler:

> The rooms are stifling. How about getting some air-conditioners that work? Also, there are flies all over the place. Do we have any flypaper?

He answered:

New air-conditioners are on order. The screens are being checked.

The two statements were lies, but constituted a written record. I yearned for flypaper. At least you could make a daily count. It might look unsanitary, but the flies loved it and stuck to it. And it could be replaced.

"You out of your head, Harry?" Foreman said. "Suppose one of the board of directors walked around and saw some flypaper in the room where his mother was sick or something?"

"That's a laugh," Rush said later when I told him about it. "I haven't seen a board member here in three years. They stop in at the front office or to have lunch. But I've never seen one of them inspect the place."

"Why not?"

"The place is too hot. They would be uncomfortable."

"Well, the summer is almost over."

"Winter is worse," Rush said, sucking on his pipe.

"Why, no heat?"

"No. Quite the contrary. There is something wrong with the valves, and the heat can't be turned off. The rooms are about ninety degrees all winter long."

As the fall days shortened and the weather got colder, the heat in the rooms mounted steadily. The temperature climbed daily till it steadied at about 93 degrees. My nostrils dried and the membranes cracked. Sick people usually sweated to death. Fluid replacement was difficult to adjust. Every so often a nurse would forget to control the flow rate and the patient would virtually drown.

Pegler considered himself the architect of one of the great geriatric and chronic disease institutes of the country.

"It's like a tropical aquarium," I told him. "My patients are becoming dehydrated."

"Obviously you don't know how to keep them under control, Harry. I had better mention that to Dr. Foreman."

"You had better maybe put some fans in the rooms or fix the fucking valves or give them the healthy air conditioner in your office or do something dramatic to cool those rooms. Because I am

285

going to note that condition with the daily room temperature on the charts."

"You try any of that shit, Harry, and you're finished here."

I didn't want to be finished there till I knew what was going to happen to Lapius.

It happened. Lapius, suffering the aches of stiffening, cold and contracting muscles, decided that he would be more comfortable in bed.

Once abed, Lapius proved incapable of using his urinal, so that morning after morning the aides would find him puddled in his own excreta.

Lapius soon developed a uriniferous skin rash. I tried to insert a catheter, but he waved me off.

"You'll develop sores, Simon. You can't lie in your urine."

"It was just an accident," he said proudly. "It won't happen again."

But it happened again. And again and again. A moist rash covered most of his back. His scrotum and buttocks became reddened, tender and inflamed with cheesy fungal deposits in the folds of his skin. I approached him again with the catheter.

"I'd rather rot," he exclaimed, "than be chained to a plastic bag by such an indignity."

"You need it, Simon."

"Harry," he pleaded, "you have to spare me this. I won't go around with a tube in my bladder."

"Simon," I reproached, "you are pissing all over yourself. You have a rash."

"Then have the aides change me more often. For my part, a catheter is an admission of failure on the part of nursing."

"Simon, your skin is macerating. Please, do it for me. Otherwise I'll be débriding your bedsore daily for six months. Spare me that."

"No, Harry! A man should die free. Not festooned to his bed by tubes in his penis, rectum, gullet and veins. Attached to bottles and sucking oxygen, and spread-eagled like Christ crucified. But what can I look forward to? What are you saving me for, Harry? Another six months, a year of rigidity and paralysis? It is not reasonable, and I won't permit it."

I became depressed.

I called Elspeth. It had been years. She remembered.

"I'm very upset, Elspeth. Just dinner. I want to talk to someone. A lot of things have happened."

"Oh, Harry. I didn't realize—sure. I'm yours for the evening."

"Dinner anyway. I'll pick you up."

She was dressed in a plaid skirt and white blouse buttoned at the neck. Her hair was flouncy in a feather cut.

"Run up and change, Elspeth. I'll take you to dinner."

"No, Harry. I've cooked up a dinner for two right here. You don't really want to go out. Candles and wine, and you know how I love to hear you talk, Harry."

I followed her into the kitchen. Two scotches with water and ice were on the counter. The smell of chicken, the beans amandine simmering on the stove, washed some of the urea smells from my nostrils.

"I didn't know you could cook, Elspeth," I blurted idiotically.

"Yes, Harry, you thought the only thing I could do was screw. A regular fucking machine. Well, why not?" she said with a laugh. "I really didn't allow you to enter my life—or allow you to know that you had entered my life, to be more accurate." We drank, and she served simply on a small kitchen table laid with a delicate cloth which I promptly stained with the rose wine she served.

"Oh, Harry, how I used to live your life so vicariously. You were so filled with the wonderment and romance of medicine, those cases you used to tell me about for hours, your research. You were a free bird in flight, so excited, so stimulated, so provocative."

"Why did you allow me to come tonight, Elspeth? It's been so long."

"Because tonight you needed me, Harry."

"I always needed you."

"Not really, Harry. You wanted me. I was your first teacher. And you were an apt student. But this is the first time you needed any other part of me."

"But you erected such a wall."

"Harry, a woman needs a man at times, but she must be wise enough to estimate the long-range possibilities. I'm older than

287

you. You weren't ready for me, or anybody, for that matter. You were having an affair with medicine. All else being equal, I could only have come out second. I had been through that once. Things are different now. I'm in love and being loved and it is good. What have you been up to?"

I told her about Lapius, the whole story up to the current impasse with the catheter. Tears welled up in her eyes.

"Oh, Simon, poor Simon."

"He was great, Elspeth. It's too bad you never really knew him."

"I knew him, Harry."

I kissed her lightly on the forehead and clasped her hands in mine.

It was a cold walk home. In revealing the totality of herself as a woman Elspeth was almost more destructive than her bitchy rebuffs when I was dancing beneath her skirts.

I tried again to have Lapius agree to a catheter.

"You like this urea smell, Simon? You think it's nice to have to wash this piss off you every morning? I want to put in that catheter."

"Nothing doing."

"I saw Elspeth last night, Simon. Remember that nurse I used to see occasionally? She wants to come and see you," I lied.

He started violently. "No, Harry. She mustn't see me like this."

"Simon, you better let me put that goddamn tube up your pecker, or she'll be here to join you for lunch. I promise you that."

With the catheter in place I encouraged Lapius to get out of bed once in a while. It was urgent, because the maceration of his skin, earned while he lay in pools of urine, had already caused a small erosion on his left hip.

I nursed his small bedsore and scuffed it daily. Checked his proteins, watched his hemoglobin, altered his diet, monitored his urine for infection, saw to it that the catheter was irrigated regularly, and changed it at proper intervals.

One morning I arrived to find Lapius immobile in bed. I scolded him. "Where's your walker? What are you doing in bed? Stay there long enough and you become petrified."

He looked up somberly and said, "I don't believe I can walk, Harry. An orderly dropped me rather forcibly and I struck the arm of the chair. My hip hurts." He rubbed his right side.

I peered under the covers. His right leg was spread like a frog's, bent slightly at the knee, the foot everted. The right femoral neck was fractured. Goddamn it.

The orthopods saw him that night. The clinical signs were unmistakable, but the X-ray was negative. They decided to keep him in bed for a week, and re-X-ray.

It happens like that sometimes. Lapius was very depressed. I didn't try to cheer him up. What for?

Lapius wasn't the only one sporting injuries. There was an epidemic of battered patients. Every once in a while on one of the three shifts an imbecile or madman gets hired. Or maybe someone turns up drunk. When that happens, the damage is noted on rounds the following morning. Spaeth had a fractured clavicle, Robbins a dislocated shoulder, Cohen two black eyes. Lapius didn't remember who had dropped him. He had never seen him before. It wasn't Bobby. The other patients were too obtunded by age to describe the incidents, their memories too distorted by senility even to remember that they had been injured.

I made notes on the charts and gave a list of the injured to Pegler. "You may have some nut loose here," I told him. "You better tell Rita to check her people. It could be almost anyone. Even a visitor. But it looks like we might have a problem."

Rita caught up with me while I was making rounds and asked me to go to her office. There she closed the door and wheeled on me. "Who the hell are you to interfere in my department? Don't you think you should have reported this to me?"

"What difference does it make who I reported it to? I told Pegler. The important thing is to find out who did it, how it happened."

"I'll find out, don't worry."

The following day I noted that my notes on each patient had been deleted from the charts. In their place were fresh sheets with Rita's careful handwriting:

Spaeth: "The patient was trying to get to the toilet and fell against the sink, thus fracturing his clavicle."

Robbins: "Patient was being led back to bed by the arm when he suddenly became violently agitated. The patient tripped, and because the orderly had hold of his arm, it was dislocated at the shoulder."

Cohen: "Patient was flailing while nurse was trying to put him to bed and struck himself in eye causing black and blue mark."

I showed the charts to Foreman. "Where the hell are my notes?" I shouted at him.

"What notes?"

"The notes I wrote on these patients, describing their injuries."

"I don't see any," Foreman said, studying each chart.

"That's what I'm trying to tell you. They are not there."

"You say you wrote notes and they are gone? I have no knowledge of your notes. All I can go by is what I see and I don't see any notes."

"I'll rewrite them."

"I wouldn't do that if I were you. It would embarrass the institution."

"What happens tonight if there is another batch of battered patients?"

"There won't be. We've fired all the orderlies on the afternoon and night shifts."

"What a group you are. You lie, delete records, close your eyes to anything wrong."

Foreman started shouting. "Why don't you grow up?" he sneered. "What do you want to do, spread this gossip all over and write it down? You have no proof of anything."

"Easy, Monty. I just described their injuries. Rita was the one who embellished the reports with spurious accounts of how they occurred."

"Good thing too, otherwise each case would be the basis of a liability suit. We have to protect the institution."

"Yeah, but who is going to protect the patients?"

The week snaked by and finally the fracture line appeared. Lapius was transferred to the orthopedic service.

A nail was driven through the femoral head to stabilize the neck of the femur. The surgery proved uncomplicated and we got him back three days later. Some of the fight was returning and he started to eat, and even talk about getting back on his feet.

"Don't rush it," I told him. "It takes about five weeks." But we did get him out of bed and into a chair.

Suddenly an area of fluctuation appeared in the suture line of his recent incision. I removed two sutures and cleaned out a pocket of pus. He was on antibiotics. I kept irrigating and débriding the wound, but it extended and pockets and fistulae kept leading to the head of a pin. I never could get it completely clean. One day he developed diarrhea, probably from the antibiotics, and then fecal material contaminated the wound. All paths led to the head of the pin. It protruded. The orthopods said the pin would have to be removed or else the wound would never heal.

"What is going to hold the bones together after you take the nail out?" I asked.

"Nothing. We'll have to put him in a well-leg cast."

I'd seen those before. Casts were applied to each leg, and a bar between stabilized the fractured leg in position against the healthy one. "He'll never survive."

"What choice do we have?"

"How about a prosthesis?"

"Come on, Harry. He's got Parkinson's, he's half paralyzed. Let's try to get some callus around the fracture, then we'll take the thing off and let him sit in a chair. It won't heal, but as long as it doesn't hurt him too much he'll get along."

I couldn't discuss it with Lapius. I tranquilized him and he was sent back for surgery.

He returned the following day in a well-leg cast—two cylinders of plaster, covering each leg from toes to hips, connected by an iron bar embedded in the plaster. The entire lower half of his body immobilized, Lapius was more than ever before dependent not only on his catheter but on human assistance for every one of his functions. He defecated into the bed. The stool encrusted the cast, and I hosed it daily. After each bowel movement, sometimes hours after, he would be moved, cleaned, his bed changed. Weeks went by. One day, without even a bowel movement in the bed, fecal odors emanated from his body.

I cut the cast down to expose the incision and found there a toilet of pus and green debris and liquefied flesh. I started again to débride and clean the putrefying wound. I was determined that whatever else happened, Simon would not entirely rot to

291

death, cruel as my ministrations might seem in that they preserved his life.

Other areas of his skin beneath the cast were starting to macerate. He lay in bed on his back, staring with fixed eyeballs at the ceiling, his cheeks sunken, his mouth parched, his skin wrinkled.

I applied soaks of one-half percent silver nitrate to his wound. I bought a sponge mattress for his bed so that other areas of skin wouldn't break down. I hired nurses round the clock, but no number of hands would now be adequate. I daily cut away slimy chunks of putrescent flesh. I plunged silver nitrate sticks into fistulous recesses from which snaky streams of pus could be expressed by pressure on his thigh and buttocks. I trimmed away rinds of skin on the undersurface of which small abscesses had seeded themselves. I transfused him with plasma and whole blood until the bare muscles began to exude a yellow gluelike serum without which no wound can heal. For weeks I was married to the wound, forgetting into whose body it had eroded. I no longer looked at Simon but became transfixed by the purely mechanical problem of cleaning the mess. Little by little the infection receded, and soon small pink mounds of highly vascular tissue began to appear, the long-sought granulation, carrying within its mysterious confines the small capillaries that would bring a new blood supply to the healing tissues. After three weeks the wound in its entirety started to heal, and for the first time I looked up and saw that in reality nothing had changed. Simon, obtunded, parched from mouth breathing, stared blankly at the ceiling. There was no chance of recovery. His bones became more prominent. As the flesh seemed daily to melt away, the skin over the bony surfaces began to develop that dusky redness and doughy quality that heralded another bedsore. Daily I listened with a stethoscope, to be rewarded finally by the fine crackling sound that indicated pneumonia. His temperature rose. I took his chart and printed across the medical order sheet: "NO ANTIBIOTICS, UNDER ANY CIRCUMSTANCES."

I wished that Father Hesu Delgado were available to comfort me.

Epitaph for Aesculapius

When S. Q. Lapius lay moribund, a physician was dying. A pivotal man bound to medicine by art and sense, intellect and love, to his patients by care and compassion, honor-bound to preserve the sanctity of life. Our goal as doctors is to become physicians. It is not a goal we knowingly achieve. We can only strive, with the hope that one day the epitaph will read "Physician."

Daily and often during unexpected hours of the night my colleagues and myself are presented with an opportunity to serve a person felled by trauma or disease. A fellow being we never met nor knew, who through the random numbers of fate or chance suddenly becomes the sacred trust of a physician and confidently submits to that arrangement.

A physician is not stranger to his fellow. "Physician" is not an isolated contemporary title, self-conferred, but an embodiment with roots that course through the dust of centuries. Our collegium is not truncated by oceans or defined by continental shelves, altered by wars or plagues or the politics of nations. Our heritage is a constant source traced to the first instance that a man kneeled to succor a stricken fellow. When one physician meets another, he knows him as an ancient friend, his honor tested, his marrow bearing the residue of a genetic chain six thousand years in length. We harbor the spiritual heritage of Egypt, Sumaria, Greece and Rome, Byzantium, the Arabic and Jewish cultures, the great European revival of learning, and the modern age, when science wedded the art of medicine. Another physician is more brother and cousin to me than kith or kin. I know what he has been through, and what he has to offer. I know his dedication and integrity. I know his bones and mind.

I departed institutional medicine for private practice, to search again for Aesculapius. Perhaps he exists in the singular affinity that develops between doctor and patient, where authority and responsibility are bound in a single passion to cure the sick, or, failing that, to make the incurable comfortable and support their death with humanity and dignity.